Flannery O'Connor

Edited by Sura P. Rath

and Mary Neff Shaw

Flannery O'Connor

New Perspectives

The University of Georgia Press

Athens and London

© 1996 by the University of Georgia Press
Athens, Georgia 30602
All rights reserved
Designed by Louise OFarrell
Set in 10/15 Galliard
by Tseng Information Systems, Inc.
Printed and bound by Thomson-Shore, Inc.
The paper in this book meets the guidelines for permanence
and durability of the Committee on Production Guidelines for
Book Longevity of the Council on Library Resources.

Printed in the United States of America

00 99 98 97 96   C   5   4   3   2   1
00 99 98 97   P   5   4   3

Library of Congress Cataloging in Publication Data
Flannery O'Connor : new perspectives / edited by Sura P. Rath
and Mary Neff Shaw.
p.   cm.
Includes bibliographical references and index.
ISBN 0-8203-1749-7 (alk. paper) ISBN 0-8203-1804-3 (pbk.: alk.
paper)
1. O'Connor, Flannery—Criticism and interpretation.
2. Women and literature—Southern States—History—20th
century.   3. Southern States—In literature.   I. Rath, Sura
Prasad, 1950-   . II. Shaw, Mary Neff.
PS3565.C57Z6679   1996
813'.54—dc20   94-48867

British Library Cataloging in Publication Data available

Dedicated to our parents,

Tara and Govind Rath

Mary Virginia Neff O'Neal and Robert A. Neff

Contents

❖ ❖ ❖

Acknowledgments

We owe debts of gratitude to a number of people in preparing this collection of essays. Professor Dennis Berthold of Texas A&M University was the first to engage our interest in Flannery O'Connor's work more than a decade ago; he has nurtured that interest all these years. Our students and colleagues at LSU-Shreveport have encouraged us to pursue this project, and the College of Liberal Arts has supported our work.

Our thanks are also to Robert Giroux, literary executor of O'Connor's estate, for permission to quote from unpublished writings of O'Connor; to *The Flannery O'Connor Bulletin* for permission to reprint a revised version of Mary Neff Shaw's "'The Artificial Nigger': A Dialogic Narrative"; to the *South Central Review* for permission to reprint Laura B. Kennelly's "Exhortation in *Wise Blood:* Rhetorical Theory as an Approach to Flannery O'Connor"; and to *Literature and Psychology* for permission to reprint a revised version of Suzanne Morrow Paulson's "Apocalypse of Self, Resurrection of the Double: Flannery O'Connor's *The Violent Bear It Away.*"

Cleatta Morris and Geraldine Toups helped transfer the hard copies of the manuscripts to computer disks, and simplified our task of copy editing. At the University of Georgia Press, our thanks are to Karen Orchard, associate director and executive editor, for her patience and encouragement; to Kelly Caudle, managing editor, and to Trudie Calvert, editor, for their help in the production process.

Finally, our very special thanks to our spouses, Manju and Buddy, for their encouragement and patience with us as we worked on this project.

Abbreviations

❖ ❖ ❖

CW   *Collected Works.* Ed. Sally Fitzgerald. New York: Library of America, 1988.

CS   *The Complete Stories.* New York: Farrar, Straus and Giroux, 1979.

HB   *The Habit of Being.* Ed. Sally Fitzgerald. New York: Farrar, Straus and Giroux, 1979.

MM   *Mystery and Manners: Occasional Prose.* Ed. Sally Fitzgerald and Robert Fitzgerald. New York: Farrar, Straus and Giroux, 1969.

Flannery O'Connor

Introduction

❖ ❖ ❖

Sura P. Rath

Early reviews of Flannery O'Connor's work were based on analysis of theme or setting. In the four decades since the publication of *Wise Blood* (1952), critical response to her fiction has passed through as many different phases. Early reviews published in popular magazines, newsletters, and newspapers simultaneously praised and condemned the novel for its grotesquerie, violence, and other naturalistic elements and judged the narrative on the basis of its contribution to the desired tone and atmosphere of the grotesque. This mixed reception led O'Connor to respond with her now famous preface to the second edition of *Wise Blood* (1962) and with letters, book reviews, lectures, and essays. Critical opinions in the 1960s brought a different perspective to the study of her fiction as readers began to examine the role of her faith in her poetics. The focus of attention shifted either to geographic realism (southern regionalism) or to Christian realism (Catholicism), but critics were still polarized regarding her dramatization of plots and characters. This was friendlier territory, but condescending and patronizing, for the local and regional emphases in critical evaluation diverted readers' attention from the universality of her themes and characters. In her essays and reviews O'Connor continued to discuss her craft and the poetics of her southern Catholicism, and her stories began to challenge earlier critical stereotyping of her work as merely southern and grotesque. In the 1970s, critical focus shifted to analyzing the function of the form and structure of her fiction in the development of her "vision," termed "redemption" by some and "apocalypse" by others. In *Critical Essays on Flannery O'Connor* (1985) Melvin Friedman and Beverly Lyon Clark collected representative essays from the second and third phases.

By the early 1980s, O'Connor scholarship had grown exponentially, largely through the publication of *Letters of Flannery O'Connor: The Habit of Being* (1979), which revealed that her strong convictions on many social, religious, and literary issues were matched by an intense interest in fellow people. The letters humanized her in the public eye. Some major scholars began to question the originality of "new" insights. Friedman and Clark acknowledged this emerging concern by citing Jerome Klinkowitz's remark that most of the current work on O'Connor was "mediocre and repetitious" (*American Literary Scholarship: An Annual/1980*, 317) and Robert Coles's call for "a bit of pause" in critical attention given her. But neither the concerned critics nor Friedman and Clark's volume prompted any moratorium in O'Connor studies; in fact, the Library of America brought out *O'Connor: Collected Works* (1988), and several collections of her primary work (letters and interviews), and revisionist readings appeared in the 1980s almost as a challenge to Klinkowitz and Coles. The *Flannery O'Connor Bulletin*, begun in 1972 at Georgia College, continued to present fresh insights on her work, and new book-length studies were published by Carol Shloss (*Flannery O'Connor's Dark Comedies: The Limits of Inference*, 1980), Frederick Asals (*Flannery O'Connor: The Imagination of Extremity*, 1982), Louise Westling (*Sacred Groves and Ravaged Gardens: The Fiction of Eudora Welty, Carson McCullers, and Flannery O'Connor*, 1985), Marshall Bruce Gentry (*Flannery O'Connor's Religion of the Grotesque*, 1986), Edward Kessler (*Flannery O'Connor and the Language of Apocalypse*, 1986), and John F. Desmond (*Risen Sons: Flannery O'Connor's Vision of History*, 1987). In addition, Lorine Getz's *Flannery O'Connor's Life, Library, and Book Reviews* came out in 1980; Carter Martin edited *The Presence of Grace and Other Book Reviews by Flannery O'Connor* (1983); Arthur F. Kinney brought out *Flannery O'Connor's Library: Resources of Being* (1985); and many fine essays appeared in the *Flannery O'Connor Bulletin* and other scholarly journals. In particular, a collection of essays, *Realist of Distances:*

Flannery O'Connor Revisited (1987), came out the year after John R. May discussed the "methodological limits of Flannery O'Connor's critics" in a *Bulletin* article. During the 1980s, seventy-nine O'Connor-related dissertations were written, fourteen of them in 1983 alone, the same number produced in 1975. These studies have synthesized the previously held piecemeal perspectives and examined O'Connor's ideology against the larger metaphysics of life as she experienced it. In these works, her art and theology are treated as integral rather than extraneous to the development of her characters, and individual elements such as the southern grotesque and her Catholicism subserve the larger design.

By 1989, echoes of some of the feelings expressed by Klinkowitz and Coles appeared in Ben Satterfield's "*Wise Blood,* Artistic Anemia, and the Hemorrhaging of O'Connor Criticism." But scholarly and research interest in O'Connor continued to present a different picture. The same year two major studies—Richard Giannone's *Flannery O'Connor and the Mystery of Love* and Robert Brinkmeyer's *Art and Vision of Flannery O'Connor*—appeared. More unpublished letters came out during all the years following the publication of *The Habit of Being:* in a special southern issue of *New Orleans Review* (1979), John R. May published O'Connor's correspondence with Father Youree Watson, and in the 1988 issue of the *Bulletin* Sura Rath brought out some of her letters to Father Edward J. Romagosa. In 1990 the Ina Dillard Russell Library acquired 168 letters totaling about 170 pages that O'Connor had written Maryat Lee during the seven-year period 1957–64. In 1992, a Flannery O'Connor Society was formed at the American Literature Association meeting in San Diego, and in 1993, *Cheers! The Flannery O'Connor Society Newsletter* was started to disseminate information about conferences, meetings, and symposia on O'Connor held in different parts of the country.

In 1993, several book-length studies also appeared. Karl-Heinz Westarp collected four early O'Connor stories in *Flannery O'Connor: The Growing Craft* (Summa) to examine her evolving craftsmanship as a novelist and storyteller. Countering the earlier critical studies that placed O'Connor directly in the tradition of the American grotesque of Poe and Hawthorne,

Anthony di Renzo proposed in *American Gargoyles: Flannery O'Connor and the Medieval Grotesque* a kinship between O'Connor's comic characters and those of English mystery cycles and medieval carnivals. In *Flannery O'Connor and Cold War Culture* Jon Lance Bacon argued that O'Connor was deeply concerned with the American popular culture of the cold war era. In *The Narrative Secret of Flannery O'Connor: The Trickster as Interpreter,* published in 1994, Ruthann Knechel Johansen drew on the narrative theories of Lévi-Strauss, Barthes, Genette, Kermode, Ricoeur, and Todorov to argue that the trickster functions as a choric device, an interpretive tool through which readers can understand O'Connor's meanings.

While scholars wait for a critical biography, a long-term project undertaken by Sally Fitzgerald, in early 1995 Susan Balée brought out *Flannery O'Connor: Literary Prophet of the South,* a life of the author in Chelsea House's children's biography series Great Achievers: Lives of the Physically Challenged. Given the role and scope of the series, and the adolescent readers for whom it is designed, the book focuses narrowly on the author's physical disability, but offers no new insight on her fiction. Also in the same year Michael Kreyling's edited volume *New Essays on "Wise Blood"* was published. Margaret Whitt's volume *Understanding Flannery O'Connor,* in the Understanding Contemporary American Fiction series, is forthcoming in late 1995. Research on several book-length studies is in progress: Sarah Gordon's study focuses on O'Connor's identity as a southern woman writer working at a particular time in southern and American history influenced by her devout traditional Catholicism; George Kilcourse's study follows up on Rose Bowen's work and examines "kenosis" as a structural principle in O'Connor's fiction.

Contrary to the criticism expressed by Satterfield and by Frederick Crews ("The Power of Flannery O'Connor") concerning her stature as a major literary figure, application of insights from new critical theories has yielded fresh and rich readings. In particular, feminist and dialogical (Bakhtinian) perspectives have contributed revisionist interpretations that O'Connor's readers in the 1960s and 1970s could not have envisioned. A common thread running through many of the new studies is Mikhail Bakhtin's dialogism. In *Flannery O'Connor's Religion of the Grotesque* (1986), for example, Marshall Bruce Gentry suggests that the grotesque serves the same positive end in O'Connor's fiction as the one Bakhtin sees in Rabelais: it brings about change, renewal, rejuvenation, and redemption. Instead of seeing her protagonists as mere puppets used for dramatic effect, he sees them as fully developed characters agonistically entangled with their author to establish their "character zone" and authority. Gentry sees redemption for them as a sometimes unconscious process. In *Flannery O'Connor and the Language of Apocalypse* (1986) Edward Kessler examines O'Connor's figurative language as a key to her apocalyptic vision, suggesting that metaphor ("as if . . .") functions as the key rhetorical strategy triggering the onset of the imaginary world. In *The Art and Vision of Flannery O'Connor* (1989), Robert Brinkmeyer contends that "much of O'Connor's greatness as a writer results from her ability to embrace the voices and viewpoints of those about and within her—in other words to give expression to the many realities" (12) that Bakhtin sees in Dostoevski and Welty sees in Chekhov. Brinkmeyer claims that "O'Connor opened herself to the multivoiced world, particularly to the voices of the southern countryside," and that by "Drawing from voices both within and without her self, O'Connor tests and challenges her self-conception and her faith, ultimately enlarging and deepening both, together with her imaginative vision" (9). Brinkmeyer believes "openness to critical evaluation of self and vision" is a crucial characteristic of O'Connor's mind and art, and he suggests Bakhtin's dialogism as a fruitful approach to her fiction.

This collection is an attempt to bring together the major new perspectives on O'Connor of the last decade and a half and to assess the directions in which O'Connor scholarship has moved. It includes essays by ten authors who approach O'Connor from a variety of thematic and narrative points of view.

A lingering question among O'Connor scholars concerns the dynamics of reader response to her fiction. In "Marketing Flannery O'Connor: Institutional Politics and Literary Evaluation" Sarah J. Fodor traces the stages of O'Connor's acceptance among readers during her life and after her death. Although several recent studies have questioned her canonical status by citing her connection to the New Criticism, Fodor holds that the history of her fiction's reception demonstrates that no single group's influence sufficiently accounts for her canonicity. She argues that although O'Connor's stories were marketed to appeal to both popular and elite audiences the academy came to consider her fiction important in the course of a wide-ranging cultural conversation about how to classify it: as southern or universal, as religious or diabolical, as masculine or feminine. Critics from a variety of perspectives found her fiction useful to exemplify their often opposed ideological views. Its ability to elude all these categories continues to fascinate readers.

Exploration of gender issues, especially the application of feminist perspectives, offers interesting new insights into O'Connor's fiction, interesting because as a southern woman author she shared the cultural myth of the South, but more important because politically she remained separate from the feminist movement. In "Women, Language, and the Grotesque in Flannery O'Connor and Eudora Welty" Jeanne Campbell Reesman argues that O'Connor's and Welty's feminine grotesques may be meaningfully compared through Mikhail Bakhtin's notion of the grotesque, which "liberates the world from all that is dark and terrifying," offering a "regenerating ambivalence" that eventually produces wholeness. In O'Connor and Welty, the conflict between addressing and defining the female body is a grotesque process that thoroughly preoccupies narrators and characters. The grotesque, like the gothic, does not necessarily emphasize the limits of female identity; it can expand them. The most important function of the grotesque in their works is the addressing of the feminine, in which the contact of women's bodies and voices with the grotesque generates unique power.

In "Gender Dialogue in O'Connor," Marshall Bruce Gentry observes that the typical O'Connor narrator is a rigidly patriarchal female who promotes gender separation, and her characters frequently find redemption as they move toward androgyny. The feminine becomes a source for the characters' rebellion, for voices that compete with the O'Connor narrator's authority. In the course of a given work, while maintaining a battle against the narrator, a female character discovers strengths that are masculine (especially by patriarchal standards), or a male character discovers his female side and the advantages of the feminine. Men and women battle constantly in O'Connor's works, but apparently critics have been reluctant to question or analyze what seems obvious: men always win. Even when Bakhtinian dialogism in O'Connor is being discussed, the battle between the authoritarian narrator and the rebellious characters is often described as a conflict based on differences in religious viewpoint, not specifically on gender differences.

In "Displacing Gender: Flannery O'Connor's View from the Woods," Richard Giannone argues that the thrust of O'Connor's displacing gender is to show that personhood is not a property of another person or a social structure or a piece of property but a property of creation. Looking beyond gender enables O'Connor to assert human worth as a function of divine activity. Her writing is then able to claim a form of feminism that inheres not in political struggle or theoretical debate but in mystical insight. From that spiritual perspective O'Connor would agree with Foucault's denunciation in *The History of Sexuality* of the habit by which Western culture uses sexual marks above all other attributes in establishing individual identity. In her writing, the male is not a male, nor is the female a female. The species is the undivided human as a created person invited by the Creator to share in yet a greater and more perfectly unified life.

O'Connor's early stories have received little critical attention except in casual reference to the potential they exhibit, yet one should go to those stories to see how her women characters evolve. In "'The Crop': Limitation, Restraint, Possibility," Sarah Gordon examines "The Crop," her only story centered on a female artist, and proposes that it suggests many of the dilemmas of the southern woman writer in the mid-twentieth century. Although O'Connor herself scrawled on the manuscript "UNPUBLISH-ABLE/FOC 1953" and although, agreeing with Frederick Asals that Miss Willerton is little more than "a stock character," we might observe that the satire is heavy-handed, the story may also be read as the young O'Connor's dialogue with herself, a powerful statement of the author's intention to exert control over her own text. Just as O'Connor allows Miss Willerton's imaginative vision to be "killed off" by the interruption of Lucia, whose request that "Willie" get to the store thrusts her back into reality, so O'Connor gives the death blow to Miss Willerton's effete idea of art and the artist, deconstructing in order to name and understand the limits and possibilities of her role as artist—as tough-minded and willing to defy notions of the "nice" and "pretty" within the constraints of her religious faith.

Like Poe and Hawthorne, O'Connor probes her characters' psyches. In "Apocalypse of Self, Resurrection of the Double: Flannery O'Connor's *The Violent Bear It Away*," first published in *Literature and Psychology* and revised for this volume, Suzanne Morrow Paulson approaches *The Violent Bear It Away* through Freud and the psychology of the divided self to suggest new possibilities for O'Connor's fiction. She rejects the traditionalist view of *The Violent Bear It Away* as a failure, proposing instead that a psychoanalytical reading centered on the doubling phenomena revealed in the interwoven but crippling relationships of the three main characters— Mason, Rayber, and Francis—offers more insights into O'Connor's work as a whole than any other approach. Her approach seems especially pertinent to O'Connor's second novel, which "turns" on events surrounding Rayber, a psychologist. An odyssey toward madness rather than salvation, the novel begins with a death and ends with a grotesque resurrection as Old Tarwater's will takes over the psyche of his young nephew, a circuitous journey suggesting that even as a religious writer O'Connor accepted Freudian truths and understood Freudian symbols because she earnestly tried to come to grips with modern times and secular thinkers.

Since the mid-1980s some rhetorical approaches to O'Connor have produced rich readings, the most visible among them being that developed by the Russian formalist Mikhail Bakhtin in the context of Dostoevski's fiction. In " 'The Artificial Nigger': A Dialogic Narrative," which appeared in the *Flannery O'Connor Bulletin* (1991) and has been revised for this volume, Mary Neff Shaw examines O'Connor's multiple manuscript drafts of "The

Artificial Nigger," suggesting that O'Connor instinctively made revisions that excised the story's monologic elements. Shaw proposes that a dialogical approach offers new insights into the story and helps the reader sympathize with O'Connor's religious intent and respect for dramatic unities. It helps explain the multiple voices underlying the seemingly authoritative voice of the narrator and offers a new view to the complexity of plot not explained by traditional analyses.

In "Exhortation in *Wise Blood:* Rhetorical Theory as an Approach to Flannery O'Connor," first published in the *South Central Review,* Laura B. Kennelly applies the discourse theory of Edwin Black to O'Connor's novel. The impatience, often outright annoyance, shown by early critics of *Wise Blood* furnishes a clue to its rhetorical genre. The clue lies in the respondents' emotionality, the psychological response consciously and carefully sought by the exhortative novel. Exhortative discourse falls outside the traditional neo-Aristotelian types which use emotion as an adjunct in appeals to reason. In exhortation, emotion does not "bias the judgment of the auditors" and thereby affect their decision; instead, emotion creates a belief. As Edwin Black theorizes in *Rhetorical Criticism: A Study in Method,* exhortative discourse has three distinguishable features: it promotes an intense conviction and "alien" view; it depends on an extensive use of emotion to inspire belief; and it relies on a clear, easily understood literary style that uses the copula and concrete description. Kennelly finds that *Wise Blood* exemplifies this discourse at its finest.

Robert Brinkmeyer examines the relationship between O'Connor's views on ascetic self-denial and her self and art in "Asceticism and the Imaginative Vision of Flannery O'Connor." Drawing on Sally Fitzgerald's suggestive remark that "Flannery seemed fated to asceticism," he suggests that "Maritain's ascetic aesthetics and Geoffrey Harpham's reading of asceticism provide a useful means for approaching O'Connor's aesthetics and her imaginative life." As revealed primarily in her letters, O'Connor embraced a rigid asceticism in both her personal and artistic life, believing that self-denial was necessary to meet the demands of faith and to combat "the sins of pride and selfishness and reluctance to wrestle with the Spirit." Likewise, her artistic calling demanded a commitment to self-sacrifice; she was, as she wrote to Maryat Lee, a "hermit novelist." Ultimately O'Connor's asceticism contained the seeds of its own destruction, for she saw its end not as disengagement from but involvement in the world—an involvement marked by loving concern and charity for others. Charity, in other words, was possible for O'Connor only through self-denial, a realization that became the cornerstone of her thinking and a central theme and narrative strategy in her fiction.

In "Flannery O'Connor and the Aesthetics of Torture," Patricia Yaeger, herself a southerner, argues that "a poetics of torture—a painful reenactment of a sadistic world whose sanity is 'hopelessly compromised' by its race and class politics—becomes the foundation of O'Connor's best work." She develops a poetics of torture based on the experience of physical pain as a grotesque means for southern women to achieve socially expected female beauty. Southern women writers appropriate the literary form of the grotesque for their own purpose, using the grotesque body to offer subversive readings of their historical surrounding. When it intrudes into a social context preoccupied with the canons of southern gentility, its rough energy shatters old norms. By focusing on the unruly orifices and openings in a character's body, or on the body's tortured doubleness and excess, southern women writers attack the conservatism of an ideology designed to close off social contradictions. Within such a context, Flannery O'Connor's stories offer intricate readings of a social system gone awry. Her fiction is the very place to describe a politicized reading of the grotesque as southern form, to drive home the point that southern literary bodies are grotesque because their authors know that bodies cannot be thought of separately from the racist and sexist institutions that surround them. Yaeger develops a phenomenology of pain in O'Connor's fiction, tracing her literary sadism as an inchoate form of readerly torture, and then relates this phenomenology to O'Connor's moment in history. Such thematic/structural studies are complemented by Freudian readings of O'Connor.

These essays continue the critical concerns of the past about O'Connor's fiction, but they break from the past in the methods used to examine the texts, the questions asked of the author and her characters, the observations made, and the conclusions drawn. The vitality and energy reflected in the published articles and conference papers owe their power to the encounter between traditional scholars, who continue to study the cultural genesis of southern literature, and new scholars who see in O'Connor's writing new horizons of relevance and meaning significant to the changed society of their time.

More remains to be done, however. For instance, very little critical work has been done on O'Connor's letters, some of which are brilliant essays in aesthetics and literary criticism; the same is true of her essays and occasional prose. One thinks of the letters Flaubert and Keats wrote in an earlier time and of those Virginia Woolf wrote earlier in this century. Application of the major poststructuralist critical theories promises new areas for prospective research. In a keynote speech at Georgia College at the thirtieth anniversary of O'Connor's death, Ralph C. Wood brought up another debatable issue—the question of race—which needs to be followed. Obviously, feminist approaches to her stories, novels, and criticism have much potential for discovery of new territory. Similarly, Freudian and Lacanian readings are likely to yield insights not yet suggested by her critics. Melvin Friedman's concluding remark in the "Introduction" to *Critical Essays on Flannery O'Connor*—"the reviews, letters, and essays have that magical touch that urges a return to the fiction" (14)—may now be revised to read that all her writing has the magical touch that urges a return to all of it.

Marketing Flannery O'Connor: Institutional Politics and Literary Evaluation

Sarah J. Fodor

Just six years after Flannery O'Connor received her M.F.A. from the University of Iowa, the New American Library issued 234,000 copies of the Signet paperback version of *Wise Blood*. Black letters on an orange band advertise "A Searching Novel of Sin and Redemption," encoding O'Connor's religious concerns in phrases that usually mark romances, thrillers, or soft porn. The picture shows a man lying on the grass in front of a mountain shack. A woman is removing his hat. This titillating scene of hillbilly sex in the field targets a mass audience, presenting O'Connor's Catholic critique of existentialism as a steamy dime novel. The cover art differs markedly from its written version in chapter 7 of *Wise Blood,* where Haze wants to seduce Sabbath because he thinks she is innocent, but he runs away in a panic once *she* actually begins to flirt with *him*.[1]

In contrast to such popular marketing, current representations of O'Connor's fiction emphasize its academic nature. Frederick Crews characterizes O'Connor's education at the University of Iowa as a "New Critical initiation," suggesting that her stories never "stray from the regnant Creative Writing mode" of her day. Crews concludes, "A cynic might say, then, that in lionizing O'Connor the American university has not so much acknowledged a literary genius as bestowed a posthumous laurel on its most diligent student" (49). Crews cynically accounts for O'Connor's academic status by claiming that New Critical theory formed her writing and that her canonization reflects not her accomplishments as a writer but her conformity to this approach. My research shows on the contrary that although the New Criticism was one important influence in O'Connor's reception, neither the power of this institutionally dominant group nor that of a monolithic "American university" is a sufficient explanation of her canonical status. Rather, the academy came to consider O'Connor important in the course of a wider cultural conversation about how to characterize her fiction: as part of popular or elite culture, as southern or universal, as religious or diabolical, as masculine or feminine. The history of O'Connor's reception elucidates both why O'Connor was canonized and what inherent and external factors make certain literature enduring.[2]

During the 1980s, several critics pointed out O'Connor's relationship to the New Criticism, though none provided an extended consideration of the role of New Critics or of New Critical values in canonizing her.[3] The timing of these statements linking O'Connor and the New Criticism, a critical approach many consider outmoded, is not accidental. The proliferation of literary theories since the mid-1970s has stimulated scholarly interest in the relationship between literary theory and writing. Do critical theories influence writing? If so, will those who value a theory value writing that in some way responds to the theory? If a writer is canonized when a theory predominates, should we reexamine the value of the writing when the theory falls from favor? Questions like these inform Crews's reconsideration of O'Connor. Yet the history of O'Connor's canonization demonstrates that the interrelationships among theory, writing, and canonization are neither simple nor direct.

Academic Support for O'Connor's Fiction: The New Critics and the New York Intellectuals

The literary academy quickly accepted Flannery O'Connor as an important fiction writer of the post–World War II era. Beginning in 1946, her second semester at the Iowa Writers' Workshop, she published short stories in *Accent,* the *Sewanee Review,* the *Partisan Review,* and the *Kenyon Review.* As early as 1961, Willard Thorpe chose "A Good Man Is Hard to Find" to appear in his historicist college literature text, *American Literary Record.* By the early 1970s, most American literature anthologies included O'Connor's stories. Paul Lauter's 1982 survey of fifty American literature college introductory courses found that O'Connor was the only contemporary woman writer to appear on these lists.[4] "Everything That Rises Must Converge" is one of four selections by women included in the Introduction to Great Books series. Finally, the Library of America, which calls itself "the only definitive collection of America's greatest writers," issued O'Connor's *Collected Works* in 1988. This series had previously featured only three other twentieth-century writers: Jack London, Eugene O'Neill, and William Faulkner. As in the Lauter survey, O'Connor was the only contemporary female author to be included.

Those like Crews who credit the New Critics with establishing O'Connor's literary status tell only part of the story. It is true that the network of contacts O'Connor made at Iowa helped her achieve initial recognition, and many of these people had New Critical connections.[5] Paul Engle, director of the Iowa Writers' Workshop, brought in southern New Critics John Crowe Ransom and Robert Penn Warren as workshop clinicians when O'Connor was a student. That both Ransom and Warren chose O'Connor's stories to discuss in the workshop sessions indicates their awareness and appreciation of her early work. In 1953 and 1954, O'Connor received two $2,000 Kenyon fellowships. Five of the nineteen stories she published during her lifetime appeared in the *Kenyon Review* under Ransom's editorship. Editors John Palmer and Monroe Spears published five others in the *Sewanee Review* between 1948 and 1962.[6]

The *Sewanee* and *Kenyon* reviews are often considered exemplary New Critical quarterlies. Ransom edited the *Kenyon* from its inception in 1939 until 1959. It served to launch his program for establishing criticism in the university, and many of the *Kenyon* essays from the 1940s exemplify a New Critical perspective. As Marian Janssen demonstrates, however, from the beginning the *Kenyon Review* included work by critics of many perspectives. New York intellectual Philip Rahv, editor of the Marxist *Partisan Review*, published his celebrated essay "Paleface and Redskin" in the *Kenyon*'s first volume.[7] In 1948, Ransom proposed a critics' symposium in which many of the leading national literary critics would describe their approaches; in a letter soliciting Van Wyck Brooks's participation, Ransom explained that he hoped to "assemble a catholic and various statement of the critic's business without presupposing any kind of thing as preferred." Ransom's tone belies the stereotyped image of the New Critic as dogmatist and reflects his own reservations about the New Criticism in the late 1940s. The 1949 symposium "My Credo" featured historical, cultural, and myth critics, including Douglas Bush, Richard Chase, Leslie Fiedler, and Northrop Frye (Janssen 175–78). Bush's participation is especially noteworthy; in his 1948 MLA presidential address, Bush attacked the New Criticism and defended historical scholarship in what Gerald Graff calls a "celebrated polemic" that constituted the "last defiant roar of the old historical scholars" (Graff 185).

O'Connor's contacts at Iowa helped her get published in short story anthologies. Paul Engle edited the O. Henry collection from 1954 to 1959 and selected O'Connor stories for four of these volumes. "Everything That Rises Must Converge" and "Revelation" won first prizes in the O. Henry volumes edited by Richard Poirier in 1963 and 1965. While Engle had New Critical connections, Poirier has been associated with New York intellectuals and with leftist perspectives. O'Connor stories were also chosen for the *Best American Short Stories* of 1956, 1957, 1958, 1962, and 1979. Inclusion in the O. Henry *Prize Stories* volumes is important because *First Prize Stories* 1919–57, 1919–63, and *Fifty Years of American Short Stories* reprinted prize-winning stories, including O'Connor's. Such collections bring an author's name before the public and serve as guides for future anthology makers. Engle's prefaces reflect New Critical values but also name other bases of literary value. In the 1954 preface, Engle sounds New Critical when he maintains that craftsmanship is important; he praises O'Connor's style, describing the narrative voice in "Greenleaf" as "authentic," "witty," and "ironic." But he maintains that craftsmanship is not enough; enduring literature must concern human values.[8] He admires "Greenleaf" for its portrayal of "economic and social pressures," using language typical of sociological and Marxist critics (*Prize Stories* 1957: 8–9). Engle's interest in social issues is more typical of the New York intellectuals than of the New Critics. His selections include writers from both groups; in 1957 he chose stories by John Cheever, Irwin Shaw, and Mary McCarthy as well as by Jean Stafford, William Faulkner, and O'Connor.

Such New Critical supporters as Engle and even Ransom were not simply New Critical; moreover, O'Connor also had important supporters among the New York intellectuals. In 1948 she met Alfred Kazin, one of the leading New York critics, during her summer stay at Yaddo, the New York writers' colony.[9] Later that year, Philip Rahv accepted a chapter from *Wise Blood* for the *Partisan Review*. In November, Rahv joined Robert Penn Warren and Robert Lowell in recommending O'Connor for a Guggenheim fellowship. What these sponsors represent is important: Rahv was a Marxist New York editor; Warren was a well-known writer and New Critic; and Lowell was a major American poet. Both Lowell and Warren had recently won Pulitzer Prizes (1947, 1948). Five years later, Rahv and fellow *Partisan* editor William Phillips chose "A Good Man Is Hard to Find" for their *Avon Book of Modern Writing* (1953). The volume signals its tie to the New York intellectuals by invoking on its title page "the same high standards set by Mr. Phillips and Mr. Rahv in their distinguished literary magazine, *Partisan Review*" and by featuring fiction, poetry, and criticism by New York intellectuals Irving Howe, Diana Trilling, and Isaac Rosenfeld. Rahv continued to support O'Connor's work; in 1963, he selected *Wise Blood* for inclusion in his *Eight Great American Short Novels,* along with works by Herman Melville, Henry James, Stephen Crane, Edith Wharton, Sherwood Anderson, William Faulkner, and William Styron. Rahv's title and his other selections claim that O'Connor is an important American writer.

One would expect the New Critics and the New York intellectuals to value O'Connor's fiction for different reasons; Engle's O. Henry prefaces exemplify these representative values when he discusses both formal qualities and socioeconomic concerns. But these critical approaches were more similar in the 1950s than they had been in the 1930s. The 1939 Nazi-Soviet pact left many leftist critics disillusioned with Stalinist socialism, and following World War II, intellectuals of varied political beliefs joined in an effort to demonstrate that the United States was not only a political super-power but a cultural leader.[10] During this period cultural and intellectual leaders increasingly became allied with universities. The New Critics had joined the university establishment by the mid-1940s, and many of the New York intellectuals, who had worked as professional men of letters in the 1930s and 1940s, affiliated themselves with universities in the 1950s and 1960s.[11] These critics valued different aspects of O'Connor's writing, but together they helped establish her work as an important contribution to contemporary American fiction.

The marketing of O'Connor follows an equally interesting track. Her fiction was well received not only by the literary elite but in popular commercial markets. "The Capture" was published in *Mademoiselle* in 1948 and reprinted in *40 Best Stories from Mademoiselle, 1935–1960*. *Harper's Bazaar* accepted four O'Connor stories between 1953 and 1958. Two of these, "Good Country People" and "Everything That Rises Must Converge," are often chosen for short story and college anthologies as well. *Esquire* included a chapter of O'Connor's unfinished third novel in 1963 and "Parker's Back," posthumously, in 1965. The stories published in popular magazines include some of the works that the academy most admires. Both popular and elite audiences valued the same stories, though perhaps for different reasons.

The marketing of O'Connor's books in paperback incorporates appeals to these varied audiences. High culture critics, authors, and New York papers provide the evaluations on these books' covers, but the pictures and blurbs sensationalize. For example, the front cover of the 1956 Signet paperback edition of *A Good Man Is Hard to Find* emphasizes sex even more blatantly than does the *Wise Blood* cover (facsimile in Farmer 19). It features a seduction scene in the hay. A pitchfork and a suitcase containing liquor dominate the background. A man, fully clothed in a dark suit and hat, reaches a clawlike hand over the foregrounded shoulder and breast of a semireclining voluptuous woman. Her eyes downcast, she wears an open-collared white short-sleeved blouse and a slim above-the-knee red skirt. Her legs and feet are bare, suggesting she has begun to undress. Presumably this is a scene from "Good Country People." The stereotypical cover art, however, gives no indication that in the story, the woman being seduced is a "lady Ph.D." who *initiates* the seduction attempt as an expression of her nihilism. The man bears little resemblance to the story's uncouth Bible salesman, dressed in a "bright blue suit and yellow socks that were not pulled up far enough" (*CS* 277). Hulga, the "large blonde woman" in the story, goes out for her date with the salesman wearing "a pair of slacks and a dirty white shirt" with "some Vapex on the collar of it since she did not own any perfume" (*CS* 284). The cover art transforms this overweight, socially inept, thirty-two-year-old blonde woman into a slender, graceful, young, dark-haired pin-up girl so as to market the book as a pulp melodrama or Harlequin romance. Her wooden leg, which plays a central role in the story, is nowhere in sight. The New American Library printed 173,750 copies of the thirty-five-cent Signet paperback; by 1961 a second printing was needed.

The back cover also addresses a mass audience:

THE SPIRIT AND THE FLESH
A criminal who took pleasure in killing
A neglected little boy who seeks love
A wife who is shocked when she becomes pregnant
A Bible salesman who steals a girl's wooden leg

These are a few
of the colorful, conniving,
well-intentioned or evil people
you will meet in this extraordinary
collection of short stories by
a young Southern writer.

These descriptions in lurid red and black read like tabloid headlines. They focus on violence and crime, sensationalizing the subjects of the stories to attract readers of pulp fiction.

Beginning in the late 1960s, when O'Connor's academic reputation became secure, the books' covers became less lurid. In 1964, the New American Library collected the two novels and *A Good Man Is Hard to Find* in the Signet paperback *Three by Flannery O'Connor*. This book offered inexpensive access (ninety-five cents) to everything she had then published, appealing to readers who specifically wanted *her* stories, not just any thrilling read. The notice, "Now complete and unabridged in one volume," targets serious readers, especially teachers who might choose this collection for their reading lists. The book's cover represents a scene from *Wise Blood*. A man, presumably Haze, drives a Model T Ford with a sign reading "Church Without Christ"; a barefooted woman, presumably Sabbath, dangles her feet out the window. The picture suggests a rural scene and a religion that is ambiguously noninstitutional, even comic. In contrast to the earlier covers, romance and sex are downplayed.

The 1965 *Everything That Rises Must Converge* has no picture, just O'Connor's name in ornamental, black letters in Gothic type and the title in shades of green, blue, gray, and black. The back cover mentions O'Connor's death twice, calling this volume a "worthy memorial." It features an evaluation of her literary contribution by Thomas Merton. Merton's name evokes the Catholic revival of the 1940s and 1950s to those who know his *Seven-Storey Mountain,* but he does not mention religion. Instead, he compares O'Connor to Sophocles, implying that her work is a masterpiece of Western civilization (Farmer 35–36). This cover offers a subtle reference to the gothic O'Connor in its choice of font and presents the volume as a monument to her achievement.

Film adaptations of O'Connor's stories also illustrate changes in the audiences targeted. In 1957, CBS broadcast a television version of "The Life You Save May Be Your Own" on its *Playhouse of Stars,* featuring Gene Kelly and Agnes Moorehead. This dramatization appealed to a mass audience by changing the story's conclusion to a formulaic happy ending. In the written version, a one-armed vagabond abandons his newlywed deafmute wife, but a New York gossip column described the show as a "backwoods love story" (*HB* 191). O'Connor's attitude toward that adaptation was self-aware, practical, and humorously cynical. When she heard that Kelly would play the vagabond in the series O'Connor pragmatically called the "Schlitz Playhouse," she wrote to friends: "A *tap dancer* by the name of Gene Kelly is going to make his tellyvision debut in it. The punishment always fits the crime" (191, 186). Clearly she was aware of the economic sources of support both for the show and for her writing. After the show aired, O'Connor's agent told her that she was investigating a Rodgers and Hammerstein–style musical version. O'Connor responded:

I can't decide if this was supposed to be a joke or not. I rather think not. I would rather see it a musical than what it was on that TV program.

> *The life you save may be your own*
> *Hand me that there tellyphone*
> *Hideho and hip hooray*
> *I am in this thang for pay.*

I will submit same to Rodgers and Hammerstein. (208)

O'Connor's wry reactions suggest that she felt she had "sold out" by participating in mass marketing but also that she believed she needed this commercial success to keep writing.

After O'Connor's death in 1964, film adaptations targeted a (at least self-styled) culturally elite audience. Between 1975 and 1977, three stories were produced for television. All aired on PBS. One of these, "The Displaced Person," was produced by Learning in Focus, Inc., as part of the American Short Story series. A companion Dell paperback, *The American Short Story*, printed the featured stories and discussed the film versions (Farmer 118). O'Connor's story is included in this series as a part of American culture which an educated person should know.

More recent paperback packaging of *Three* (1983) clearly aims to live up to its billing as a Signet *Classic*. The back cover describes O'Connor's achievement and the individual volumes collected here. The opening section appeals to an intellectual audience: "Flannery O'Connor's strong, fiercely comic, powerful fiction has won unanimous critical acclaim." But the book summaries appeal to a mass audience in their focus on character and plot:

WISE BLOOD
evokes a terrifying world as it reveals a weird relationship
between a sensual young girl, a conniving
widow, and a young man who deliberately blinds himself.

THE VIOLENT BEAR IT AWAY
tells of a strangely decadent family—three
generations of men obsessed by guilt and driven to violence.

EVERYTHING THAT RISES MUST CONVERGE
is a collection of compelling stories about eroding
family relationships, individuals grappling with their sense
of place in a changing society, race relations in the new
South, and a powerful vision of death and divine revelation.

The downplaying of O'Connor's religious concerns in these descriptions is striking, especially in the summary of *The Violent Bear It Away,* a book about prophecy whose central action is a baptism. The only mention of religion on the entire cover is the single phrase "divine revelation." In their emphasis on sex, decadence, and guilt-obsessed generations of men, these could be descriptions of Faulkner. The description of *Everything That Rises Must Converge* names key social issues of O'Connor's era, presenting her as a powerful cultural critic. This cultural emphasis, important to many literary critics of our own time, is made explicit in the citation of Alfred Kazin's *New York Times Book Review* article: "[O'Connor] has expressed something secret about America, called 'the South,' with [her] transcendent gift for expressing the real spirit of a culture." Kazin, who admired O'Connor's work even before she published *Wise Blood,* is not a New Critic or a Catholic critic but a New York cultural critic with a cultural point to make.

The textual apparatus of the volume appeals to a student audience. Sally Fitzgerald's lengthy introduction includes biography and explication. Fitzgerald discusses religious issues in O'Connor's fiction but feels she must persuade the reader to remain open to these meanings: "I would ask only that you keep in mind some of the references I have proposed to you, in order to deepen your understanding of what underlies the marvelous surface of Flannery O'Connor's tales" (xxxiv). Unlike previous editions, the book concludes on a strikingly academic note with a one-page bibliography of O'Connor's works and criticism.

Throughout O'Connor's career, her books were marketed to both popular and academic audiences, although the balance shifted from a predominantly sensational popular appeal to a more clearly academic claim for her canonicity. Historically, the academy disdains popular culture, but these examples demonstrate the importance of the literary marketplace in keeping an author's work before the public, which includes academic readers. It seems no coincidence that Robert Penn Warren and Albert Russell Erskine selected "The Life You Save May Be Your Own" for their *New Southern Harvest* (1957) two years after its television dramatization.

Region, Religion, and Gender

Once O'Connor had established reliable publishing connections, reviewers began to evaluate her place in the literary scene, classifying her fiction in a variety of ways. Many reviews included New Critical praise for formal attributes, especially style. For example, John Simons praises O'Connor's "taut, dry, economical and objective prose" in his 1952 review in *Commonweal*. He characterizes *Wise Blood* as "an important addition to the grotesque literature of Southern decadence. It is also a kind of Southern Baptist version of 'The Hound of Heaven'" (297). Even though Simons was writing for a Catholic magazine, his review places O'Connor in a southern tradition rather than identifying her as an important new religious writer.

Many early reviews place O'Connor as a regional writer, joining Faulkner, Erskine Caldwell, and Carson McCullers in the "school of the Southern grotesque." The alliance with Caldwell emphasizes O'Connor's grotesque, seamy, backcountriness as well as social and economic issues in her writing. Citing McCullers allies O'Connor with a woman writer of the grotesque. Naming Faulkner makes a larger claim because recent events had established Faulkner's reputation as a "serious" literary figure in the academy.[12] Reviewers invoke these names both to interpret O'Connor's fiction and to establish its significance by relating it to the southern literary renaissance.[13] O'Connor's regional identity remained important throughout her career; she is more likely to be included in southern anthologies and discussed at greater length in southern literary histories than in general collections.

Early reviewers who appreciated O'Connor's religious concerns often cite religious issues as evidence of her universality and insight, defending her against "mere" regionalism. Sylvia Stallings writes about *Wise Blood,* "Some of the power of Miss O'Connor's writing comes from her understanding of the anguish of a mind tormented by God" ("Young Writer" 3). In her review of *A Good Man Is Hard to Find,* Stallings explains that O'Connor "is a regionalist in the best sense of the word; that is, she understands her country and its people so well that in her hands they become all humanity" ("Flannery" 1).

Many early reviewers noticed O'Connor's religious themes but seemed unsure about her attitudes toward these issues. Influenced by New Critical aesthetics, they attribute the difficulty of her early books to her failure effectively to structure symbolic resonances. For example, the *Time* reviewer of *A Good Man Is Hard to Find* seems confused about O'Connor's religious intentions because of what he sees as ineffective symbolism: "Only in her longest story, 'The Displaced Person,' does Ferocious Flannery weaken her wallop by groping about for a symbolic second-story meaning—in this case something about salvation. . . . Such arty fumbling . . . also marred . . . *Wise Blood*" ("Such Nice People" 114). The reviewer suggests O'Connor is unsure of her own intentions. His mocking alliterations call attention to the art of his journalism while suggesting he admires O'Connor's "power" but believes her symbolism is esoteric and unnecessary.[14]

It was not until O'Connor had published her first two books that reviewers began to defend her religious perspective. After she announced,

"I see from the standpoint of Christian orthodoxy," in her 1957 essay for Granville Hicks's *Living Novel* (162), critics increasingly quoted O'Connor to explain religious meanings in her work. Typical of reviews in the 1960s, this conjunction of biography and evaluation illustrates the waning power of W. K. Wimsatt and Monroe C. Beardsley's interdiction against the "intentional fallacy" (1946, rpt. in *The Verbal Icon* in 1953). Granville Hicks, who in the 1930s and 1940s was an exemplary Marxist critic, wrote a 1960 review that discussed O'Connor's Catholicism (Leitch 10). Hicks unabashedly begins his review with biographical information: "Flannery O'Connor is a Southerner and a Catholic and both of these facts are important. Her material, up to a point at any rate, comes from her region, and is roughly of the sort described as Southern Gothic. Her attitude towards the material derives, as she has herself pointed out, from her religious convictions" (18). Hicks also includes a passage from "The Fiction Writer and His Country," quoting O'Connor to explain her use of the grotesque in *The Violent Bear It Away*. One would expect Hicks's use of biography and the author's statements to disturb hard-line New Critics. But Hicks also shows that he shares the New Critical focus on language, praising O'Connor's "breathtaking first sentence" and "strong, supple prose."

Donald Davidson also relies on information about O'Connor to explain her intentions, even though he was a lifelong friend and critical ally of Ransom and Tate. His 1960 review of *The Violent Bear It Away* begins: "Flannery O'Connor's new novel, like her preceding works, is strong medicine, but now we know, as we did not earlier, that the medicine is for the soul, and is not just realistic Southern calomel and Epsom salts." Immediately following this claim, he quotes the Bible verse, printed on the novel's title page, from which the title is taken. Davidson's conclusion that "now we know . . . that the medicine is for the soul" could be based solely on "the text itself," but the certainty of his statement suggests that his new understanding of O'Connor's intentions relies on more than a single biblical citation. After all, religious allusions do appear in the titles and texts of O'Connor's earlier stories. For Davidson, knowing O'Connor's intentions takes her work beyond mere regionalism and constitutes "an invitation to read the novel for a religious, even allegorical meaning" which Davidson nonetheless finds difficult to decipher (4).

Some reviewers cited regional affiliations to demonstrate O'Connor's contribution to a literary movement; others discussed her religious intentions as evidence of her insight and universality. Another series of comments described O'Connor's style in masculine terms to characterize its powerful effect. In a 1958 *Critique* issue on O'Connor and J. F. Powers, Louis Rubin describes her style as "precise, bounded, direct, oddly masculine" (14). William Goyen goes further, commenting on the violent, perverse pleasure he perceives in the narrator of *Wise Blood:* "The stark dramatic power of the scenes is percussive and stabbing, but Miss O'Connor seems to tell her story through clenched teeth in a kind of Tom-boy, Mean-Moll glee" (4). O'Connor does not resist this masculine or androgynous professional identity. As Sandra Gilbert and Susan Gubar point out, O'Connor chose "Flannery" as her professional name rather than her given "Mary Flannery" (241) with its feminine, southern, Catholic associations.

The marketing of O'Connor's stories takes advantage of these gendered evaluations. For example, the British version of "A Good Man Is Hard to Find," quotes Evelyn Waugh: "If this is really the unaided work of a young lady, it is a remarkable product." This jacket also quotes *Time:* "She packs a punch that for sheer sardonic brutality recalls the early Graham Greene" (Farmer 15). These comments ally O'Connor simultaneously with masculine power and with established British Catholic authors. The American Signet paperback version cites *Time*'s comment: "Highly unladylike . . . a brutal irony, a slam-bang humor and a style of writing as balefully direct as a death sentence" (facsimile rpt. in Farmer 19). These statements gender O'Connor as masculine both to account for the power readers perceive in her narration and to claim a broader audience for her work. O'Connor's "masculinity" may also help explain why anthologists chose to include her fiction in textbooks and classes over that of other women writers with "feminine" styles and concerns.

Early Critiques and Defenses
of O'Connor's Literary Reputation

Readers in academic and popular circles valued O'Connor's work for its contribution to the southern literary renaissance, its religious vision, and its masculine power. Others used the same categories to criticize her fiction. From the mid-1950s through mid-1960s a series of critiques and defenses of O'Connor's position in the literary world appeared. For example, a *Time* review of *The Violent Bear It Away* begins with an attack on its author: "Author Flannery O'Connor is a retiring, bookish spinster who dabbles in the variants of sin and salvation like some self-tutored backwoods theologian. She is an earnest Roman Catholic who raises geese and peacocks on the family farm near Milledgeville, Ga., which she rarely leaves; she suffers from lupus (a tuberculous disease of the skin and mucous membranes) that forces her to spend part of her life on crutches" ("God-Intoxicated Hillbillies" 118–19). This writer exaggerates biographical information, religious belief, and regional stereotypes in rejecting O'Connor's fiction. He admits that O'Connor reads books and knows theology but implies that she is not really knowledgeable because she lives on a farm and is self-tutored; she is not serious but only dabbles. Her interest in religion is obsessive, reflecting the naive earnestness of her beliefs. The headline suggests that both O'Connor and her characters are illiterates who are drunkenly addicted to religion. But no wonder O'Connor pursues this religious habit: she is not married and has no social life. This is perhaps owing to her disease, which sounds horribly disfiguring. Her oddity is exacerbated by her strange hobby of raising fowl. In short, the reviewer turns O'Connor into one of her own grotesques as a way of dismissing her fiction.

Unlike most other major periodicals, both *Time* and the *New Yorker* printed only short, negative, or mixed reviews of O'Connor's books while she was alive. *Time* opens its 1952 review, "Seasons come, seasons go, but Southern novels just keep rolling along" ("Southern Dissonance" 108). The *New Yorker* disposes of *The Violent Bear It Away* in a single paragraph, calling it "a dark, ingrown Gothic tale about a monosyllabic teen-age boy from the Tennessee backwoods" (179). O'Connor's southernness was usually an asset in her reception, but these reviews in New York periodicals dismiss her fiction because of its region.

Responding to such reviews, writers such as Caroline Gordon, Andrew Lytle, and Robert Fitzgerald, who knew O'Connor well and shared her beliefs, published influential articles that helped establish her reputation and encouraged religious perspectives on her fiction. In 1955 Gordon reviewed *A Good Man Is Hard to Find* for the *New York Review of Books*. Unlike those who connected O'Connor to Faulkner and other southerners, Gordon makes larger, international claims by comparing her to James and Maupassant. For Gordon as for other New Critics, James's fiction is a paradigm of craftsmanship, narrative point of view, and style. Citing James's evaluation of Maupassant, Gordon maintains that O'Connor shares Maupassant's "precision, density, and an almost alarming circumspection." But she also has what James says Maupassant lacks: an "account of the moral nature of man." Gordon locates O'Connor's power in her "moral, even theological" perspective while she New Critically praises her style, realistic rendering of detail and speech, and use of symbolism (5).

In the 1958 *Critique* O'Connor/Powers number, Gordon confronts the issue of O'Connor and the southern grotesque by comparing her to Truman Capote. She finds O'Connor's fiction superior to Capote's because of the clarity of her moral judgment and her theological frame of reference. Rather than praising O'Connor for New Critical objectivity and ambiguity, Gordon places her in the older, established tradition of Hawthorne and Balzac. Like these canonical authors, O'Connor makes her moral judgments implicit by providing a clear "frame of reference." Her fiction demonstrates that this tradition is still vital: "Miss O'Connor's talent, occurring in such a milieu, is as startling, as disconcerting as a blast from a furnace which one had thought stone-cold but which is still red-hot" (6).

In a move that emphasizes O'Connor's New Critical connections, both Brooks and Warren and Gordon and Tate chose her "A Good Man Is Hard to Find" for the second editions of their college texts (*Understanding Fiction*, 1959; *The House of Fiction*, 1960). As one might expect, Brooks and

Warren's study questions on O'Connor's story ask the reader to consider theme, character, and structure. Gordon and Tate's commentary, however, echoes Gordon's articles, comparing Capote and O'Connor to point out the superiority of O'Connor's moral perspective. Their recent conversions to Catholicism may explain why they focus more directly on religion than did Brooks and Warren. In any case, Gordon and Tate depart from strictly formalist New Criticism by straightforwardly basing their evaluations on ethical issues.

Andrew Lytle, O'Connor's adviser at Iowa and fellow writer, also valued her religious perspective. He helped establish O'Connor's importance by planning a *Sewanee* issue around her work. In 1961, Lytle wrote Tate that he felt both O'Connor and Peter Taylor had "reached that stage where they need a concentrated appraisal." Following Tate's response, which is unpublished, Lytle expanded: "I know what you mean about Flannery's reputation. But she is good, and the wrong kind of thing that is being written about her must be corrected and this *Review* is the place to do it. By the way, what is Robert Fitzgerald's most recent address?" (Young 314–15). The O'Connor issue, which appeared in the summer of 1962, featured her novella "The Lame Shall Enter First" and essays by Robert Fitzgerald ("The Countryside and the True Country") and John Hawkes ("Flannery O'Connor's Devil").

Because Lytle follows his comment by requesting Fitzgerald's address, and Fitzgerald's essay appears in the special issue, Fitzgerald's article can be considered an example of correcting the "wrong kind of thing." Fitzgerald critiques the 1955 *Time* review which admires the "wallop" of "Ferocious Flannery" but believes "The Displaced Person" is weakened by "arty fumbling" that has "something to do with salvation." He argues that this review illustrates the reviewer's lack of insight, not O'Connor's artistic flaws. Asserting that the "displaced person" refers not only to the Polish refugee but also to Mrs. Shortley, Mrs. McIntyre, and many others among O'Connor's characters, Fitzgerald concludes: "[Her stories] not only imply, they as good as state again and again, that estrangement from Christian plenitude is estrangement from the true country of man" (393).

Fitzgerald provides a close reading of "The Displaced Person" from a Catholic perspective. Moreover, by emphasizing the *Time* reviewer's inability to read O'Connor's fiction adequately, he resists a popular reading of her work and reclaims it for the academy.

The companion article to Fitzgerald's, Hawkes's "Flannery O'Connor's Devil," introduces a controversial issue that engaged O'Connor critics for the next twenty years. Hawkes argues that O'Connor's fiction features diabolical voices and, further, that the narrator—and by extension O'Connor herself—often speaks from this diabolical perspective. Critics well into the 1980s felt the need to express their position on this issue of holy versus diabolical, discussing whether characters were saved or damned. The 1962 issue of *Sewanee* served a double role: it clarified the religious intention in O'Connor's stories and revitalized scholarship about her. Hawkes's article in particular led to additional studies in academic journals and located a canonical position for her that does not depend on a New Critical or a Christian reading.

O'Connor's Fiction and Institutional Politics

O'Connor has remained canonical in the academy precisely to the extent that her work has engaged a variety of readers of diverse critical perspectives. Crews's counterargument that O'Connor was canonized because of her New Critical training is anticipated by several mid-century accounts of post–World War II fiction. These studies point out the relationship between critical approaches and the literature published and praised by those associated with these approaches. O'Connor's fiction serves as a convenient example in these ideologically charged discussions. In 1954 Malcolm Cowley published a sociological description of the "new fiction," which, he argues, corresponds like the "new poetry" to the New Criticism. This new fiction attempts to provide a "moral realism" that deals with "permanent human situations" (52). But Cowley argues that it bears little relationship to people's lives and concerns: it is "non-social," "non-political," and "non-historical" (44).

Cowley does not mention O'Connor, who in 1954 had published only *Wise Blood* and the individual stories that make up *A Good Man Is Hard to Find,* but two years later John Aldridge listed her along with other writers associated with universities whose names appear "in issue after issue of the quarterlies." Aldridge contrasts writers such as Randal Jarrell, Mary McCarthy, Eudora Welty, Saul Bellow, Elizabeth Hardwick, O'Connor, Jean Stafford, Katherine Anne Porter, and Robie Macauley with those who "remained free of affiliation except to their craft"—Norman Mailer, James Jones, Irwin Shaw, and Gore Vidal. Aldridge argues that the quarterlies ignored the latter group not only because they were not associated with a university but also because "their novels had to do with such subjects as war, race, prejudice, sexual aberration, social maladjustment, neurosis, and insanity, or simply the way it was in 1945 or the winter of 1947, and these— now that the academy had attended to the burial of both the older realism and naturalism—were considered outside the province of the novel" (22). Like Cowley, Aldridge views attention to writers as part of an ideological struggle based on the writer's subject, treatment, and institutional association.

Aldridge focuses specifically on O'Connor in his criticisms of the *Kenyon* and *Sewanee* fellowships. He calls O'Connor a "distinctly minor novelist" and accounts for her receiving two Kenyon fellowships by suggesting that she has become the "official 'younger Southern novelist'" of the quarterlies: "In a sense, Miss O'Connor does for the academic intellectuals what Truman Capote does for the pseudo intellectuals of the flossy New York fashion-magazine world—she provides them with tone or chic, a little sprinkling of fake old magnolia blossoms" (59). Aldridge shows little evidence of having read O'Connor's fiction: her work is a useful example for his purposes because it has been widely published by the quarterlies he attacks. He structures his argument along ideological lines; O'Connor's stories serve as ammunition in this battle.

In a 1965 review, Irving Howe echoed the partisan nature of Cowley's and Aldridge's criticisms and prefigured Crews's 1990 questions about the value of O'Connor's fiction. His review demonstrates how he positioned himself in opposition to the New Critics and in support of writers associated with the New York intellectuals. Howe criticizes O'Connor's use of irony: "Miss O'Connor clearly intends us to savor a cluster of ironies; her sensibility as a writer of fiction was formed in a milieu where irony took on an almost totemic value. But there can be, as in much contemporary writing there is, a deep failure of ironic perception in a writer's unequivocal commitment to irony" (16). Anticipating Crews's argument, Howe identifies O'Connor's education with New Critical values. Academic readers in the mid-1960s would know that Howe was targeting Brooks and Warren in particular for their elevation of irony as a literary standard. He believes O'Connor's stories are too predictably ironic. For example, in "Everything That Rises Must Converge," "one [knows] that some kind of ironic reversal will occur in the relationship between mother and son." Crews uses the same phrase in his description of "the classroom formula of [O'Connor's] day": "point everything toward one neatly sprung ironic reversal" (49).

Howe acknowledges that O'Connor is "in control of the narrative line from beginning to end, and by the standards of many critics, that is the consummation of her art." But he is "moved by something more than control" in the stories of writers such as Delmore Schwartz, Norman Mailer, and Bernard Malamud. In their work, "there comes a moment when the unexpected happens, a perception, an insight, a confrontation which may not be in accord with the writer's original intention and may not be strictly required by the logic of the action but which nevertheless caps the story" (16).

Howe contrasts a New Critical emphasis on control and craftsmanship with the greater imagination he finds in the artists he names. That all three are Jewish New Yorkers, however, suggests that Howe's preferences are based on party ties.[15] He ends the review by lamenting O'Connor's early death, acknowledging that she "began to break past the fences of her skill and her ideas" in the late stories "Revelation" and "Parker's Back." Howe may be justified in preferring "Revelation" to "Everything That Rises Must Converge," but his language and examples indicate the difficulty of separating literary evaluation from institutional politics. Those like Aldridge,

Howe, and Crews who criticize O'Connor's fiction as a way to discuss larger ideological issues contribute to her canonicity. Surprisingly, despite Howe's reservations about her work, from 1972 to the present he has included "The Displaced Person" in his international *Classics of Modern Fiction*. Even more so than Rahv's *Eight Great American Short Novels*, Howe's title indicates that he believes O'Connor's novella is canonical.

Literary Histories and the Proliferation of Critical Approaches

A crucial transition in O'Connor's reception occurred when critics began to identify her work with categories outside the initial three: southern gothic, Catholic, masculinely powerful. R. W. B. Lewis was one of the first to place O'Connor's fiction in a broader frame. In a 1953 review of several novels, including *Wise Blood, The Old Man and the Sea,* and *Invisible Man,* Lewis argues that memorable American characters are "ec-centrics," outsiders. He maintains that despite claims about the death of the novel, these novels are alive for three reasons: they share this vital "outsider" theme; they are content "to exist—and not to atone for some truculence in nature or to affect the course of tomorrow's politics"; and they connect in an appropriate way with their literary predecessors. Even though Lewis uses O'Connor's fiction in a project of myth criticism, his argument retains New Critical traces in the value he places on these books' aesthetic distance from nature and politics.

In the late 1960s, literary historians began to discuss O'Connor's work in their treatments of the contemporary period. In *Radical Innocence* (1961), Ihab Hassan characterizes the heroes and antiheroes of post–World War II American fiction as rebel-victims "born under the shadow of nihilism" who share a trait of "radical and redemptive innocence." O'Connor's Haze Motes is one of these heroes; the "idea of the grotesque" is not southern but national. In the contemporary literature section of the 1963 revision of Robert Spiller's *Literary History of the United States,* Hassan concludes that O'Connor's irony and black humor ally her with other figures of the period: "Writers as different as Berger, Bellow, Hawkes, Burroughs, Heller, Purdy, and Flannery O'Connor shared a grotesque and ironic view of man. Through irony the fictional imagination endeavored to redeem reality" (in Spiller 1413, 1421–23; Hassan 78–79). Using existentialist vocabulary, Hassan gives New Critical value to irony and to the spiritual role of literature.

A flurry of critical studies of O'Connor's fiction appeared in the years following her death in 1964. The posthumous *Everything That Rises Must Converge* got sympathetic reviews even from those who had previously been negative. In contrast to its earlier one-paragraph dismissals, in 1965 the *New Yorker* printed a four-column treatment of *Everything That Rises Must Converge*, New Critically praising O'Connor's "powerful, economical, and elegant style" as her "most striking literary asset" (220). The reviewer insists that O'Connor "is not a provincial writer. Or if she is, her province is Christendom rather than the South" (220). O'Connor's southernness and Christianity are no longer the liabilities they were for *Time* and the *New Yorker* before her death.

Between 1969 and 1980, thirteen book-length studies of O'Connor were published. In the early 1970s she headed the list of the number of doctoral dissertations on fiction writers after 1930. In 1974, James Justus reported in *American Literary Scholarship:* "With four new books (and several more on the way), the usual spate of articles and notes, and the founding of the *Flannery O'Connor Bulletin,* the O'Connor industry now promises to rival that of Salinger years ago" (274). Justus laments that critiques of the New Criticism notwithstanding, most treatments of contemporary writers are still New Critical (264). More recent theoretical perspectives influenced O'Connor scholarship of the 1980s, such as Frederick Asals's psychoanalytic approach (1982), Louise Westling's feminist treatment (1985), Marshall Bruce Gentry's and Robert Brinkmeyer's Bakhtinian studies (1986, 1989), and James Mellard's Lacanian reading (1989).

During this period, several reconsiderations of O'Connor's canonicity also appeared, primarily focusing on her religious concerns. Critical studies by Josephine Hendin (1970), Martha Stephens (1973), and Carol Shloss

(1980) question whether an atheist can make the inferences about religious meanings O'Connor says she intended. In 1988 Ben Satterfield reflected the persistence of New Critical values when he argued that O'Connor's statements about her religious intentions have misled readers, giving her an academic stature her fiction does not deserve: "It is time to recognize that no sound artistic reason exists to continue inflating her reputation, and it is past time to cease stuffing critical (and not so critical) journals with glowing anagogical interpretations that use her fiction as a springboard for a dive into mystical speculation that is not justified by the work itself" (48). Satterfield's attack on O'Connor based on "the work itself" is strikingly New Critical.

Frederick Crews agrees that "O'Connor's stock is due for what Wall Street calls a correction. After all, the religious neo-orthodoxy of the post World War II university has long since evaporated." Crews insists that O'Connor's religious worldview is central to her fiction. It cannot be ignored or explained away through the use of sophisticated theoretical models. Instead, "in a time of rapidly expanding ethnic and egalitarian sentiment in the universities, O'Connor's provincial conservatism, especially with regard to the race issue, will probably come to seem harder to discount" (49). Like Howe, however, Crews finds himself testifying to "the power of Flannery O'Connor" even as he identifies the limitations of her work.

The variety of approaches to O'Connor's fiction over the past forty years is no doubt a testimony to critical ingenuity. Yet the history of her reception shows that her canonicity is based on much more than its fit with whatever New Critical values she learned at the University of Iowa and absorbed through the literary quarterlies. Recent literary histories demonstrate the range of value readers continue to find in her work. Three different writers discuss her fiction in the *Harvard Guide to Contemporary Literature* (1979) under the rubrics of southern literature, black humor, and experimental fiction. In the 1988 *Columbia Literary History of the United States,* Raymond Federman considers O'Connor an important precursor of the self-reflexive fiction of the 1970s; Malcolm Bradley includes her work as an example of neorealist fiction; and Larry McCaffrey compares the social alienation of the "most significant writers of the 1950s," including O'Connor, to the situation of the 1980s. What a New Critic would call the richness, tensions, contradictions, and "meaning on many levels" of O'Connor's work may testify both to the continuing institutional power of the New Criticism and to the ability of O'Connor's fiction to generate a response in many different readers. Her stories have engaged popular and elite audiences, naturalistic and religious readings, and a variety of critical approaches, but in the end it may be their ability to elude all these categories that continues to fascinate readers.

Notes

1. David Farmer's bibliography provides descriptions of the editions of O'Connor's books through 1979, including *Wise Blood* (10).

2. My analysis builds on recent studies of canonicity which argue that aesthetic value is constructed rather than absolute. Barbara Herrnstein Smith demonstrates that our literary judgments are economic and social, reflecting personal and public needs, desires, and experiences. Michel Foucault's discussion of discursive practices that work both to include and exclude literary works and William Cain's treatment of the role of literary histories in justifying Melville's canonization have helped me formulate questions about canon. Sharon O'Brien's study of Cather's reception illustrates how Cather's style has been described as feminine to place her as a "minor" writer.

3. These include Asals (1982), Spivey (1987), Ragen (1987), and Paulson (1988).

4. O'Connor appeared on four syllabi. Only five other women were included: Dickinson (in twenty courses), Wharton (eight), Chopin (eight), Jewett (six), and Bradstreet (six) (Lauter 19 n. 2).

5. As Jane Tompkins maintains in *Sensational Designs*, such connections are crucial in the making of literary reputations. Yet acknowledging the role of others in attracting attention to one's work does not necessarily denigrate its quality or indicate a conspiracy to make or break certain authors.

6. The New Critical orientation Allen Tate established when he edited the *Sewanee Review* from 1944 to 1945 retained an important influence on his successors. Andrew Lytle, *Sewanee* editor from 1942 to 1944 and 1961 to 1973, was also

an Agrarian writer and close friend of Allen Tate. Tate and Lytle continued on the editorial board throughout the 1950s and 1960s. In the spring and fall semesters of 1947, Lytle worked as fiction adviser in the Iowa Writers' Workshop, supervising O'Connor's work on *Wise Blood*.

7. Both contemporaneous and current accounts of the critical milieu identify the New Critics and the New York intellectuals as the dominant critical groups of the 1950s. These groupings are based on shared critical tenets and literary associations, but like any description of artistic and critical "schools," these labels emphasize group tendencies rather than individual differences.

8. Engle mentions O'Connor's "earnestness of theme" mixed with "warm humor" in "Greenleaf" but does not comment on the story's or author's religious concerns. Others such as Andrew Lytle, Robert Lowell, Robert Giroux, Robert and Sally Fitzgerald, and Caroline Gordon and Allen Tate valued O'Connor's religious perspective but did not present her as a religious writer until the late 1950s.

9. Kazin and Robert Lowell, who was also working at Yaddo, recommended O'Connor's work to Robert Giroux, who was to be her editor throughout most of her life.

10. Several critics discuss the formation of this cold war consensus, including Donald Pease in his study of liberal ideology and the American Studies movement, Lawrence Schwartz in his history of Faulkner's reception, and Gerald Graff in his institutional history, *Professing Literature*.

11. Howe became a professor at Brandeis in 1953; Rahv joined him in 1957; when William Phillips joined the faculty at Rutgers in 1963, the *Partisan* moved with him from New York (Leitch 113).

12. These include the publication of Cowley's *Portable Faulkner* (1946), Faulkner's successful publication of *Intruder in the Dust* (1948), the 1949 Nobel Prize, and the reissue of Faulkner's novels of the 1930s (Schwartz 66–70).

13. Southern is of course not equivalent to New Critical, but many influential New Critics such as Ransom, Brooks, Warren, Tate, and Gordon grew up in the South and valued writing by other southerners. The confluence of aesthetic, regional, and other affiliations is difficult to sort out. Did Warren and Erskine choose "The Life You Save" for *The New Southern Harvest* in 1957 because it was southern? New Critical? religious? familiar? Warren and Erskine also included sociological, even Marxist selections by Harriet Arnow and James Agee, attesting to the importance of southernness over and above other shared ideologies.

14. See Isaac Rosenfeld's *New Republic* review of *Wise Blood* for a similar criticism that the symbolism is imposed, not organic.

15. Louis Rubin's 1966 essay "Southerners and Jews" describes these competing literary groups. Reviewing several novels, including O'Connor's *Everything That Rises Must Converge* and Bellow's *Herzog,* Rubin explains, "It now transpires that it is not the Beats who apparently threaten the Southern hegemony. It is the Jews. Saul Bellow, Karl Shapiro, Bernard Malamud, Howard Nemerov, Norman Mailer, Philip Roth, Herbert Gold, Alfred Kazin, even 'Howl' Ginsberg, the Zen Talmudist—where did they appear from, and what are they about? I ask this question both as a Southerner and a Jew, which is to say, as one with a foot in each camp" (697).

Women, Language, and the Grotesque in Flannery O'Connor and Eudora Welty

Jeanne Campbell Reesman

A clubwoman in Jackson, Mississippi, once asked Eudora Welty to "just come and tell us one of your stories in your own words" (Welty, *Conversations* 256). Thus this essay begins with two beginnings. First, the opening lines of Flannery O'Connor's "Good Country People":

Besides the neutral expression that she wore when she was alone, Mrs. Freeman had two others, forward and reverse, that she used for all her human dealings. Her forward expression was steady and driving like the advance of a heavy truck. Her eyes never swerved to left or right but turned as the story turned as if they followed a yellow line down the center of it. She seldom used the other expression because it was not often necessary for her to retract a statement, but when she did, her face came to a complete stop, there was an almost imperceptible movement of her black eyes, during which they seemed to be receding, and then the observer would see that Mrs. Freeman, though she might stand there as real as several grain sacks thrown on top of each other, was no longer there in spirit. As for getting anything across to her when this was the case, Mrs. Hopewell had given it up. She might talk her head off. Mrs. Freeman could never be brought to admit herself wrong on any point.

And then, from Eudora Welty's "Why I Live at the P.O.":

I was getting along fine with Mama, Papa-Daddy and Uncle Rondo until my sister Stella-Rondo just separated from her husband and came back home again. Mr. Whitaker! Of course I went with Mr. Whitaker first, when he first appeared here in China Grove, taking "Pose yourself" photos, and Stella-Rondo broke us up. Told him I was one-sided. Bigger on one side than on the other, which is a deliberate, calculated falsehood: I'm the same. Stella-Rondo is exactly twelve months to the day younger than I am and for that reason she's spoiled. . . . So as soon as she got married and moved away from home the first thing she did was separate! From Mr. Whitaker! This photographer with the popeyes she said she trusted. Came home from one of those towns up in Illinois and to our complete surprise brought this child of two. Mama said she like to made her drop dead for a second. . . . "How?" says Mama, but all I says was "H'm!" There I was over the hot stove, trying to stretch two chickens over five people and a completely unexpected child into the bargain, without one moment's notice.

O'Connor and Welty brilliantly and unrelentingly invoke the grotesque, with characters talking their heads off, dropping dead, stretching chickens over five people and one child. Recent approaches to the related topics of the body as *topos,* of voice in women's writing, and of the "dialogics" of narrative suggest new roles for the grotesque, and such a combined approach to reading O'Connor and Welty reveals the multifaceted nature of their grotesques as social as well as personal and spiritual phenomena.[1]

Why, as has often been asked, does southern literature contain so much grotesque? Clearly frontier society is a factor, for marginality gives rise to the grotesque. The experience of a decadent society has accentuated southerners' eccentric status outside the mainstream; the degree to which Old South society was built on oppressive race, class, and gender designations is the degree to which it is grotesque, and this has been the subject of the "classics" of southern literature. But arising from frontier days is a cruder southern tradition, the folk literary tradition of the Old Southwest—that of Augustus Baldwin Longstreet, Johnson Jones Hooper, and Joel Chandler Harris. Here there is a relentless focus on the grotesque boundaries of human or animal bodies and their conjunctions (Rickels 155–66). Bodies in this enduring tradition are profoundly anticlassical; they emphasize reduction, enlargement, deformity, mutilation, death, eating, drinking, digestion, defecation, sexuality. The humor of the Old Southwest often portrays the body in terms of self-deprecation and self-praise at the same time, as in the characteristic hillbilly story of shooting an elusive prey while defecating in the woods. Thus grotesque southern literature can be tied to an individual's sense of positive power and to the celebration of individual freedom. At the same time, the "classical" grotesque illustrates an individual's or a society's distortion, that is, its distance from some ideal state. The grotesque simultaneously—and dialogically—acknowledges the social and spiritual realms in which the individual resides; through negative example, the grotesque reasserts an outraged individual or social norm.

O'Connor and Welty adapt these dual southern grotesque traditions to their own purposes, which, though not identical, are parallel, especially in their invocation of a feminine grotesque. Whether asserting the individual or the society, the grotesque inhabits borders and displays tolerance for borders and for crossing them. Indeed, the grotesque is at its most characteristic when it enjoins us to reexamine borders between individual bodies and their environments. The spiritual or transpersonal located within physicality is explored by Edgar Allan Poe, Mark Twain, William Faulkner, Truman Capote, Walker Percy, and James Dickey in their treatments of southern marginalities of race, class, and identity, but in O'Connor and Welty, and to a lesser extent in such southern women writers as Katherine Anne Porter, Carson McCullers, or Zora Neale Hurston, the grotesque takes on a dimension larger than the southern cultural one: it is revealed most of all as a gender issue.

Most of O'Connor's and Welty's characters are women who have their eyes opened to some truth about themselves. Yet it may be better to say that their ears are opened, in that in their work the grotesque—historically a visual event—becomes a visual device verbalized. Women in these stories talk and talk in seemingly endless clichés about subjects at once everyday and cataclysmic: sexuality, birth, deformity, abuse, death. In their talk of survival, the disjunction between subject and tone can only be described as grotesque. Characters' and readers' ears too are opened to the unexpected in the midst of the banal.[2]

The objectifying of women's bodies in southern fiction is obviously connected to the question of the ownership of the body in the South. Unable for the most part to escape the conventions that historically allowed ownership of the bodies of African Americans, these women cannot escape those conventions that own *them*. O'Connor and Welty suggest that whatever women in the South have had to say on the subjects of racism and sexism has for the most part been unsaid or deflected; characters' speaking in clichés is an unconscious attempt to draw attention to their sense of powerlessness. Their conscious or unconscious awareness of the traditional South as itself grotesque is coupled with their sense of themselves as unaddressed others and is reflected in their speech. An "empty" language thus reflects an emptiness.

But in O'Connor and Welty this empty language harbors the grotesque, which leaks out as it must. O'Connor's and Welty's women load their conversation with visual images that highlight the clash between conventionality and reality, and if we take literally some of their visual clichés, whether voiced by characters or the narrator, as I believe we are meant to, then what is being said is anything but empty. Through metaphors of yelling your head off, being fit to be tied, dropping dead, being born twelve months apart, the grotesque dimension reverses the usual figurative effect of literary language, creating a new and uncanny plane of meaning on which metaphors threaten to become real. This alarming effect points to what one scholar of the grotesque calls "play with the forbidden," a "temporary gratification of banned desires" as "a means of expressing a perceived lack of control" (Cassuto 135, 138, 140). Such multiplicitous reversals of categories as I have been describing have inhabited the grotesque since its beginnings.

Something is grotesque when it violates our notions of reality by combining the dissimilar elements of horror and humor, whether termed the uncanny and the comic (Steig 259) or the ludicrous and the fearful (Ruskin 126). Generally features of the human body are startlingly combined with features of animals or plants, or, in the modern world, machines. Incongruity is the key. Our ambivalent laughter stems from what Philip Thom-

son calls a "clash between incompatible reactions" (2–3) and Wolfgang
Kayser terms "an estranged world" that is also one of "secret liberation"
(Kayser 188). In addition to disharmony, the grotesque features extrava-
gance, exaggeration, abnormality, and very often the physical sense of
something protruding into another space. The grotesque may take the
form of—though it is never identical with—satire, the absurd, the bizarre,
the macabre, caricature, parody, irony, or the comic, but it is always the
"ambivalently abnormal" (Thomson 27–28). It is, in short, the grotesque's
sense of *otherness* that informs all its manifestations. It always retains its
visual nature, marginality, and corporeality derived from its origins in depictions of human bodies featuring animal or vegetable body parts. These
depictions are found in the prehistoric cave paintings at Lascaux, but the
later appearance of grotesque murals in the "caves" or "grottoes" of ancient
Roman palaces unearthed during the Renaissance gave the grostesque
its name.

The grotesque in O'Connor means, as she noted, that "it is the extreme situation that best reveals what we are essentially" (*MM* 58), and
certainly her stories are all concerned with exposing the mysteries of the
buried inner life (Vande Kieft 45). But this inner life exists within more
contexts than just that of the individual, and it is in the end not to be
simply "exposed." The inner life in both O'Connor's and Welty's work is
in constant contact with spiritual and social worlds, and contact is made
through the grotesque. The feminine grotesques offered by O'Connor
and Welty simultaneously address the personal, spiritual, and social realms
of existence, joining them dialogically through their multiple referential
capacities.

Similar as they are, O'Connor's and Welty's treatments of the spiritual
grotesque are not identical (Lawson, Sloane).[3] Not "seeing" is the central
sin in O'Connor's stories, but in violent visionary moments, sinners can
see themselves in relation to God better than believers in complacent pi-
eties. Indeed, the grotesque has the odd effect of pointing the finger at
everything that is not (or does not consider itself) grotesque and making it
so. Richard Poirier describes O'Connor characters who are damned "pre-

cisely to the degree that they lack Miss O'Connor's own 'measure' of their trivialities." At the same time, O'Connor "can show in people who have been almost preposterously flat a sudden visionary capacity" (Poirier 46). In O'Connor's mind the regional and religious grotesques are intimately connected. She remarked, "Of course, I have found that anything that comes out of the South is going to be called grotesque by the Northern reader, unless it is grotesque, in which case it is going to be called realistic" (*MM* 40). She continues, "Whenever I'm asked why Southern writers particularly have a penchant for writing about freaks, I say it is because we are still able to recognize one. To be able to recognize a freak, you have to have some conception of the whole man, and in the South the general conception of man is still, in the main, theological" (44).

Welty does not share O'Connor's severe religious argument. But Welty does rely heavily on her knowledge of mythology, and, as in O'Connor, this cosmic dimension is sometimes shockingly yoked together with the particulars of everyday life in nature and in human society. Alice Walker relates how a young student described his study of O'Connor under Welty's direction: "'I don't think Welty and O'Connor understood each *other*. . . . For Welty's part, wherever we reached a particularly dense and symbolic section of one of O'Connor's stories she would sigh and ask, "Is there a Catholic in the class?"'" (Walker 56). Though Welty's humanist approach is very different from O'Connor's religious one, at the heart of both is the idea of *relationship:* first the exploration of the individual heart, then how personal identity, operating under often unexamined cultural codes, couples with the body of society, and finally how the individual can be said to be part of a spiritual body as well. The function of the grotesque in O'Connor and Welty—especially O'Connor—has been well-described by many critics as a personal and a metaphysical phenomenon, but what has been lacking is analysis of the social function of the grotesque for female protagonists in these authors' fiction.[4]

The most rewarding theorist to keep in mind in analyzing these authors is Mikhail Bakhtin, whose notion of the grotesque "liberates the world from all that is dark and terrifying" by offering a "regenerating ambivalence" that produces wholeness. For Bakhtin the "carnival laughter" of the grotesque is the universal laughter "of all of the people" (*Rabelais* 47, 11–12, 20–21). The body's margins (mouth, genitals, breasts, phallus, nose, potbelly) take on special grotesque meaning. Though grotesque realisms may "degrade, bring down to earth, turn their subject into flesh," what "ambivalent" laughter degrades it also "materializes." It is "always conceiving," for "to degrade is to bury, to sow, and to kill simultaneously, in order to bring forth something more and better." This is why actions that involve copulation, birth, or defecation are dwelled upon in the grotesque: "To degrade an object does not imply merely hurling it into the void of nonexistence, into absolute destruction, but to hurl it down to the reproductive lower stratum, the zone in which conception and new birth take place." The body through its protuberances and entries, its transgressing limits, its *contact* with the rest of the world, "discloses its essence as a principle of growth" (315, 19–22, 26–27). The primary grotesque scene for Bakhtin is birth, the act that distinguishes the female body.[5]

The word born of the grotesque, then, is *fertile,* and in the case of the women in O'Connor's and Welty's stories, it is often the only way they are able to address their tenuous social status. Bakhtin argues that because all language is "dialogic," a living event between real people, it is also an area of social conflict in which words are saturated with the various perceptions of other words. Discourse may disrupt and subvert the authority of prevailing ideology. Even more than language in general, literary language *addresses* rather than defines. Bakhtin calls the power of the word to overturn fixed realities a "carnivalizing" function, for he compares it to the overturning of hierarchies of power that occurs in carnival, in which the people of a community express both their sense of being victims of power and their own power to subvert or overturn oppressive institutions, such as the king. But it is an indirect attack, much like those of the women of O'Connor's and Welty's grotesque worlds.

When we put together the marginalized word attempting to address and relativize the king figure—aristocratic, masculine, oppressive—with the feminine grotesques uttered by O'Connor's and Welty's women characters, Bakhtin's relevance for reading southern women writers can be seen in their grotesque dialogics of the body. Certainly O'Connor and Welty are practicing in their grotesques Bakhtin's *heteroglossia* in the literalized clichés their characters utter. The stories of O'Connor and Welty are structured dialogically in scenes that portray failed and sometimes successful attempts at communication in the characters' "own words."[6] In interviews Welty has repeatedly characterized her writing technique as "listening" or writing "by ear." As is true of O'Connor, dialogue is the most complex part of her work: "Dialogue has to show not only something about the speaker that is its own revelation, but also maybe something about the speaker that he doesn't know but the other character does know. . . . Dialogue is action" (*Conversations* 279).[7]

In O'Connor's "Good Country People" the grotesque arises from jarring juxtapositions, radiating from Joy/Hulga's artificial leg, which symbolizes her artificiality of self, that is, its lack of borders. The story opens not with her but with the comparison of Mrs. Freeman's face to a truck and the clichéd description of Mrs. Hopewell "talking her head off," literalized by the grotesque dimension. These women are in danger—of youthful and hasty marriage, of boredom, of depression, of physical injury, of scorn by family members, of spiritual emptiness, of being swindled, of being raped—and the grotesque in their language and the narrator's alerts us to such urgencies.

In the opening passage and later in the story the traditional grotesque animal/human or plant/human imagery is partially replaced by mechanical/human figures. The reference to the grain sacks not only helps us to see Mrs. Freeman's lumpy body but ironically connects the truck image to primeval fertility goddesses. Joy/Hulga later responds to her mother's addresses "in a purely mechanical way," and one of her visions is of "the ugly sweating Vulcan who stayed in the furnace and to whom, presumably, the goddess had to come when called," a vision Joy/Hulga associates with her name, her "highest creative act." Indeed, she knows "her mother had not been able to turn her dust into joy," and Mrs. Freeman's "beady steel-pointed eyes" have not penetrated far enough to find her own "secret infection" or "hidden deformity" of the spirit, though they have gone far. Mrs. Freeman does enjoy hearing "at any time as if it had happened an hour ago" the details of how Joy/Hulga's leg had been shot off by her father (*CS* 274–75). Later the "obscenity of the suggestion" from the Bible salesman that Joy/Hulga remove her leg is made even more mysterious by Mrs. Freeman's inquiries (288). What Joy/Hulga does not see is that her grotesquerie and Mrs. Freeman's are connected.

Standing "against the wall and roll[ing] her head from side to side" (273), Joy/Hulga does not talk with anyone unless she has to because she is convinced that meaning does not exist—until, that is, she is confronted by the Bible salesman. Juxtaposed to the grotesque physical description of Joy/Hulga are Mrs. Freeman's and Mrs. Hopewell's empty conversational clichés, some of which arise from their talking around Joy's deformity: " 'Everybody is different,' Mrs. Hopewell said. 'Yes, most people is,' Mrs. Freeman said. 'It takes all kinds to make the world.' 'I always did say it myself' " (273). But *how* different?

O'Connor apparently believed that being set apart from society could sometimes have positive effects on the deformed one. She marked Mircea Eliade's passage in her copy of *Patterns in Comparative Religion:* "Thus ugliness and deformities, while marking out those who possess them, at the same time makes them sacred" (Feeley 24). But who is deformed and who is sacred in this story? The grotesque violation committed upon Joy/Hulga has the effect both of humanizing her and of spiritualizing her and her view of the world. Is she the only one against whom a grotesque act is committed? We quickly forget, when confronted with Manly's aggression, her own urge to seduce and humiliate him. We have trouble seeing these characters.

The ocular metaphor in "Good Country People" is important, the pattern coming to fruition when Joy/Hulga loses her eyeglasses at the end of the story, but her internal vision has been readjusted. It is in many ways a story about looking and not seeing, with great stress laid on the repeated references to watching, eyes, or inner vision. But from Joy/Hulga's squint to Glynese's sty, vision in this world is faulty, perhaps the reason her father accidentally shot off her leg when she was a child. Joy tells us that she sees from afar or "through to nothing," but Manly's eyes are described as "steel spikes" (*CS* 289), and after all he carries a glass eye he got from a previous conquest. Vision itself is grotesque.

Opposed to reductive ocularity is a host of verbal images. Mrs. Hopewell lies about having "the Word" in the house, and of course Manly tries to make Joy/Hulga say she loves him. The cliché of the title becomes terribly ironic; the literalizations of grotesque clichés acknowledge truth, as Joy/Hulga hopes when she renames herself. And when Manly, whose speech is the most countrified and awkward to start, asks Joy/Hulga whether she is shy, he dialogically moves right to the point, so to speak. He reveals himself in language, not appearance: when he says he believes in nothing we believe him. At the end Joy/Hulga stumbles blindly with his final words aching in her ears.

O'Connor's characters' self-hatred of the female body is sometimes overcome and sometimes not (Kahane "Maternal" 2). Joy/Hulga's rage against her femininity is grotesquely turned against itself, perhaps to heal her. O'Connor holds out hope for those who are able to see and address their grotesque selves; Joy/Hulga, "her face purple and her mouth half full," earlier demands of her mother, when she can stand no more of her and Mrs. Freeman's advice that "a smile never hurt anyone," " 'Woman! do you ever look inside? Do you ever look inside and see what you are *not?*' " Joy/Hulga has the opportunity to do just that, and in encountering her violation we not only witness her startling moment of self-knowledge, but also, through the story's grotesqueries, we find the boundaries blurred between our own worlds, inner and outer, verbal and visual. If Joy's "weak heart" is strengthened and her deformity overcome by a grotesque violation, we must continue to ask about the grotesque world in which this occurs, a world that goes on in Mrs. Freeman's and Mrs. Hopewell's inane conversation at the story's conclusion. How much of their conversation masks the violations of women that occur daily in their society? How much of what they say *is* a violation? O'Connor leaves us, like Joy/Hulga, waiting for answers.

We all seem to remember the grandmother's death in "A Good Man Is Hard to Find," though we do not give much thought to the deaths of the other family members. This is a grotesquerie in ourselves, notwithstanding that the other family members are presented in graphic animal and vegetable images. Readers vary in their reactions to the grandmother, but it is easy to reject her daughter-in-law, who has a "face as broad and innocent as a cabbage" and who wears "a green head-kerchief that had two points on the top like a rabbit's ears" (CS 117). Her son, Bailey Boy, with his yellow and blue parrot shirt, is even less likable. The grandmother embodies some of the worst and best of what O'Connor presented as feminine, but what is important is that she is described as a voice and not another "dumb animal." Like Joy/Hulga, she is violated and asks the right questions of the violator; in the process, she finds truth. Her verbal touch is deadly to the Misfit's love of meanness, his failed antidote to truth.

A cat—which the grandmother brings along because it might be asphyxiated by the gas stove jets if left at home—causes the immediate trouble in the story by flinging itself onto Bailey's back as he drives the family car. In the end the Misfit is remade through an animal image, when the grandmother's touch galvanizes him as though a snake had touched his chest instead of her hand. But the humans are all adequate generators of the grotesque themselves, as we see in the case of Red Sammy Butts, whose highway sign advertises, "TRY RED SAMMY'S FAMOUS BARBEQUE. NONE LIKE FAMOUS RED SAMMY'S! RED SAM! THE FAT BOY WITH THE HAPPY LAUGH! A VETERAN! RED SAMMY'S YOUR MAN!" (120–21). The monkey in the chinaberry tree seems only an extension of the grotesqueness of Red Sammy himself; after all, Red Sammy's stomach is described as swinging like a full sack of meal. We are also told that when the grandmother "told a story, she rolled her eyes and waved her head and was very dramatic," as when she tells how she was courted by a man, Mr. Edgar Atkins Teagarden of Jasper, Georgia, who would write "E.A.T. Well" in watermelons he got for her (120). Certainly the grotesque focus is on appearance, even the Misfit's "scholarly look." Yet the grandmother "recognizes" him under his "look" (127–29).

According to O'Connor, the grandmother occupies the "most significant position" the Christian life offers, the moment of facing death, and she does not do it alone: her "gesture . . . is unlike any other in the story. . . . [It is] both totally right and totally unexpected," both "in character" and "beyond character." Reality is something to which "we must be returned at considerable cost," and a person in a desperate situation will often reveal "those qualities least dispensable in his personality, those qualities . . . he will have to take into eternity with him." The grandmother's action has entered the Misfit's heart like a mustard seed and will grow into "a great crow-filled tree in the Misfit's heart, and will . . . turn him into the prophet he was meant to become" (*MM* 109–11, 114).

In an important way the story is about how her redemptive power arises from the grandmother's femininity. It was the grandmother who wanted to avoid Florida and visit some of her "connections" in Tennessee. She is still seeking connections, still the " 'talker' " in the end, talking of "babies" and "children"; through her grotesque nurturing act she is both destroyed and redeemed. Her real children, already dead in the woods, are too late for her redemptive mothering—they are dead because of her desire to re-experience her own childhood. But like the Misfit, who killed his father, she is never on her own, especially in death.

The heroine of Welty's "Petrified Man" is similarly outcast but in community. Welty says she sent "Petrified Man" "all over to every magazine in the U.S.A." but everyone sent it back. Welty burned it. When the *Southern Review* reconsidered, she rewrote it from memory: "But that was a 'by ear' story," she says, one she "could just listen to . . . and click, could play it back as if it were on a tape" (*Conversations* 257–58). "Petrified Man" is a story about storytelling; the plot is structured around a series of conversations, mainly voiced by and focusing on the beautician Leota, for whom storytelling is the means "of creating community," as Libby F. Jones notes. Leota attempts through speech to combat the isolation she experiences inside her lavender booth; she has only a single inadequate relationship with her husband, who "lays" around the house "like a rug," to sustain her (Jones 65, 67–69). Despite Leota's efforts, "Petrified Man" is a story of inarticulate rage.

Peter Schmidt rightly finds it odd that critics are seemingly unanimous "in blaming the women in the story for the perversions of sexuality that it depicts." Instead, we should examine how the story draws connections between "representations of women in advertising and violence toward women in society." He describes Leota's beauty parlor as "an elegantly appointed torture chamber with the female body as its victim" and notes the phrases Welty uses to indicate how the beauty parlor can remake nature: there are "aluminum wave pinchers," hairdrying machines that "cook" their occupants, one's natural hair shape is given a new "body" called a "permanent" (which of course is not really permanent—Mrs. Fletcher speaks of her "'last permanent'"), and makeup that changes a natural smile into a "fixed" one (Welty, *Collected Stories* 18, 28). Sexual relations in the story cause everything from dandruff to pregnancy, and it seems far better to be "gratified" in one of the booths. Leota spells out "'p.r.e.g.,'" as though it cannot be named aloud, and then asks Mrs. Fletcher, "'how far gone are you?,'" implying that pregnancy is a kind of dying (20). Significantly, Schmidt notes, the freak show is right next door to the beauty parlor, and it further comments on their grotesque view of themselves. But the most dangerous deception in the beauty parlor is that it is a place where women can exert some power by mocking their men; of course, they really have no more power there than they do anywhere else (Schmidt 83–87). Talk seems to be the only way out of this mirror game, the only satisfying way of mediating reality—suspect as talk may be.

From Leota's opening words, "'Reach in my purse and git me a cigarette without no powder in it if you kin, Mrs. Fletcher, honey. . . . I don't like no perfumed cigarettes'" (*CS* 17), to Billy Boy's wonderful last ones, "'If you're so smart why ain't you rich?'" (28), "Petrified Man" offers an even stronger reliance on voice and a rejection of ocularity than many of Welty's other works; its perfection of ear is astonishing. Giving rise to the many grotesque statements of the characters are the grotesque situations in which they find themselves: the rituals of the beauty parlor, the freak show, the identification and capture of the "petrified" rapist, Mr. Petrie— all powerfully visual but presented in hilariously idiomatic language. Until Billy Boy, male characters are offstage and unheard from, and male-female violence is described by the female voice (see Prenshaw xvi). The women's talk also carries extreme tension. An important theme is Leota's grotesque reversal of pride going before a fall, yet the story's disturbing undercurrent of violence and sexual hatred amounts to more than that.

With women around them "half wound for a spiral," Leota and Mrs. Fletcher discuss Mrs. Fletcher's unwanted pregnancy and Leota's new friend Mrs. Pike. The focus is on grotesque juxtapositions between humans and machines, as Leota asks Mrs. Fletcher, "'Now go git under the dryer. You can turn yourself on, can't you?'" (23). There is violence: "Leota was almost choking her with the cloth, pinning it so tight, and she couldn't speak clearly. She paddled her hands in the air until Leota wearily loosened her" (24). Leota likes Mrs. Pike because she keeps "'a sharp eye out'" (17). When Mrs. Fletcher angrily discovers that it was Mrs. Pike who told Leota she is pregnant, Leota tells her, "'Mrs. Pike ain't goin' to bite you.'" To mollify Mrs. Fletcher, Leota tells her they visited the freak show, especially remarking on the twins in the bottle. Already the violent grotesque juxtapositions—Mrs. Fletcher's pregnancy and the twins in the bottle, for one—are accumulating faster than they can be dealt with. Leota goes on to describe "'the teeniest men in the universe,'" the freak show's pygmies who can "'just rest back on their little bohunkus an' roll around an' you can't hardly tell if they're sittin' or standing. . . . Just suppose it was your husband!'" The description of the petrified man, whose joints are supposedly turning to stone, is the climax that connects the personal and interpersonal levels of the story into social ones: "'A course he *looks* just *terrible*'" (20–21). So do the blowsy Leota and the tight-ringleted Mrs. Fletcher, whose hennaed hair falls for most of the story like a frazzled storm cloud. Beauty is important to these ladies, and they are ugly; the spiritual adviser and fortune teller Lady Evangeline may have the "sixth mind," according to Mrs. Pike, but she has "'the worst manicure I ever saw on a living person'" (22). None of them directly addresses men as the oppressors (as creators of the beautiful images the women strive for), but they get some revenge: their description of the petrified man unconsciously neutralizes his threat, and Mrs. Pike's sharp eye and tongue allow her to recognize him and name him as the rapist to win the reward posted in *Startling G-Man Tales*. After all, we must recall that his being "petrified" is a literalized version of the Medusa myth. He has looked at the freaks who look at him, as it were, and has been reduced by the female gaze; and furthermore, he is *named* by the women who gaze at him.

As though to express their repressed anger, the women's clichés take on a more and more peculiar literalism as the story progresses, for example, Leota's description of the woman in labor who wants a permanent wave before she goes to the hospital: "'She yelled bloody murder, too, but she always yelled her head off when I give her a perm'nent'" (24). Newly pregnant, Mrs. Fletcher plots her abortion. There are other strange juxtapositions: "''Honey me an' Fred, we met in a rumble seat eight months ago and we was practically on what you might call the way to the altar inside of half an hour,' said Leota in a guttural voice, and bit a bobby pin open. 'Course it don't last. Mrs. Pike says nothin' like that ever lasts'" (23). Sexual grotesquerie reaches its crescendo when the ring of "wild-haired ladies" (28) futilely beats Billy-Boy.

Despite their victory over the rapist, little changes. The women still seek to attract and are repulsed by their husbands, and Leota loses hers in the process of the story, along with the reward money for the rapist masquerading as the petrified man—the money and possibly the husband go to Mrs. Pike. Giving voice to their inarticulate awareness of their situations, the women are defeated in the end by the stinging words of a little boy abandoned by his mother to a weird community of outraged women.

We might not at first think of "A Worn Path" as a grotesque story, for it is gentle, lyrical, and affirmative. Marshall Bruce Gentry writes of O'Connor that almost never are her characters "considered admirable *because* they are grotesque" ("Eye vs. Body" 488); his remarks apply just as well to Welty, especially in regard to this story. Gentry identifies O'Connor's grotesque redemptions as arising from "the action of the individual [character's] unconscious" so that physical distress or degradation or even annihilation can be a transformative, redemptive experience. Because it represents as well as perceives, it is also a positive, even ideal or religious, activity (*Religion* 4, 10–11). Similarly, in "A Worn Path" we *perceive* grotesque representations at the same time that our understanding normalizes what is presented as grotesque. The story illustrates divisions in society even as it brings members of its world together.

In a discussion of *The Golden Apples*, Lowry Pei says reading Welty's stories is like experiencing "that other subjectivity . . . something we can see (for a moment) but cannot share." Language is the means by which we attempt to bridge the gap between "the accustomed subjectivity that is over here and the bewildering one that is over there." Welty often models this communicative function on the gap between nature and our perceptions of it (Pei 415–18, 429). She uses a particular grotesque language to do this, most effectively through a female speaker who is close to her own perception of the world. Phoenix gives us that "other" that is "over there" in her communion with the natural world around her as she goes to get medicine for her grandson's terribly scarred throat, but she gives us back ourselves in the world, too, through her marvelous voice. Her throat is well, and it can heal others.

Phoenix's speech contains grotesque references, such as to the two-headed snake, but its gentle, poetic eloquence contrasts sharply with the edginess of the instrumental and patronizing speech she hears from the white people she encounters. Its realistic folk language frees the narrator "for a kind of surreal lyricism" that reinforces sympathy for the characters as well as achieves the goal of poetry, according to Ronald R. Butters. Furthermore, Phoenix's speech is devoid of the standard markers that show phonological deviation to indicate folk speech; that is, though it contains many features of black English, such as double negatives and the invariant *be*, these features are softened because of the absence of "eye dialect," such as deliberate misspellings ("kin" for "can" and the like). Phoenix is sympathetic in ways that neither the narrator of "Why I Live at the P.O." nor Leota of "Petrified Man" is, for their speech is heavily peppered with such stigmatized lexical items. Welty deliberately elevates Phoenix's speech (Butters 34–37).

In Phoenix the grotesque is moved away from the main character and directed outward into the world; grotesque juxtapositions occur between Phoenix and the whites she encounters, between her frailty and her act of will, between that effort and the probable sad outcome of her grandson's condition. What is *not* sharply contrasted in juxtaposition are Phoenix and the natural world around her. She addresses the thorn bush, the alligators, the other animals and plants and fences and ditches of the woods. She passes "big dead trees, like black men with one arm," and enters a corn field that "whispers" to her. When she trips and falls, she lies there like " 'a June-bug waiting to be turned over.' " Animal imagery further accentuates her essential wholeness rather than any grotesque dualism. For example, her cane tapping the frozen ground as she makes her Christmas walk to town to get medicine is likened to "the chirping of a solitary little bird." In contrast, the young white hunter carries a game bag with one "little closed claw" hanging out, one of the bob-whites Phoenix previously greeted, "its beak hooked bitterly to show it was dead" (*Collected Stories* 142, 144–45). Our emotional identification with Phoenix is strangely coupled with a sense of both our distance from her and our communion in the natural world with her.

Perhaps that is the end result of the grotesque, after all, as Bakhtin would argue: the urge to connect across a gulf. The grotesque can lead to renewal and rebirth, if not of the flesh then of the restless spirit that resides within it. Phoenix and her little grandson are, she says, " 'the only two left in the world.' " But he has a " 'sweet look,' " wearing a scrap of quilt from behind which he " 'peep[s] out holding his mouth open like a little bird,' " and he will be glad for his medicine and the little paper windmill his grandmother brings him (148–49).

Notes

1. Leonard Cassuto has explored the grotesque as a cultural rather than personal phenomenon. Cassuto identifies the grotesque as *socially* constructed to explain why different societies find different things grotesque. The grotesque does not just transgress the limits of the body but of society, too, often furnishing "trenchant social criticism." The more serious the violation, "the greater the danger, and the more fearful the grotesque." As he concludes, "The [grotesque] gesture thereby becomes a miniature attempt to organize and control the world" (113, 93–94).

2. O'Connor's and Welty's fictions beautifully fit Joyce Carol Oates's description of how an essentially "arch" tone can reveal a "black comic-naturalism" made all the more realistic by its presentation within the "chatty life" of everyday existence. "What shocks us about this art," Oates writes of Welty, "is its delicate blending of the casual and the tragic, the essential femininity of the narration and subject, the reality, which is narrated" (71–74).

3. On this point see also Gentry ("The Eye vs. the Body"), Kessler, Muller, and Neuleib.

4. An exception to this lack is that in his analysis of *Wise Blood,* Marshall Bruce Gentry observes that while the displaced grotesque character is displaced from a hostile society, at the same time "the grotesquerie of a character is a sign of that character's participation in the redemption of his community" ("The Eye vs. the Body" 489). The issue becomes the character's inner displacement as well as outer alienation. As O'Connor put it, grotesque characters "have an inner coherence, if not always a coherence to their social framework. Their fictional qualities lean away from typical social patterns, toward mystery and the unexpected" (*MM* 14).

5. Claire Kahane has described the imaginative exploration of the boundaries of the body in the gothic genre as an issue of "relation to power, sexuality, and the maternal body"; O'Connor's characters, for example, stare or are stared at as they approach discovery of the "dark secret center" of the body, "as if looking were a matter of life and death" (Kahane "Maternal" 243–44).

6. Cleanth Brooks identifies Welty's use of dialect with something like Bakhtin's social analysis of language when he refers to her characters' talk as "rich and exuberant" because spoken in a variety of voices: "male and female, gentle and quiet or aggressive and domineering, querulous and argumentative or ironic and conciliatory; but they are all voices of the folk and speak the characteristic folly or wisdom, joy or melancholy, of such a community" (Brooks 102). Robert H. Brinkmeyer, Jr., has linked O'Connor and Bakhtin, particularly as they address the "differing reali-

ties" within characters: "There is no transcendent, defining order looming behind the interactions of people; there is not one reality, but many, each stemming from a living person." The relation to O'Connor's religious belief is plain: "Such a dialogic dismantling of the self frees it from the tyranny of its self-image, allowing for . . . growth and understanding." Thus O'Connor resists imposing her Catholicism on her fiction monologically, for to do so would be detrimental to art. Instead she was highly conscious that religious faith must be tested, that one's faith "must be continually probing and searching out other perspectives of reality," an activity she called "Christian skepticism" (Brinkmeyer 13–18, 24).

7. Southerners are born narrators, Welty believes: "In the South so many things are going on simultaneously, and many stories are being told at the same time. Sometimes two different people are telling the same story in two different parts of the room. That's challenging!" (*Conversations* 279).

Gender Dialogue in O'Connor

Marshall Bruce Gentry

Men and women battle constantly in O'Connor's works, but apparently critics have been reluctant to question or analyze what seems obvious: men always win. Even when Bakhtinian dialogism in O'Connor is being discussed, the battle between the authoritarian narrator and the rebellious characters has been described as a conflict based on differences in religious viewpoint, not gender specifically. Perhaps this silence is because Bakhtin seems to have a blind spot regarding feminism (Booth 154).[1] I believe that women win frequently, however. After arguing that the typical O'Connor narrator is a rigidly patriarchal female who promotes gender separation, I will show that O'Connor characters frequently find redemption as they move toward androgyny. The feminine becomes a source for the characters' rebellion, for voices that compete with the narrator's voice for authority. In the course of a given work, while maintaining a battle against the narrator, a female character discovers strengths that are masculine (especially by patriarchal standards), or a male character discovers his female side and the advantages of the feminine.

O'Connor typically claimed that she did not care much about gender. To her correspondent called "A," O'Connor wrote on 22 September 1956: "On the subject of the feminist business, I just never think . . . of qualities which are specifically feminine or masculine. I suppose I divide people into two classes: the Irksome and the Non-Irksome without regard to sex. Yes and there are the Medium Irksome and the Rare Irksome" (*HB* 176). Louise Westling has argued that O'Connor allied herself with masculine authority more than with other women ("Revelations" 19). After reading Westling's arguments about O'Connor's complicated sense of her own gender, one can easily conclude that when O'Connor's fiction is dialogic, gender is one of the areas of dispute, and one is likely to take seriously O'Connor's concession to her correspondent "A," in a letter dated 2 August 1955: "You are right that I won't ever be able entirely to understand my own work or even my own motivations" (*HB* 92; *CW* 944).

Frederick Crews, who has portrayed O'Connor in the *New York Review of Books* as an overly conscious crafter of stories that fit the academic model of her time (49), says that "nowhere" in her fiction does he find O'Connor's irony directed at her narrators (50), so perhaps it is worthwhile considering a couple of examples in which mockery of a narrator is fairly explicit. In a letter to Sally and Robert Fitzgerald dated 20 December 1952, O'Connor ridicules one of the local farm wives who narrates the story of another farm wife. I quote the passage with Sally Fitzgerald's editorial insertions in *The Habit of Being* (the passage was revised slightly for its publication in *CW* 905–6):

Mrs. P. [farm wife] met Mrs. O. [former farm wife] wandering around downtown yesterday. They didn't take to each other atall but Mrs. P. never loses an opportunity to get any information about anything whatsoever so she stopped her and asked if Mr. O. was working *yet*. Well, says [his wife] (whine), dairy work is so reglar, we decided he better just had get him a job where he could work when he wanted to. Mrs. P. has not got over this yet. She never will. She manages to repeat it every day in [Mrs. O.'s] tone of voice. (50)

Here ridicule is directed at a narrator for repeating with malicious glee the words of another. At the same time, however, we notice O'Connor's own glee in repeating the words of both these women. Surely she is also poking fun at herself for her own delight in recording and ridiculing others' speech. This passage from a letter is comparable to a passage in "The Displaced Person," where Mrs. McIntyre complains to Mrs. Shortley about all the "sorry people" (*CS* 202) Mrs. McIntyre has had on her farm. Mrs. Shortley refuses to acknowledge the insult to herself, thinking, "Neither of them approved of trash" (203). Most readers with whom I have discussed this passage see satire directed not just at Mrs. Shortley but also at Mrs. McIntyre for her spitefulness; I question whether the O'Connor narrator can be excused for expressing a similar attitude with one more narrational layer of distance from the characters.

The early story "The Crop" provides another example of a narrator within the story who is ridiculed throughout, Miss Willerton. As Ruth Fennick has pointed out, after creating a sharecropper and his wife and starting a fight between them in a story she is writing, Miss Willerton enters her own story, "adopting the role of God (or His angel)," and she "strikes down the evil wife and rescues Lot from imminent death" (47). Miss Willerton is laughable, but one reason the reader is amused is instructive: humor results because Miss Willerton cannot maintain her commitment to this implausible wish fulfillment she creates, *not* because she momentarily becomes the equal of her characters. Her fantasy of entering her own story is the only point at which Miss Willerton indeed seems a writer; when she goes to the grocery store at the end of "The Crop" and once again considers herself superior to people like the characters she has created (*CS* 40–41), Miss Willerton deserves ridicule once again.

These two clearly ridiculous narrators, the farm wife Mrs. P. and Miss Willerton, are, of course, both women, and when I in the past have described an O'Connor character as a version of the typical O'Connor narrator, that character was another female, Sarah Ruth Cates from "Parker's Back" (*Religion* 80). This woman disapproves of cars (*CS* 510) and even considers "churches . . . idolatrous" (518); like the typical O'Connor narrator, she is "forever sniffing up sin" (510). Robert H. Brinkmeyer, Jr., however, has pointed to a male character, Julian in "Everything That Rises Must Converge," as one who resembles the O'Connor narrator: "In their efforts to show people up, both Julian and the narrator distort and demean; they manipulate to teach a lesson, simplifying the complexity of human experience to validate their own—but no one else's—integrity. A central irony of the story lies in this mirroring of Julian and the narrator, for because of their close identification, Julian's downfall implicitly signals the narrator's even if the narrator remains unaware of it" (72).

Most of O'Connor's writers are male, and most of her writers receive ridicule; along with Julian, one thinks of Asbury Fox in "The Enduring Chill," Thomas in "The Comforts of Home," Calhoun in "The Partridge Festival" (though Calhoun does have a female counterpart, Mary Elizabeth), and Rayber in *The Violent Bear It Away*. But O'Connor's women also frequently tell stories, orally rather than in writing. The issue of whether the typical O'Connor narrator is male or female can be resolved, I believe, through the positing of a composite figure: a female narrator espousing patriarchal, masculine values.

I should provide an explanation about the narration in the stories I have been discussing. I do not wish to claim that Miss Willerton dialogically rivals her narrator for authority in "The Crop"; I consider Miss Willerton as much of a joke as Ruth Fennick does. Miss Willerton's failure to win the reader's sympathy is one reason this story looks like an apprentice story. In "Everything That Rises Must Converge," the narrator resembles a woman as much as a man. The narrator's satire is like the lightning bolt of judgment delivered by the black mother who hits and perhaps kills Julian's mother for patronizing the black child.

In most of O'Connor's works, narrators who represent patriarchal authority have their authority undercut; the characters they mock are capable of strength and self-transformation that the narrators underestimate and misinterpret. The battle is more complicated than a matter of male patriarchy in the narrator versus female rebellion in the characters. Dale M. Bauer, in discussing the ways Bakhtin opens his theories to feminist uses of them, says, "The feminist struggle is not one between a conscious 'awakened' or natural voice *and* the voice of patriarchy 'out there.' Rather, precisely because we all internalize the authoritative voice of patriarchy, we must struggle to refashion inherited social discourses into words which rearticulate intentions (here feminist ones) other than normative and disciplinary ones" (2). Surely all of O'Connor's characters have internalized the voice of patriarchal authority; that is why their strategies for redemption, their battles against the narrator's authoritarian and totally conscious patriarchy, must be carried on unconsciously. If O'Connor's characters understood their rebellion against patriarchy, they generally would not want to rebel and could not if they did want to.

Two more examples of characters who resemble the typical O'Connor narrator are Mrs. Pritchard of "A Circle in the Fire" and Mrs. Freeman of "Good Country People." These characters do not use theology to rationalize their malicious glee for narration, but its lack may simply indicate that theology is not necessarily the ultimate basis of the narrator's persona. Mrs. Pritchard is willing to "go thirty miles for the satisfaction of seeing anybody laid away" (175), and she can easily imagine the landscape "flattened to nothing" (178). She feels "satisfaction" when she says to Sally Virginia Cope (who thinks herself capable of handling three delinquent boys), "They'd handle you" (187). Mrs. Pritchard smiles in "an omniscient rewarded way" when she reports a misfortune (188), she cannot "stand an anticlimax" (189), and she is "charged" by the story's climactic fire (193). Mrs. Freeman, equally fond of the grotesque, also resembles the O'Connor narrator in never admitting she is wrong while telling a story; she mechanically follows her tale, her eyes "turn[ing] as the story turn[s]" (271). It is also interesting that the narrator of "Good Country People" starts referring to Joy Hopewell as Hulga at precisely the point at which we are told that Mrs. Freeman enjoyed taking the liberty of calling her Hulga (274).

Perhaps the best example of a character who resembles the O'Connor narrator is one who does bring in the religious dimension: the nun at the end of "A Temple of the Holy Ghost." Although the nun never speaks, she literally forces patriarchy into the face of the young female protagonist, "mashing the side of [the child's] face into the crucifix hitched onto [the nun's] belt" after "swoop[ing] down on her mischievously and nearly smother[ing] her in the black habit" (248). As if the association of the nun with negative aspects of patriarchy is not obvious, the child protagonist recalls her mother's statement that the nuns at the convent school "keep a grip on" the "necks" of their female students so that the young girls will not "think about boys" more than is allowable (236).

Regarding the typical narrator as a female spokesman for patriarchy clarifies the ways characters rebel. In work after work, O'Connor's characters resist the patriarchal authority represented by the narrator, finding their own unorthodox routes to redemption. One form of resistance has to do with gender. While narrators promote gender differences, satirizing women who are masculine and men who are feminine, the characters move toward androgyny and hermaphroditism. Such dialogue was surely important for O'Connor personally, for her position in society made her able to understand what it is to be both dominant and marginal. Her class made her position in Milledgeville very respectable, and her personal dogmatism allied her with religious authority, but she also knew the limits that could be imposed on her by her gender, her disability, even, in some contexts, her southernness.[2] Consider what it must have been like for O'Connor to face her community's expectation that she would want to be a southern belle. And, of course, what we know of O'Connor's mother makes it plausible that she would be a female voice for patriarchal authority in O'Connor's life and thus a model for a female narrator. Mrs. O'Connor exercised control over her daughter's entire adult life, and apparently she was the constant dispenser of judgments the daughter wanted both to accept and reject. Thelma J. Shinn says, "The alternatives to growth for [O'Connor's] women are a hated dependency on mothers or a perpetual but socially sanctioned dependency on a heavenly Father" (90). In stories in which the patriarchal female narrator is victorious and succeeds in imposing monologic control over the text's potentially disruptive voices, O'Connor's female characters find themselves subject to the authority of both the mother and the father.

In her study of correspondence between O'Connor and the person called "A," Louise Westling has thoroughly demonstrated that O'Connor was properly open to the raising of questions about gender in her fiction ("Revelations"). And O'Connor did tell "A," in a letter dated 6 September

1955, "Of course I do not connect the Church exclusively with the Patriarchal Ideal" (*HB* 99; *CW* 952). But in *Sacred Groves and Ravaged Gardens,* Westling's study of the traditional association of southern womanhood with the landscape, she concludes that O'Connor could not "envision any positive, active life for women of her own generation" (176). Shinn states a similar view: "O'Connor's presentation of women is very pessimistic, even hostile. The only women who offer any values are the Southern ladies, and their truths have become empty clichés" (90).

Claire Kahane finds in "A Temple of the Holy Ghost" a sort of solution to gender issues for O'Connor in which the sideshow hermaphrodite promises "a symbolic resolution to the problem of gender limitation" ("Gothic" 350). For Louise Westling, "A Temple of the Holy Ghost" is something of a copout ("Revelations" 18), but for Kahane, the female as hermaphrodite "restor[es] to women at least conceptually the breadth of human potential" ("Gothic" 350). The child protagonist learns to value that sinful pride that makes her mockingly imitate the Baptist preacher in town (*CS* 243), in spite of her conscious sense that the rules of the church forbid such malicious glee in using another's words and that the rules of the community forbid any rudeness on the part of little ladies. Insofar as "A Temple of the Holy Ghost" is inspired by Carson McCullers's dream of powerful, androgynous females, as Westling and Kahane have demonstrated (*Sacred* 138–43; "Gothic" 347–50), it may seem an exceptional story for O'Connor. In a letter to Beverly Brunson dated 13 September 1954, O'Connor surprisingly rejects the idea that the story has to do with sex or even with power for women: "The point is of course in the resignation to suffering, which is one of the fruits of the Holy Ghost; not to any element of sex or sexlessness" (*CW* 925). The child character in "A Circle in the Fire," Sally Virginia Cope, has fantasies of masculine strength that are even more explicitly drawn than are the fantasies of the child in "A Temple of the Holy Ghost." Although Sally Virginia cross-dresses and carries toy pistols, she is finally unable to solve the problems presented by the three boys who threaten to destroy her mother's farm.

O'Connor also creates many other female characters who achieve masculine strength. Ruby Turpin of "Revelation," Mrs. Shortley of "The Displaced Person," and perhaps even Mrs. May of "Greenleaf" and Sally Virginia's mother, Mrs. Cope, in "A Circle in the Fire," are good examples of females overcoming patriarchal authority through private strategies. Each may appear to suffer a chastening in the course of the story, but they can also be read as creators of alternate, unorthodox, personal religious systems that give them as much control over their lives as men have over theirs. It is no coincidence that many of O'Connor's female characters have taken the "man's place" on a farm.

Many female characters in O'Connor's fiction are associated with masculine divinity. This pattern is surprising; one might expect O'Connor to compare women to female divinity, and occasionally the image of the Virgin Mary does come up. Sabbath Lily Hawks in *Wise Blood*, after a night of fornication with Hazel Motes, presents herself as the Madonna, carrying a stolen, shrunken mummy and telling Hazel, "Call me Momma now" (*CW* 106). Sarah Ruth Cates's pregnancy mystifies O. E. Parker in "Parker's Back" as if she had been impregnated supernaturally. The hermaphrodite in "A Temple of the Holy Ghost" wears a blue dress and submissively says, as the Virgin could, "This is the way [God] wanted me to be and I ain't disputing His way" (*CS* 245). Sally Virginia Cope has a rather appropriate age and the perfect middle name. And Lucynell Crater in "The Life You Save May Be Your Own" is called "the sweetest girl in the world" and "an angel of Gawd" (149, 154).

But such characters are ultimately the objects of effective satire as they are victimized by men or stuck in unenlightened positions. Such characters as Mrs. Greenleaf or Mrs. May in "Greenleaf" or the child in "A Temple of the Holy Ghost" might be exceptions to the pattern. But generally, I think O'Connor resists equating her heroic female characters with the Virgin/Madonna because of her deep disgust for the prescribed repression and bland perfection of the southern belle, that corruption of and substitution for the Virgin Mary. Kathryn Lee Seidel discusses the background for such an equation of the belle and Mary, saying, "Repression is the requisite personality trait for the girl who wishes to be the madonna-angel of male fantasy" (67), and the "exaggerated notion of the belle's purity is a Protestant analogue for the inviolateness of the Virgin Mary" (140).

Rather than risk the possibility of seeming to honor southern woman-hood in the form of the belle, O'Connor made many of her females into versions of Christ and other male religious figures. Consider the similarity of Sarah Ruth Cates's eyes to those of Jesus, the prophetic abilities of Mrs. Shortley in "The Displaced Person" and of Ruby Turpin in "Revela-tion," Joy/Hulga's identification with the god Vulcan in "Good Country People," Mary Fortune Pitts's identification with the Christ-like trees in "A View of the Woods," the equation of Hazel Motes's mother with Jesus in *Wise Blood,* and the female child preacher in *The Violent Bear It Away,* Lucette Carmody, who is obsessed with Jesus. Even in "A Temple of the Holy Ghost," where the child protagonist identifies with the madonna-like hermaphrodite, the story's final image, of a sun like "an elevated Host drenched in blood" (*CS* 248), suggests an equation of the child's maturing body with the body of Christ. Although I accept Martha Chew's persua-sive argument that O'Connor's characterization of Lucynell Crater is an attack on "the traditional role of the Southern woman" (17), I also believe that O'Connor's hatred of the belle led her to find ways to affirm women who are able to take on positive masculine attributes.

Two problematic figures, Ruby Hill of "A Stroke of Good Fortune" and Joy/Hulga Hopewell of "Good Country People," for whom the battle with narratorial authority is less successful, require special attention. One might construct a reading of O'Connor's works in which the association of females with masculine divinity is taken as always justly and purely satiri-cal. These two stories might seem to prove the case indirectly by demon-strating that two women who try to become like men deserve punishment precisely because they ought to be purely feminine. Perhaps "A Stroke of Good Fortune" deserves to be attacked; Karen Fitts has proposed that this story should be taught so teachers can expose and refute O'Connor's patri-archal biases. Critics like Westling and Kahane are inclined to emphasize that the protagonist, Ruby Hill, can achieve a remarkable amount of reader sympathy in the course of her defeat. I would argue that neither story is typical of O'Connor. Ruby Hill ridiculously dreams of self-destruction rather than of freedom and power. Perhaps Joy/Hulga's fantasies of herself as a goddess submissive to a man (Hulga-become-Joy/Venus submissive to Manley Pointer as Mars) are too patriarchal, finally; perhaps Hulga is an androgynous character guilty of dreaming that she can become a belle. More likely, the narrator punishes Joy/Hulga because the character is simply too close to home for O'Connor. A strategy for self-transformation by a character, if it is to work, probably has to remain beyond the conscious reach of that character. For O'Connor to understand, well enough to write a short story, the psyche of a character so like herself, perhaps she could not allow that character's unconscious strategy to succeed.

It is even more interesting to discover that gender ambiguity seems to allow males to achieve redemption more easily than females in O'Connor. Many of her male characters achieve redemption, it seems, because their personal strategies involve assuming what they perceive as female roles. The feminization of men became more pronounced and more valuable over the course of O'Connor's career. In the posthumous collection *Everything That Rises Must Converge* gender is one of the things that must converge. Asbury, for example, finally manages to imagine himself in the position of a victorious Leda about to be raped by a godly bird. Although Asbury misquotes Yeats early in that story, he apparently remembers the possibility in "Leda and the Swan" that Leda "put[s] on" the god's "knowledge with his power."[3] Similarly, we may read "The Comforts of Home" as a story in which Thomas, far from succumbing to masculine advice from his father, botches his consciously intended plans for incriminating a woman to demonstrate to himself how much he has in common with Sarah Ham and his mother.[4] Despite serious efforts to achieve redemption, other male characters may ultimately fail because they finally reject the femaleness with which they engage in dialogue. Examples are Mr. Fortune in "A View of the Woods," Julian of "Everything That Rises Must Converge," and Sheppard in "The Lame Shall Enter First," characters who ought at least to admit their similarity to women rather than trying to force females to become masculine. Mr. Fortune ends up killing his granddaughter, and Julian might be considered responsible for the death of his mother in a manner less transformative than that in the scene in which Thomas kills his mother.

Before considering "The Lame Shall Enter First," we must consider the novel *The Violent Bear It Away*, in which the protagonist, Tarwater, is ready to become a child evangelist after he is raped; it is certainly possible for the rape of a man by a man to have nothing to do with women, but we can also say that within the set of ideas about gender that one might expect Tarwater to have, part of the insult of rape is that it puts him in the position of being dominated, a position he would associate with being feminized. O'Connor apparently intended the rape scene to dramatize pure evil; Jean W. Cash has published and analyzed an uncollected letter dated 27 August 1962 in which O'Connor says the scene "can only be understood in religious terms" (69). But a statement of conscious intent does not eliminate other, less conscious meanings for the scene, as O'Connor herself admitted. Certainly Old Tarwater taught the boy that bad people are asses and whores (*CW* 355); Tarwater probably thinks his rape makes him both. And the rapist, whom Tarwater wholly or partly creates, is a stereotype of effeminacy. It is probably significant that when Tarwater does become a prophet as the novel ends, his role model is most likely a female. Lucette Carmody, the evangelist Tarwater hears in the middle of the novel, preaches as a child and preaches in the city so we might say that she is more like what Tarwater will become at the end of the novel than is Old Tarwater.

If *The Violent Bear It Away* is regarded in such a manner, it is easier to know what to make of that devilish story "The Lame Shall Enter First," in which the young male delinquent Rufus (a character clearly related to Tarwater) becomes a substitute for both the son and the wife of the protagonist, Sheppard. When Rufus claims that Sheppard made "immor'l suggestions" (480), we may recall that Rufus has been given the dead wife's room and has danced about the house in her corset (456) and conclude that Rufus's claim makes some sense. I suggest that the feminization of a male character in this story fails to produce redemption because the story belongs to Sheppard ultimately, not to the feminized Rufus. Robert H. Brinkmeyer, Jr., has called Rufus "a double to the narrator" (97) in this story, but Sheppard is clearly the protagonist. Although I do not think Sheppard desires Rufus sexually, there may be a connection between Sheppard's adoption of the role of purely masculine dominator and the disastrous ending of the story.

O'Connor's first collection has less feminization of males and fewer good men. A good man is hard to find because being masculine gets in the way of being good. In this collection there are many almost purely masculine characters—the Misfit, Mr. Head, Gen. Sash, Mr. Shortley, and, of course, that most masculine and vicious of characters, Manley Pointer. It is to this collection that I would apply Josephine Hendin's description of "much of O'Connor's work" as taking place in a world where "men are either old, asleep, dead, diseased, or mutilated, or murderers and thieves" (121). The clearest Christ symbol among O'Connor's male characters, Mr. Guizac of "The Displaced Person," is not feminized. He is clearly masculine from the moment he shocks Mrs. Shortley with a kiss on the hand of Mrs. McIntyre at the beginning of the story. But there are hints of the valuable feminization of males in some of O'Connor's early works. Gabriel in the seldom discussed story "Wildcat" equates the prowling of the wildcat with Gabriel's meeting the Lord and even with Gabriel's feminization: when the wildcat is about, Gabriel is encouraged to stay with women for protection. But the feminized characters in the early works are typically boys, not men. In "An Afternoon in the Woods," the revised version of "The Turkey" that almost made it into the collection *A Good Man Is Hard to Find,* a young character, again named Manley (perhaps the original Manley), is trying hard to become fully masculine but finally imagines himself pursued by a "Something Awful" (*CW* 772) that may dominate, feminize, and rescue him. And in "The River," the protagonist Harry/Bevel in a sense faces a choice between two captors who will dominate him: Mr. Paradise, associated with a dominating pig and the three male children who have sadistically introduced Harry/Bevel to the pig, or that man Mrs. Connin introduced Bevel to, Jesus in the form of "the waiting current . . . like a long gentle hand" (174) taking Bevel to death by drowning. Surely Harry/Bevel selects the more feminizing choice, though both choices have potential in that direction. If one decides that O'Connor associates childhood with androgyny, one can also develop a reading of the late story "Parker's Back" in which O. E. Parker is feminized as he is redeemed, for when Sarah Ruth Cates beats him with a broom at the end of the story, he cries "like a baby" (530).

Wise Blood handles the protagonist's gender with a high level of complexity. The protagonist is called Hazel, a feminine name, as well as Haze, a more masculine-sounding name. Hazel is drawn powerfully to—indeed, haunted by—memories of his mother and the homestead and landscape she dominated, and he spends much of the novel apparently trying to become another Manley Pointer by preaching blasphemy and dominating and destroying others. An important scene in the novel involves his murder of his double, who is significantly named Solace Layfield. The name suggests a lay in the field and the solace that goes with it. The scene in which Hazel insists that Solace undress before Hazel runs over him with his Essex surely has a sexual dimension.[5] After Hazel watches Solace die, Hazel sees himself adopting a dominated, feminized role, and he senses that such a role is somehow proper for him too. We might conclude that Hazel becomes feminized when he conjures up a patrolman to dominate him and destroy his car. Probably the most positive effect Hazel has on any character is his influence on Mrs. Flood, his landlady, who also makes a woman of him. Even if one is reluctant to make much of the fact that she wants to "penetrate" his "darkness" (*CW* 127), or that she envisions him finally as a "dark tunnel" (131), surely when Mrs. Flood thinks of marrying Hazel after he blinds himself, she plans to play the dominant role.[6] I have in the past written that Enoch Emery, Hazel's disciple, and Hazel "follow complementary paths toward redemption" (*Religion* 136), but one aspect of Enoch's private religion seems to be that he is trying to move farther and farther toward masculinity. Perhaps Enoch's putting on of Gonga's ape suit in his final scene demonstrates that Enoch cannot adopt Hazel's androgyny. Perhaps it is his androgyny that makes Hazel's rebellion against his narrator's presentation of him effective.[7]

One benefit in examining gender dialogue in O'Connor is that it helps preserve our sense of the characters' wonderful individuality. Dale M. Bauer warns that in many works with dialogue between genders, the voices of women eventually "die out" (xiv). O'Connor's women and men refuse to become a mass of identical, silenced souls as they work out their redemptions; one might recall Ruby Turpin's vision, at the end of "Revelation," of diverse humanity on a ladder to heaven, still odd, still grotesque, still "shouting and clapping" (*CS* 508). As Michael Holquist says, society for Bakhtin is "a simultaneity of uniqueness" (153), a description that also fits O'Connor's fictional world. Another interesting aspect of this approach is that the narrator becomes, like most O'Connor characters, somewhat "freakish": the narrator is a patriarchal female who tries to deny to characters the very compassion desired by the narrator as well as by the real Flannery O'Connor. In considering the complexity of the narrator, one recalls Parker's "suspicion" about Sarah Ruth Cates that maybe "she actually liked everything she said she didn't" (*CS* 510), along with the line in "Good Country People" about the pleasant Mrs. Hopewell, who "had no bad qualities of her own but she was able to use other people's in such a constructive way that she never felt the lack" (272).

Although it is important to separate O'Connor's narrator from O'Connor herself, the narrator generally reflects parts of O'Connor's own character that she wanted to transform. In a study on the Bakhtinian carnivalesque and grotesque (among other things), Peter Stallybrass and Allon White make a generalization that suggests the extent to which the O'Connor narrator might also be involved in something like the characters' search for redemption through a shift in gender: "A recurrent pattern emerges: the 'top' attempts to reject and eliminate the 'bottom' for reasons of prestige and status, only to discover, not only that it is in some way frequently dependent upon that low-Other . . . but also that the top *includes* that low symbolically, as a primary eroticized constituent of its own fantasy life" (5).

None of my argument is intended to suggest that O'Connor's conscious intentions were markedly different from what she said they were. O'Connor would not have written what she did if she were not an orthodox Catholic. But whereas Louise Westling argues that O'Connor's "ambivalence about being a woman" ("Revelations" 15) interfered with her art, I believe O'Connor produced her best art when her emotions caused her works to overflow their containers, cracking the molds intended to control and shape them. As Claire Kahane has suggested, even the nun in "A Temple of the Holy Ghost" suggests a Catholic version of hermaphroditism ("Gothic" 350).

O'Connor's apparent definition of woman as that which is dominated may be very troubling, though I would answer that she understood fully the extent to which women receive unfair treatment. I prefer to raise gender questions about O'Connor's fiction (and what perhaps must follow, more analysis of O'Connor's sense of her own gender) to the inclination on the part of some critics to demonstrate that she was perfectly "normal" in order to "save" her from investigations of gender issues. Rather than concluding tidily our investigations of O'Connor's sense of herself as female with details about her occasional close male friend, I would rather claim that she was willing to sympathize and identify with all of her characters, to investigate the mysteries of gender and the need for androgyny, even if doing so might drive her toward despair.

Notes

1. Bakhtin's most important texts for an understanding of dialogism are "Discourse in the Novel" and *Problems of Dostoevsky's Poetics.* In *Flannery O'Connor's Religion of the Grotesque,* I have discussed the relevance of Bakhtin's theories on the grotesque (in *Rabelais and His World*) and on novelistic narration to the study of Flannery O'Connor, arguing that her stories typically dramatize battles between an excessively authoritarian narrator and grotesque characters engaged in unconscious strategies for redeeming themselves, strategies the narrator mocks in vain. This essay reconsiders the argument in my "Flannery O'Connor's Attacks on Omniscience," where I suggest that the battles may be seen as gender disputes as well, with the narrator a male and the typical character a female (or feminized male). Although I am now inclined to label the typical O'Connor narrator female rather than male, I still want to insist that she uses her narrator to express a point of view

she wants to transcend. There are important differences between O'Connor and the narrators of her fiction. See pages 6–9 of *Flannery O'Connor's Religion of the Grotesque* for my discussion of how Bakhtin's theories of novelistic narration can be most usefully adapted to the study of O'Connor. For a discussion of feminist attacks on Booth's feminism, see Bauer (173–74).

2. Nancy Glazener refers to "the peculiar position of women who (if they are bourgeois) can be both dominant and marginal" (129).

3. Patricia S. Yaeger argues, in a Bakhtinian reading of Eudora Welty, that Welty turns the patriarchal values of Yeats's poems upside down in *The Golden Apples*. I see a similar feminist inversion of Yeats in "The Enduring Chill."

4. See my "The Hand of the Writer in 'The Comforts of Home.'"

5. For an argument that Hazel and *Wise Blood* are generally asexual, see J. O. Tate.

6. Compare the "long penetrating look" Manley gives Joy/Hulga in "Good Country People" (*CS* 288) or the "white penetrating stares" (*CS* 179) the three boys turn on Mrs. Cope in "A Circle in the Fire." Claire Kahane has made a strong case that Hazel's self-blinding finally achieves his desired escape from women and all they represent in the novel ("Comic" 116–17).

7. Mary Frances HopKins provides a thorough analysis of the specific stylistic techniques by which *Wise Blood* becomes dialogic, but HopKins never considers the narrator's authority to be called into question.

**Displacing
Gender:
Flannery
O'Connor's
View from
the Woods**

*Richard
Giannone*

In her treatment of gender, Flannery O'Connor
may turn out to be a feminist. If so, O'Connor
would be a feminist despite herself for she avows
fidelity to a patriarchal church and culture. Her convictions ring with univocal consistency. She states
her aim to be the accurate naming of things to engage the reader with stable meanings; she reiterates
a neocritical bias for organic unity that makes her
strive for precisely structured wholes; and behind
the art lies O'Connor's trust that her Christianity
provides an inviolable vantage point from which
"to see and judge" the "life of this age" (*MM* 117).

These securities locate O'Connor at a far remove
from postmodern sensibilities, and yet from that
antipode of traditional and Christian aesthetics
O'Connor speaks in a lasting voice to successive
waves of secular and religious readership.[1] Within
this steady confluence of interest there lies a quiet
appeal to our present concern for the distinguishing strength and loyalty of women writers that critics have begun to investigate.[2] I wish to build on
this inquiry through a brief consideration of the
theology anchoring O'Connor's remarks on gender and to proceed to a reading of "A View of the
Woods," the story that puts the gender issue in perspective.

Leaving aside subtle theoretical distinctions
about oppression (Gayle Rubin 307–8) to survey
O'Connor's fiction, we can see that the usual di-
chotomy between female weakness and male toughness does not give final shape to O'Connor's action.
Cruel exercise of power fills her short stories and
novels without harsh burdens falling along gender

lines. Mothers manipulate daughters and sons; arrogant sons and insolent daughters retaliate by controlling their parents. Fathers and uncles indiscriminately tyrannize their dependents. Landladies and landlords alike push workers around by their rights as property owners. Nowhere in O'Connor's work do we find women dramatized in what Barbara Johnson deplores as the repeated literary state of "simulacrum, erasure, or silence" (40). O'Connor simply does not replicate the cultural or language patterns that efface females. Nor do cultural forces wipe out her males. Oppositional critics who insist that we define ourselves against a dehumanizing culture will find that O'Connor is with them. All of her characters stand outside the circumference of American society's definition of acceptable women and men and children, and none want to enter it.

Domesticity holds great importance within the outlying places where O'Connor's characters work out their displaced lives. As is the case with many women writers, family life generates the conflicts in O'Connor's fiction; but in her world the tables are always turning in household arrangements of power. Anyone can be crushed by the adaptations required by family life. Physical abuse crosses gender lines. A wife brutalizes her husband on their porch as readily as a mother takes it on the chin from her son at a bus stop. The balance of positive treatment is also in flux, for there is no telling who answers the basic needs for care and security that all the characters seek. A young father willingly tends the hearth after his wife deserts their home and afflicted child. And yet O'Connor sings of arms and the woman. In one story a girl of twelve equips herself to fight off dangerous male intruders on her mother's place.

Finally, we will look in vain for evidence of bonding by gender among O'Connor's characters. Her southerners skip this phase of socialization in favor of a code of primitive survival and self-interest. In a physician's office a young woman flings a book across the room at an older woman before biting her on the neck. The outdoors is more perilous. Crimes of hatred casually erupt along the Tennessee and Georgia byways. In one backwoods a male driver rapes a teenage male hitchhiker. The only blood brothers and blood sisters we find are those who join in complicity without regard for gender to do in a convenient, unsuspecting victim. And so it goes in the gender free-for-all of O'Connor's fiction.

Scrambling extends into the otherworldly precinct, where O'Connor hurls her oppressors so that they may feel the ultimate portent of their inhumanity. In this realm lies personal and divine judgment (but, to our horror, not social justice). Wherever divine intervention corrects human perception, there lies grace. Freely and universally given, supreme truth disarranges the roles assigned by gender and age so as to overturn the power wielded by these differences. The faithful gentleness of a boy with Down's syndrome delivers a censure to his murderer that anticipates the denunciation leveled against the killer by a large, granitelike woman. The task of prophecy, like that of judgment, also defies age and gender. Death may still the bellow of an eighty-four-year-old hermit, but soon the blazing voice of a crippled little girl of eleven or twelve rises to renew his condemnation of our age, an age of wrath.

By driving the story toward a sacred view of human violence, O'Connor drastically dislocates our usual sexist way of seeing. She forces us to see with Saint Paul in Galatians 3:27 a condition in which "there is no longer male and female." For Paul such unity comes through baptismal equality; for O'Connor the cancellation of any division by sex marks the fulfillment of God's promise. Her characters' death march in all of the stories serves as an entrance into the grand consummation of the world and of history. This theme underlies all of O'Connor's stories. And this completion with its radical disclosure of each character's destiny unites all differences into one saving action.

In the end, for the end, all kinds of figures discharge the sacred duty of attending the countless maimed and wasted victims to their final rest in death. A grasping, starchy bourgeois landlady keeps vigil over her bizarre, self-mortifying tenant. A black woman wails over the corpse of a white prophet, whose grave is dug by a black man. A wizened Irish priest anoints the mangled body of a Polish refugee and then ministers to the slow death of the woman who conspired to kill the Pole. The more grave the disaster in the fiction, the more astonishing is the reversal of gender roles.

In one notorious ending a prim grandmother consoles a serial killer as he pumps three rounds into her chest. The old social signs of femininity (her straw hat, white gloves, and genteel speech) fall away as the doomed woman takes bullets and gunman into her bosom. However gruesome and irrational, her clemency expresses divine inwardness by overcoming wanton hatred; and as with God, who is without gender, the new life to come, in behalf of which the grandmother acts, knows no gender.

Yet O'Connor's egalitarian treatment of race and gender is frankly inconsistent with certain of her well-known rigidities. Even the times cannot excuse her refusal in 1959 to meet James Baldwin, whose work she respected, on the grounds that in Georgia "[it] would cause the greatest trouble and disturbance and disunion" (*HB* 329). On this occasion O'Connor, the chronicler of trouble and disturbance who can find love in mass murder, acquiesced to racial bias. O'Connor's letters and essays are univocal on local manners: she follows the custom of her country, the Deep South not yet changed by the civil rights movement, and gives white males supreme power over blacks and white females. Other loyalties commingle with O'Connor's consent to the status quo: she draws heavily on the Hebrew Bible and confesses to Roman Catholicism.[3]

Nevertheless, an intelligent woman writer with the highest professional aims, who is a religious minority in the Protestant South and as a white woman is a minority within the controlling majority, could not help but think about her status in her society and church. She does, in fact, reflect on both, paying more attention to defining herself as a woman of faith than as a woman of action. While writing within male structures, O'Connor remarked on gender as early as the mid-1950s. She was urged to declare herself by her Atlanta correspondent "A," whose searching questions on social and religious topics catalyzed some of O'Connor's richest observations.

O'Connor's comments on gender are few. Each responds to rather than initiates the discussion. All are of a piece in denying the essential difference between male and female. In one exchange, "A" brings O'Connor to clarify her notion of male/female concurrence. "What you say about there being two [sexes] now brings it home to me," O'Connor explains. "I've always believed there were two but generally acted as if there were only one" (*HB* 136). To prod O'Connor out of this undifferentiated anthropology, the feminist in "A" has apparently cited the bridal imagery in the Song of Solomon as a way of putting gender on the scriptural grounds that are congenial to O'Connor's thinking. If "A" believes that the Hebrew Bible's showing that God chooses Israel as one selects a bride, or even that Paul's figure of Christ's wooing the church into a final union (Ephesians 5:22–32) will sexualize O'Connor's imagination, "A" is mistaken. "I've never spent much time over the bride-bridegroom analogy," O'Connor notes. "For me, perhaps because it began for me in the beginning, it's been more father and child" (*HB* 136). Whether her response expresses a measure of sublimated sexuality or a reaction to her father's death when she was sixteen or an early conditioning by tradition, O'Connor finds more spiritual security in a parental than spousal relation to God, particularly in the fatherhood of God that allows the child unconditionally to trust.

O'Connor's emphasis on the fatherhood of God is telling for two reasons. To begin with, she could respond to God as mother. This understanding is part of an honored tradition with which O'Connor was familiar. A woman spiritual writer would find the maternity of God a source of insight, as did Julian of Norwich. In describing the deep reality of the divine that comes to her in visions, Julian evokes a full theology of divine life by balancing the power of divine fatherhood with the tenderness and supportive love of Mother Jesus. Julian's *Showings* (or *Revelations* as the record is also called) of the fourteenth century is prescient of the feminine theological teaching that we now require and are uncovering. Julian sees that "God rejoices that he is our Mother" (279). "The mother's service is nearest, readiest and surest: nearest because it is most natural, readiest because it is most loving, and surest because it is truest" (297).

The second point to be made about O'Connor's reference to God as father is its inadequacy as a guide to her own practice. O'Connor's canonical presentation of God's dealings with humankind shows that God does act as mother. God proves to have loving breasts to nourish her brood ("A

Good Man Is Hard to Find"), gentle hands to protect her young ("The River"), and warm arms to embrace her lost offspring ("The Lame Shall Enter First"). As O'Connor thinks "more and more about the presentation of love and charity" in her fiction (*HB* 373), her characters increasingly experience the plenitude of God's motherhood. The cumulative result of O'Connor's sustained contemplation of "the image at the heart of things" (*MM* 168) is her recognition of the feminine share in the total mystery of God.

The feminine side of O'Connor's theology remains obscured from our immediate appreciation by the spectacular violence through which grace operates. From first to last story brute force blasts the divine entry into her characters' lives, leaving in the aftermath mangled bodies to fascinate us. By training we interpret the physical might causing these blows as masculine; and in the same categorizing move we assume that power precludes tenderness. Such conditioned habits get in the way of our understanding O'Connor and the true nature of grace. One of the meanings in Latin of *gratia* is a favor done, a service, a kindness. Etymology, then, supports the rich feminine source of grace, whereas its operation in human affairs combines humble service with great upheavings that we associate with masculine warriors. This full expression of grace underlies O'Connor's inclusive portrayal of God.

To get at another sense of gender totality in O'Connor's thinking we should return to her exchange with "A." O'Connor's letter of 13 January 1956 responds to her friend's belief that women are superior to men. "You may be right that a man is an incomplete woman. It don't change anybody's external destination however, or the observable facts of the sex's uses (a nice phrase)" (*HB* 129). The issue of gender superiority neither challenged O'Connor's religious orthodoxy nor stimulated her moral imagination. She summarizes her position with more than usual plainness in a letter of 22 September 1956. "On the subject of the feminist business. I just never think, that is never think of qualities which are specifically feminine or masculine. I suppose I divide people into two classes: the Irksome and the Non-Irksome without regard to sex. Yes and there are the Medium Irksome and the Rare Irksome" (*HB* 176).

For all her folksy amiability, O'Connor's eradicating gender as a basis for human identity would be controversial even if expressed by a feminist. Coming from a staunch Catholic woman writer who is highly circumspect on sexual and political issues, the remarks are startling. If translated into action for institutional reform, such disregard for gender would under-mine the patriarchal structure of O'Connor's church. Her position points up the altogether human paradox of the believer who can be at once socially conservative and theologically provocative. Such a person simply defers justice by laying her or his unlived life and unrelieved sufferings onto the future—or in the case of O'Connor, detonating her explosions in her art. And so the tension between social injustice and its spiritual correc-tion brings us back to Galatians 3:27 in which Paul radically declares the kingdom open to pagans and yet insists that domestic slaves must stay in their place. O'Connor does not draw upon Paul's harmful legacy of toler-ating slavery or misogyny, but she does share in the apostle's dependence on his belief in a resurrected life to gather up the pain of flesh and an-guish of sexual desire and in his envisioning the form of this renewal as the genderless mystical body of the Creator.

Having made these preliminary observations, I would offer a general statement about O'Connor's scattered comments on gender. O'Connor's habit of mind, as I see it, is to submit gender to three successive dis-placements. She begins by dismissing as a basis for distinction the obvious anatomical differences between female and male in favor of the impact of character, notably that of irritation and disgust. Without fleeing from fixed gender identities, as Virginia Woolf does to survive as a woman, and without having a stake in the feminist project of destroying the bi-nary of femininity and masculinity, O'Connor with her respect for human and divine totality comes close to Carolyn Heilbrun's concept of an "un-bounded and hence fundamentally indefinable nature" (xi). After blurring the feminine and masculine, O'Connor in her second move replaces inner character with moral judgment as a basis for identity. Finally, she dislodges moral judgment from the social and political world to locate true human integrity in the ungendered future. Transcendence secures humankind in its permanent and inescapable orientation to God. Eternity resolves all disharmonies and contradictions and confers freedom and life.

In displacing gender as a basis for identity and source of dignity, O'Connor does not ignore the painful disparities and strifes that females and males endure in the sexist condition of the dramatic present. As a writer determined to point out the evils of our age, she could not do so and sound the moral deep of how we live now. The action of grace in O'Connor's fiction is frequently in the sexist territory held largely by the devil. Displacing gender supports her larger aim to disorient our conscience by wrenching our gaze to a prospective view of a final union with God that is incalculable but intimately felt by her characters.

Though otherworldly mystery intrudes at the end of O'Connor's narratives, the preceding action never concerns esoteric phenomena set high above the earth. God's interventions make up O'Connor's this-worldly grief. Her conflicts are lowdown, raw. And they arise through O'Connor's attention to what it means to be female and male in conservative, patriarchal southern families. The task for readers now that O'Connor's reputation looms so high centers on the ways her assumptions about gender infuse her artistry. O'Connor herself would be coolly undisturbed by such insistent questions. Nevertheless, a consideration of O'Connor's practice offers the reward of seeing how a spiritual woman writer contributes to the gender debate. After all, it is not every day that we encounter a writer who displaces gender by subsuming the issue into theological finality.

A good way into the subject is through "A View of the Woods." This prize-winning 1957 story, collected posthumously in *Everything That Rises Must Converge* (1964), is pure O'Connor. As usual, a bucolic title belies unspeakable wickedness. The view of these Georgia pine trees is so tied to the self-worth of the good country people that they torment and kill for it. Whereas murder is common in O'Connor's writing, the configuration of forces leading to bloodshed in this story is shocking even for her.

There are two killers, and they kill each other in an act of retribution. The fatal balance concluding this "little morality play," as O'Connor calls her tale (*HB* 186), dramatizes the destructive hatred born of gender warfare. So that even the most myopic reader can see the evil, O'Connor exaggerates the conflict by making the female opponent a young girl of nine and the male opponent an old man of seventy-nine. O'Connor binds them as granddaughter and grandfather. Their kinship is a story of unrelieved ugliness. "A View of the Woods" provides a glimpse of O'Connor the artist of extremity taking gender across ordinary borders to explore gender politics in a weird backwater of her particular domain of wrath.

O'Connor's border crossing brings us to a penal colony occupying eight hundred acres in the Georgia hinterland owned by Mark Fortune, a spoiled brat of seventy-nine who believes that a deed to land entitles him to absolute power over his family. As befits the old man's airs, the narrator customarily uses the alternate title for master when referring to *Mr.* Fortune. Mr. Fortune bolsters his gerontocracy through the egoist's desperate maneuver of extending himself beyond death by founding a new town. A supermarket, a motel, a gas station, and a drive-in picture show will rise out of his land to transform an undeveloped patch on a clay road fifteen miles from the paved highway into Fortune, Georgia, a memorial to his gumption and foresight.

Mr. Fortune may be "a man of advanced vision" (338) in town planning, but he sees people through the timeworn lens of white male domination. Most of those under his thumb remain nameless because they have no meaning to him, are but minor characters in the soap opera of male ingenuity and progress into which Mr. Fortune projects himself as the builder-hero. Two subjects, however, do menace his patriarchate: Pitts and Mary Fortune. The male rival Pitts, who is Mr. Fortune's son-in-law, for ten years has been living on the old man's place trying to make a go of a dairy business and farming to support his wife, Mr. Fortune's daughter, and their seven children. No matter how hard Pitts works, he remains a tenant, a low-status dweller with a temporary hold on his dignity before his family as a male provider. The old man cuts a hard deal: "What Pitts made went to Pitts but the land belonged to Fortune and he was careful to keep the fact before them" (336). The rivalry for the position of dominant male deepens into hateful stalemate with the incapacitated old man gloating in systematically humiliating his younger competitor, who retains the upper hand by virtue of physical power. Mr. Fortune sits at the head of the table at meals; Pitts sits at the side in angry awareness that the seating arrangement enforces lower status. The older man enjoys the delusion of male adequacy so long as the younger male takes the position of domestic impotence.

Pitts is too shrewd in the ways of male territorial combat to aim his anger directly against Mr. Fortune. Younger and stronger, Pitts knows that the best way to deal with a tyrant is to outlive him. Until that time comes, Pitts gets at the old man indirectly by beating his daughter Mary. His intention is to make the old man feel the emotional and physical impotence that lies beneath Mr. Fortune's legal power.

O'Connor does not hold back in presenting Pitts's savage abuse of his daughter. The sacrifice of the girl is so established and essential to the stability of the household structure that its violence no longer seems violent to the family and its horror no longer incites resistance against the commanding officer Pitts or defense of the innocent victim Mary Fortune. Whenever Pitts feels Mr. Fortune's control (mealtime for this family brings out the hunger for pain), he gets up from the side of the table where Mr. Fortune has put him down and takes his daughter to the woods to whip her.

To note Pitts's sexism in picking on the vulnerable female child that Mr. Fortune cherishes is merely to touch the surface of Pitts's psychopathology. For a writer known to savor the unseemly but to eschew its sexual aspects, O'Connor manages to encompass Pitts's evil with a rapid glance at his sadism. Through an understanding of Pitts's seamy underside O'Connor provides an understanding of Pitts's politics. His liturgy of paternal domination follows a prescribed obeisance to Priapus, the god of male procreative power. This ritual adds the male-female disciplinary system to the parent-child disciplinary system. Such doubling of force turns

Mary Fortune's punishment into a method of instruction. Its action is simple. "Time and again" Pitts would "abruptly, for no reason, with no explanation jerk his head at Mary Fortune and say, 'Come with me,' and leave the room, unfastening his belt as he went." Trained to submit to her father, Mary Fortune, with a look resembling "cooperation" (340), follows her handler as would an animal on an invisible leash. Pitts then drives his daughter down the road to a pine tree out of the family's earshot where he "methodically" belts her around the ankles for about three minutes "as if he were whacking a bush with a sling blade" (340). The master asserts his power by engraving his law into the body of his dependent.

O'Connor's presentation of the scene through the viewpoint of Mr. Fortune brings out the politics of Pitts's discipline. Mr. Fortune observes the punishment from behind a boulder a hundred feet away, and there the titular patriarch manifests concealed submission and terror before actual brute male power. Mr. Fortune receives the intended lesson of terror and helplessness from the flogger, and the old man's knowledge contains the lesson that the eight other younger victims around the table learn from the punishment. The instruction begins with a public display of Pitts's phallic power and gains force with Mary Fortune's reciprocal assent. The instruction culminates as both the disciplining ritual and its subject disappear into the woods where the warning leaves the everyday world to enter the dark of consciousness both of the girl and of those who must imagine the pain Pitts forbids them to see.

The clandestine beating brings the action across the threshold of domestic secrecy into the horror of silence. Instead of screaming, O'Connor's language is flat. Her steely calm forces the reader to feel the law of paternal power being internalized unimpeded by victim, observer, or authorial emotion. The forfeiture of authorial response parallels Mary Fortune's loss of her rights and her will and integrity. She is Pitts's property to be used to keep everyone in line: "'She's mine to whip and I'll whip her every day of the year if it suits me'" (341). For a redneck ox, Pitts is an astute political tactician who establishes authority by implementing a harsh, unjust sentence on his young daughter's body. The girl and the family learn to live with a ceremonious indignity that has always been the pride of a misogynistic world.

Subdued anguish that is deprived of a saving human witness permeates "A View of the Woods" and shows its damage most fully in the character of Mary Fortune. She lives under two oppressive male regimes—a grim patriarchy superimposed on a feeble gerontocracy. Whether Mary Fortune is the prime target of the patriarch's free-floating rage or a prize for the older man's manipulative affection, the girl's life as a child and a female is degrading. Her value depends on the inhuman use of her humanity by others, and her femaleness lowers the worth of her service and as she grows up increases the poignancy of her exploitation. Her very birth is a form of extortion. Pitts and his wife arrive on the Fortune place ten years earlier with six children. Knowing that Mr. Fortune resents their presence, the couple soon announce that his daughter is pregnant and that they will name the new baby Mark Fortune. The newborn will be donated to the old man as a human *ex voto* offering by dutiful subjects. The bribe backfires. The old man spurns the linking of his name to that of Pitts. To sharpen the disappointment all around, the baby turns out to be a girl, and femaleness is low coinage in a patriarchy. By genetic chance, however, the girl resembles Mr. Fortune. Vanity wrests some kindness from the old narcissist's heart, and the girl receives the name Mary after Mr. Fortune's mother, who died bearing him. Now Mary Fortune Pitts is the namesake manqué for Mark Fortune, but she becomes his soulsake complete by dint of their close companionship. Mary Fortune takes on the aggression and willfulness to match the light blue eyes, the florid complexion, and the wide forehead that she shares with her grandfather.

Their age difference and equivalent dispositions make for a confused familial relationship because his eugenic myth imposes an intimate and brutal discipline on her. He sets the rules and roles for her conduct. Mr. Fortune on occasion plays a "suitor trying to reinstate himself" (347) after the two quarrel; he can wax ambiguously solicitous in asking " 'sister' " (350) what bothers her; and with his Cadillac he serves as complaisant chauffeur. His adoration for Mary Fortune follows from the old man's designating her as his heir. Her right to inheritance not only isolates the girl from her parents and siblings, it also imposes on her the political identity of future boss of the place. Mr. Fortune serves Mary Fortune so that she will serve him as posthumous instrument of revenge against the family. With the egoist's talent to reminisce about life after he dies, Mr. Fortune savors the prospect of Mary Fortune making them all "jump" (337) to her orders. The old man's devotion to his granddaughter is another bribe, and she knows it. That knowledge is Mary Fortune's power over Mr. Fortune, and her legacy will be her power over Pitts. The fact of being born female may expose Mary Fortune to the tyranny of two generations of male parents, but it does not finally determine her relation to power.

In sum, the opponents in "A View of the Woods" are old, rich, nasty and irksome, middle-aged, dispossessed, brutal and irksome, and young and irksome. Their convergence in the woods through a series of violent encounters dismantles the power structure that makes daily life a living hell. If we consider the first and last scenes of the story, we can see the operation of O'Connor's displacement of gender. O'Connor's precision of detail guides us. To follow her concrete particulars, however, we will need to augment our usual way of observing gender conflict "with the anagogical way of seeing" (*HB* 180). If we train our eye to see several realities in one image or one situation, we can appreciate how O'Connor goes deeper into fact to get closer to mystery. Another letter to "A" directs our attention to the locus of O'Connor's interest. To put the domestic violence into perspective, she notes, "some prediction of hell for the old man is essential to my story" (*HB* 187). That forecast comes through O'Connor's use of Dante, the seer into mystery who teaches her how to plumb the unseen and whose anagogical mode here serves O'Connor's collapsing gender differences.

The story begins with the making of hell out of the earth's plain loveliness. The destruction is the work of Mr. Fortune, whose damage to the local ecology goes hand in glove with his patriarchal abuse of his human environment. To guarantee that the Pittses do not feel that the land is theirs, Mr. Fortune sells off twenty-five acre lots to various developers. The scheme now under way is a fishing club by a new lakeside. Each morning for a week the old man drives Mary Fortune in his mulberry-colored Cadillac to watch the excavation. Everything in Mr. Fortune's surroundings speaks to feelings of mastery and entrepreneurial know-how. He especially enjoys observing the bulldozer dig a huge hole in the ground where the old pasture that Pitts managed to clear of bitterweed used to be. With his whole being dilating in an atmosphere of seniority, Mr. Fortune uses these inspection tours to teach Mary Fortune how to rule others, especially their family, through ownership of property.

But title-deed and the privilege it gives deceive Mr. Fortune. His power and sadistic pleasure in disfranchising people are demonic delusions. The reader's anagogical eye can discern that the activity gratifying Mr. Fortune is really ruinous and disgusting. The big bulldozer gorges itself on the red soil and then "with the sound of a deep sustained nausea" (335) spits up the fine-grained particles. The machine's blade makes the natural red Georgia clay hemorrhage over the corrugated hole, and that hollow makes the site a peril. The excavated pit before Mr. Fortune and Mary Fortune warns them of the abyss that oppression is creating in the family, a chasm that can and does swallow them up. Like the moist sloping cavity, power is slippery. Both Mr. Fortune and Mary Fortune are physically at risk of falling down the embankment of the pit that has the very conical shape of Dante's inferno.

The paradox of economic power applies to gender relations. Though Mr. Fortune believes that selling off parcels of land enhances his prestige over Mary Fortune and the family, the physical positions that the old man and young girl instinctively assume suggest that the situation is otherwise. From the moment Mr. Fortune wakes, Mary Fortune is on top of him pulling the reins. She bestrides his chest in bed, ordering him to hurry so that they can see the concrete mixer at the construction site. At the new lakeside he sits on the car bumper, and "she sat on the hood with her bare feet on his shoulders" (338). When she wants to shift the direction of their verbal tilts, she stamps his shoulders with her feet to spur him. The old man must prove himself to the young girl. By laying his unlived life on Mary Fortune's youth, Mr. Fortune gives her power over him. He is under her feet.

The tableau of dispersed gender power sends forth a still sharper image to the anagogical eye. It takes the form of a three-part eyesore: Mary Fortune straddling the Cadillac hood with Mr. Fortune sitting below on the bumper. Female and male faces enclosing the car grill reproduce Dante's Cerberus, the three-throated dog with blood-red eyes and greasy black beard in Canto VI of the *Inferno*. Cerberus's job is to flog the souls being punished for gluttony as they wallow in filth and are pelted by fiery rain. As voracious eating fills Dante's scene, ravenous greed fills O'Connor's picture. The bulldozer first "systematically ate a square red hole" (335) in the earth and then stuffed the clay in its "big disembodied gullet" (335). As Mr. Fortune savors this gorging, he battens on his power to humiliate Pitts by selling the land out from under him. Dante's dog-devil registers O'Connor's censure of abusive power. She adds machinery to the monster's nature to update its political office in Georgia's burgeoning backwoods. On the Fortune place the ugly jumble dehumanizes as it devours victims.[4]

Power relations affect the needs of the human body. Everyone feels deprived. They hunger, eat, and remain starved. Mary Fortune has grown "stout" (346) trying to control her own life, but the girl cannot reclaim her body and spirit from her family's dominance. She understandably looks at the bulldozer with "complete absorption" (336) while it ingests and spits up soil. The mechanical rhythm catches her repeated efforts to satisfy an appetite for freedom only to be sickened by restraint. When the bulldozer threatens to go beyond the stake, the roaring girl lurches after the machine, again like a dog on a chain or leash. Whereas Mary Fortune's pale eyes seek freedom, Mr. Fortune's eyes crave to possess. He stares "sometimes for hours" (335) at the digging and building without reaching the bottom of his desire. And it seems unlikely that Mr. Fortune will grasp his essential human need. Having substituted wealth for power and power for human companionship, the isolated old man lives in vanity. This vanity is the emptiness portrayed in Ecclesiastes 4:8 in the person "who has no one" and feels "no end to all his toil" because "his eyes are never satisfied with riches."

One week before the story begins, during their last visit to the new lakeside, Mr. Fortune confides in Mary Fortune that he is negotiating to sell the lot in front of the house to a developer named Tilman for a gas station. This deal is no typical bit of devilry because this section is no ordinary piece of land. The property for sale lies not on the outskirts of the place but at the front door of the house, and the new gas station would imprison the Pittses by depriving them of their beautiful " 'lawn' " (342). Mary Fortune's daddy grazes his calves on the open space, and everyone enjoys the liberating view of the pine trees that rise across the road. The obliteration of their view of the woods is intolerable to the family, who experience Mr. Fortune's latest blight on their lives as the act of ecological terrorism he intended the sale to be.

Mr. Fortune tells the family about his plan at high noon during dinner. The unpalatable fare dished out by the old man sickens everyone and stirs the Cerberus instinct in Pitts. Pitts goes berserk with heaving rage. He blames his daughter for the sale of the lawn, summons her to the woods, and beats her with Cerberus's determination. Soon a self-sustaining process of abusive power runs its course. Pitts's impotence speaks to Mr. Fortune's impotence; then spite begets spite, and wrath speeds the male conflict to an unspeakable and mortal confrontation between old man and young girl. Mr. Fortune closes the transaction with a handshake at Tilman's, at which moment Mary Fortune fights for her family's interest by hurling bottles and whatever else is available at Tilman and her grandfather. This public tantrum of insubordination by a girl of nine outrages Mr. Fortune's sense of seigniory. As with Pitts, the affronted male ego closes its mind to anything but its own power. The Cerberus in the old man takes over. Mr. Fortune dumps the girl in his Cadillac to discipline the "hellion" (353) once and for all. Since Pitts by his flogging has endowed the young female body with the value of ownership and importance, his rival Mr. Fortune competes for rank by borrowing the penal practice he thinks the female subject respects. Mr. Fortune brings the girl to the exact spot where Pitts flogs her to reclaim his investment in Mary Fortune's obedience and to overmaster Pitts by means of his own effective method—the belt.

But the power generated by Mr. Fortune's feeling of rightful ascendancy again tricks him, this time into assuming that Mary Fortune's compliance with her father's beatings lies in her femaleness that bows by nature before all male discipline. In this story, however, male power is no single thing. Pitts's domination of Mary Fortune is based on the rule of father that keeps the daughter isolated and therefore despairing of aid to control her behavior. Mary Fortune survives by publicly giving in to Pitts's punishment but privately denying that it happens. She sends a mannequin to the post. " 'Nobody's ever beat me in my life,' " she snaps to her grandfather right after he sees her whipped, " 'and if anybody did, I'd kill him' " (351). This is not the weaker sex speaking. She means what she says.

By splitting her wounded body from her scarred psyche, Mary Fortune keeps her life intact. The social fact of the girl's untenable position leads to a political event. The very denial of her father's strappings compels Mary Fortune to examine her lowly status as victim and thereby toughens her resolve against abuse from any other source. Her determination is the tremendously empowering part of Mary Fortune's subjugation as a female child. It is this precise understanding of what abuse she will not take that brings about a stunning reversal of the crushing flow of destructive processes that make her oppression seem irresistible. In a world governed by leather jesses, Mary Fortune's protected anger stands out as a clearly marked locus of predetermined action to protect her body by getting rid of the laws put on it and to assert her freedom.

She repeats her death threat to her grandfather when he takes off his belt to reprove her for her rampage at Tilman's. The instant his belt slaps her ankles, the blow throws a switch located in Mary Fortune's guarded humanness, and her force cuts the current that has sustained the sinister hold over her. In a flash Mary Fortune is on top of the old man, pummelling his chest. Her sitting on Mr. Fortune repeats the position she takes on his shoulders at the beginning and later on his bed, but the playful aggression of those earlier scenes turns into fiendish hostility. The Cerberus in Mary Fortune comes alive. Nothing is more marked than her mouth with its vociferous appetite for revenge against Mr. Fortune and the absent male who initiated the beatings. Mary Fortune bites the side of Mr. Fortune's jaw. When he begs for mercy, she gnaws more deeply. Then with a sense of triumph she declares, " 'I'm PURE Pitts' " (355). Again power proves to be a delusion. Another stunning reversal occurs when Mary Fortune momentarily loosens her grip and the old man rolls over, mounts the girl, and grabs her neck. To mark the calculated horror of Mr. Fortune's action, the narrator counts carefully with the old man as he "once" pounds the child's head against a rock and then brings her skull down "twice more" (355). He kills her without remorse. He takes "two steps" and dies of a convulsive heart attack.

"A View of the Woods" ends with an indictment of all power relations. After years of physical abuse by her father, Mary Fortune lies dead with her skull cracked against a rock by her grandfather. The devaluation of the female child under mortal patriarchal domination by two male parents serves as an attack on sexist ideologies. Victory does not resolve power relations. Death does. At best, male physical power allows Pitts and Mr. Fortune to strike the pose of manhood confected by a sexist society. At worst, male power is killing and, in Mr. Fortune's case, self-destructive. But power in this story is not androcentric or exclusively misogynistic. Mary Fortune, at the cost of her life to be sure, betters the old man to the point of near death. O'Connor repeatedly says in her letters that holiness costs; this story shows that integrity costs. Besides, Mary Fortune brings down the entire place.

The ending of "A View of the Woods" is really three scenes engraved on one another like so many layers of a palimpsest. In the foreground the spot in the secluded woods on the Fortune place erupts into a calamitous double homicide, and depth on depth behind the bloodstained earth are the hellish exhibition of gluttons devouring each other and the apparition of violent sinners receiving the torment of their own brutality. O'Connor presents the maiming and killing of the girl and old man so that their cruelty is part of some vast process of sin and retribution that involves the entire universe and takes all time to complete. Another way to appreciate the ending is to see it as a spatial movement from the dark Georgia woods to the adjacent dismal wood of Dante's circle of gluttony (the third ring in upper hell) down to the circle of violence (the seventh ring in lower hell). The monstrous dog-devil Cerberus of the upper region intrudes his flesh-eating bulk in each of the scenes. Just before Mr. Fortune dies, he desperately looks around for help and finds only "one huge yellow monster which sat at the side, as stationary as he was, gorging itself on clay" (356). Except for the yellow color the hideous shape is unrecognizable, but we know from O'Connor's previous noting Mary Fortune's dress as yellow that the masticating figure is the corpse of the girl. She and Cerberus unite to open the jaws of hell before Mr. Fortune. In this ugly permutation Mr. Fortune sees his own "conquered image" (355). He who intends to give a good lesson gets back what he sends out, and he receives the lesson on his body, which now becomes the body of his knowledge of his doom. As a basis for a relationship between grandfather and granddaughter, power amounts to a gnawing on the humanness of the other.

The fact that in the shame of his soul Mr. Fortune cannot recognize Mary Fortune brings out the effect of his avarice. His greed renders all the members of his family invisible except as they serve his wealth. Money is his only real power and identity. The yellow of the chewing monster emblematizes the gold of Mr. Fortune's desire in the way that Dante's violent usurers (Canto XVII) are recognizable only by the escutcheon on their moneybags. Usury is another way of understanding O'Connor's handling of Mr. Fortune's evil against female and male alike. Usury is a sin against human industry and identity insofar as it reproduces only the material it begins with—in O'Connor's story, clay producing clay, a parody of productivity.

Dante puts the violent against nature along the outer margin of the seventh circle where they sit despondently in burning soil trying to fend off a rain of fire. A purse (one purse is yellow) hangs on the neck of each, and the eyes of these violent shades feast upon their moneybags. The moral climate of Dante's seventh ring prevails in "A View of the Woods" to vivify the condition of O'Connor's prediction of hell. After Mr. Fortune and Mary Fortune leave the courthouse with the sale papers ready for Tilman's signature, the sky darkens with a "hot sluggish tide" thickening the air, "the kind felt when a tornado is possible" (351). The old man rushes to Tilman's shed to beat the storm and wants the whipping of Mary Fortune over with before the "downpour" (354). If only the old codger had as good a country sense of emotional climate as he has of physical weather, he might duck the gale; but the eye of the turbulence lies within, and there is no escaping the several cyclonic waves of his own making. He and Tilman are first buffeted by Mary Fortune's flying objects. Shortly afterward in the woods "a pack of small demons" bombards Mr. Fortune in the form of Mary Fortune's fists, feet, and teeth. It is his own will to harm that plays the demon in him. Mary Fortune is the old man's retribution, his satanic wrath returning to him as the girl makes him "dance" under a "rain of blows" pounding his stomach. Like those damned in Dante's *Inferno* by their own violence who squirm in a burning tempest, Mr. Fortune rolls on the ground "like a man on fire" (355). A bizarre mud-wrestle in the red Georgia clay redescribes Dante's burning ground.

The forecast of hell is a foreboding of life without love, and love is the law of O'Connor's universe. By Mr. Fortune's abuse of love for Mary Fortune he engenders his doom. After nine years of power overwhelming her innocence, Mary Fortune ends triumphantly victimized. As he deprives his family of the status of their labor and the comfort of the environment, so Mary Fortune dispossesses Mr. Fortune of all he owns and any reward for his machinations. Though this young female is battered and killed by a rigid male system of control, Mary Fortune at nine seizes power decisively to defy the man at the center of oppression. O'Connor does not discriminate in depicting the physical balance of their combat; female and male share equally in destruction. Nor does she sentimentally quiver over the girl's daring and death; in a letter O'Connor flatly says the girl is "saved" (*HB* 190).

There is intensity behind O'Connor's treatment of gender hostility. Because her trust lies in Christianity as a prophetic faith rather than a civic religion, her zeal leaps over the barricade of social protest to the judgment that renders all gender power null and void. What remains at the end of "A View of the Woods" is the tract of woodland. This grace gift endures in sacred reserve. As the final scene opens, the long, thin pines "appeared to be gathered there to witness anything that would take place" (353). The trees alone, O'Connor states, "are pure enough" to put the carnage into moral perspective (*HB* 190). The trees escape the old man's exploitation and transcend the Pittses' desire for beauty. These evergreens indicate a judgment fixed from the foundation of all time, a prospective justice that resolves the destructive forces surrounding it and corrects the sexist distortion of Mary Fortune's humanity.

The trees are a consecrated landmark against which to measure the extent of human frailty and the expanse of an ungendered horizon. The woods offer a view that shows the two sexes in relation to each other not as two distinct entities but as two parts of a whole. This view is the hallowed ideogram expressing O'Connor's position on gender totality. It is the mystical feminism of a spiritual woman over against the civility of the humanist feminist, the grandeur of the theoretical feminist, the excitement of the proletarian feminist, and the common sense of the rebel feminist.

O'Connor shares with feminists the insistence that literature is tied indissolubly to reality. Unblinking before the oppression of our time, O'Connor puts before us the carrion of misogyny. And equally a realist of the invisible, O'Connor sees the spoils in the woods to be a shadow of God's final design and mutability as prefigured in Paul's world of Galatians 3:28 where there is "neither male nor female." Such a promise partakes of the countercultural force that gave rise to Christianity as a subversion of Rome's imperial structures. The eschatological unity evoked at the end of "A View of the Woods" carries a religious encouragement of social change here and now for both the theology and politics of the story assail the power relations generated by avarice and the death-dealing opposition between male and female. Subordination of Mary Fortune is an unjust violation of a female's original equality in creation. The view beyond her crushed skull into the future of justice and mercy calls for a restoration of the pristine plan for creation. From that measureless distance the pure woods disclose a condition of shared renovation beyond gender and the text.

If we take feminism to mean work that is "consistently political in its approach" to the task of destroying (Moi 167), then O'Connor's fiction could not be considered feminist. The hierarchical South suited her. Within its confinements she lived a sheltered life that brought a deep sense of belonging and an unflappable dignity. In contrast to her sexist time and place, O'Connor was serenely confident that women were equal to men. The artistic recognition she sought came and strengthened O'Connor as a woman writer and a woman of faith. In her faith the majestic Father of the Hebrew and Greek Bibles remained unchallenged as Lord and God; but as O'Connor's faith intertwined with her literary exploration, she came to write as though there were no gender differences.

The thrust of O'Connor's displacing gender is to show that personhood is not a property of another person or a social structure or a piece of property but a property of creation. Looking beyond gender enables O'Connor to assert human worth as a function of divine activity. Her writing is then able to claim a form of feminism that inheres not in political struggle or theoretical debate but in mystical insight.

From that spiritual perspective O'Connor would agree with Michel Foucault's denunciation in *The History of Sexuality* of the habit by which Western culture uses sexual marks above all other attributes in establishing individual identity (27). Biology may divide humans into two sexes, and Western culture may raise that division into favored fixity, but O'Connor does not use male/female as *the* dimension of identity. In her writing male is not a species, nor is female. The species is the undivided human as a created person invited by the Creator to share in yet a greater and more perfectly unified life. O'Connor's view of gender is a glimpse of liberating totality. The tragic balancing of power under the Georgia pines points toward the future unanimity in God. Curiously enough, by sidestepping the gender issue, O'Connor contributes to it through her great hope for final unity.

Notes

1. One measure of interest in O'Connor is the response to *Flannery O'Connor: Collected Works* edited with notes by Sally Fitzgerald (New York: Library of America, 1988). The first printing of twenty thousand copies sold out soon after publication in September 1988. Another twelve thousand were printed in November 1988 and in July 1989, another twelve thousand. At the time of publication, O'Connor's *Collected Works* was the most contemporary writing brought out by the Library of America. The volume continues to be among the most popular in the series. Sales figures and print runs for the many cloth and paper editions of O'Connor's fiction, letters, and essays by Farrar, Straus and Giroux, New American Library, and Harcourt, Brace are not available.

2. O'Connor has her feminist detractors and sympathizers. The overriding issue among these readers has been the relationship between mother and daughter. The close interdependency between O'Connor and her mother, Regina Cline O'Connor, makes this focus necessary and inevitable. For a sampling of responses to the filial and maternal pressures in the art of this powerful daughter written under the manorial roof of this powerful mother, see the titles by Lisa S. Babinec, Josephine Hendin, Claire [Katz] Kahane, Claire [Kahane] Katz, Louise Westling, and Margaret Whitt. In these discussions gender issues remain subordinate to women's issues, and "A View of the Woods" is not taken up.

3. On the issue of her church's patriarchy, O'Connor maintains a remarkable openness that anticipates current feminist thinking. She does not confuse faith with power structure based on gender. On 6 September 1955 she wrote to "A": "Of course I do not connect the Church exclusively with the Patriarchal Ideal. The death of such would not be the death of the Church, which is only now a seed and a Divine one" (*HB* 99).

4. O'Connor's use of food and hunger and her special attention to the mouth go back to ancient beliefs that the sin of Adam and Eve was not a sexual act but rather, as Peter Brown states it, was "their lust for physical food that had led them to disobey God's command." O'Connor extends this idea of hunger and rapacity to define the characters' need to free their bodies from the restraints of avarice and dominance, which in her economy overrides sexual desire. For a brilliant discussion of the subject see Brown, 220.

"The Crop": Limitation, Restraint, and Possibility

❖ ❖ ❖

Sarah Gordon

"To measure what is the flesh, the natural, the humanly given, and what are the mediating forces of personality, convention, culture is like weighing water with open hands. The 'semantics of biology'—the ways in which we codify, interpret, and experience our carnality, our mortality, the world of storm, stones and chromosomes— defy an easy reading."

—Catherine Stimpson as quoted by Carolyn Heilbrun, *Hamlet's Mother and Other Women*

Flannery O'Connor would doubtless have been chagrined to see her master's thesis stories included in the 1971 volume *The Complete Stories*. That thesis, "The Geranium: A Collection of Short Stories," was completed in 1947, dedicated to her teacher at the University of Iowa, Paul Engle, and largely put behind her as Flannery O'Connor moved on to complete *Wise Blood*. Although O'Connor used a later version of "The Train" as the opening chapter in *Wise Blood* and continued to rewrite her first published story and the first story in the collection, "The Geranium," until the end of her life, the other four stories in the thesis collection are slight, clearly the work of a young writer experimenting with form and voice. Indeed, until the late 1970s, critics largely ignored the six thesis stories, although their inclusion in the 1971 collection with its illuminating introduction by Robert Giroux would seem to have whetted scholars' interest. Indeed, to this day most commentators note the uncharacteristic absence of O'Connor's religious themes in these stories, citing "The Turkey" (and its later, more successful version, "An Afternoon in the Woods") as the most indicative of fictional interests and strategies of the mature writer. Although several commentaries on the thesis stories appeared before 1982, Frederick Asals's *Flannery O'Connor: The Imagination of Extremity* was perhaps the most noteworthy discussion of the early work, attempting to connect the subject, theme, and technique of these stories to the later work.

Among the thesis stories, only "The Geranium," "The Turkey," and "The Train" were published in O'Connor's lifetime. "The Barber," "Wildcat," and "The Crop" were published in the early 1970s by permission of the author's literary executor at the time, Robert Fitzgerald, who, in the case of both "The Barber" and "The Crop," appended a note explaining that the stories' shortcomings obviously resulted from their being early works. "The Barber" is of interest to critics largely because of its satire of the liberal intellectual, a theme that dominated the later work. "Wildcat," obviously indebted to Faulkner's "That Evening Sun," is usually cited as indicative of the young O'Connor's search for subject and voice. "The Crop," which has received no extended critical attention, may well be the most important story in the thesis collection.

On one draft of "The Crop" O'Connor scrawled, "UNPUBLISHABLE/ FOC 1953," (Dunn and Driggers 8), certainly a clear indication that the maturing writer saw the story's limitations. In 1948, however, O'Connor had tried to get the story published; she notes in a letter to Elizabeth McKee that the story is "for sale to the unparticular" (*HB* 6), and, later in that same year when a revision had been rejected, she wrote to McKee, "I should not write stories in the middle of a novel" (*HB* 7). In his note to the posthumous publication of the story (1971), however, Fitzgerald observed that "although it is obviously far from her best work, 'The Crop' would never be mistaken for anyone else's production," adding that "we enjoy a small caricature of that shady type, the imaginative artist," and that the "exacting art, the stringent spirit, and the sheer kick of her mature work are promised here" (Fitzgerald qtd. in *CS* 551).

Few would claim that the choice of subject matter in "The Crop" is propitious; in fact, a hallmark of the novice storyteller is the attempt to write about writers and writing, perhaps a necessary though self-conscious step in the evolution of self-confidence. Of course, Western literature is filled with successful examples of such writerly self-consciousness, and O'Connor was certainly familiar with many of them. Joyce's *Portrait of the Artist as a Young Man,* for example, exerted great influence on O'Connor, most particularly in her satiric portrait of the artist Asbury in "The Enduring Chill." In fact, O'Connor's scathing attack on her "artist" figure in that story is a subversion of the Joycean religion of art and the artist and of the romantic figure of the intense, sensitive, and alienated writer, superior to his surroundings and to the claims of family and familial duty. "The Enduring Chill," the work of the mature and focused O'Connor, is anticipated by "The Crop," the only O'Connor story that presents the artist as female. In spite of its superficial texture, this thesis story is noteworthy as a revelation of O'Connor's acknowledgment of the forces over which the female artist must have control; in some measure O'Connor is here revising Woolf's *Room of One's Own.* If the genuine confidence of a writer emanates from a real sense of control over material, the apprentice's story of the writer grappling with subject matter and with the basic questions of the relationship of art to life can be seen as an implicit acknowledgment of the territory to be conquered. Flannery O'Connor's "The Crop," although a sharply satirical account of a would-be artist, is just such an acknowledgment. Furthermore, this story suggests many of the dilemmas of the southern female artist in the middle of the twentieth century by implying the author's own questions of range, form, and content.

At the conclusion of "The Crop," we are certain that Miss Willerton will never complete a story. Having discarded several fanciful plots, including one in which she herself becomes involved as a character, Miss Willerton is ready to take up the subject of the Irish. The last sentence shows clearly that she knows no more about the Irish than she knows about the foreign bakers, teachers, or sharecroppers she has earlier considered for her subject matter: "Miss Willerton had always admired the Irish. Their brogue, she thought, was full of music; and their history—splendid! And the people, she mused, the Irish people! They were full of spirit—red-haired, with broad shoulders and great, drooping mustaches" (*CW* 41). (As we smile at the superficiality of Miss Willerton's knowledge of the Irish, we note also that the Irish "people" are present in her mind as a male stereotype. O'Connor is probably not satirizing Miss Willerton's neglect of the female population of Ireland; more than likely she herself thought in terms of the primacy of the male, a common enough practice at the time she wrote the story.)

Obviously, here O'Connor is satirically delineating the problems of a writer who seeks to write about a world of which she has little knowledge or experience. Moreover, O'Connor indirectly attacks the emphasis in mid-twentieth-century fiction on social and economic realism, especially as exemplified in the work of fellow Georgian Erskine Caldwell. Caldwell's stories of sharecroppers and other impoverished characters would certainly have fulfilled Miss Willerton's ideal: "Miss Willerton had never been intimately connected with sharecroppers but, she reflected, they would make as arty a subject as any, and they would give her that air of social concern which was so valuable to have in the circles she was hoping to travel!" (*CW* 35). Early on in the story we perceive Miss Willerton as a ludicrous figure, shallow and unfulfilled, preferring to escape to the dream life momentarily afforded her by her own fanciful creation, the story of Lot Motun.

Asals observes that "The Crop" points up the age-old theme of the difference between art and life; that although Miss Willerton "is no more than a stock character" (Asals *Flannery O'Connor* 16), she is nevertheless the first of the "comic authorial self-projections" presented throughout O'Connor's fiction; and that the story finally hints at O'Connor's own rejection of both "fashionable 'subjects,' elaborated by free-floating fantasy" (17) and the subject matter of everyday life *anywhere* (16–17). Asals's observations are certainly valid, but, in my view, they do not go far enough. That this story concerns a female writer, or would-be writer, is crucially important, for, although one can argue that O'Connor's scathing attack on Miss Willerton later culminates in such characters as Joy/Hulga Hopewell of "Good Country People," Julian in "Everything That Rises Must

Converge," and Asbury in "The Enduring Chill," we do well to remember
that Joy/Hulga is not a writer, or even a would-be writer, and that Julian
and Asbury are male. To be sure, Mary Elizabeth, Calhoun's double in
"The Partridge Festival," is an aspiring writer, but Miss Willerton is the
only female artist given center stage. As O'Connor's only treatment of the
myriad problems of the woman writer, "The Crop" anticipates her later
technique and her territory.

I believe that this early story constitutes a dialogue with herself for it
is a powerful statement of the author's attempt to exert control over her
own textuality, even as it describes, albeit in fiercely humorous fashion,
the attempt of a woman writer to exert that same control. And just as
Miss Willerton "kills off" the female protagonist in the sharecropper story
so that she may enter the plot as the replacement of that female character (an obvious attack on the notion of art as therapy or fulfillment for
the emotionally starved), so Miss Willerton's imaginative vision is "killed
off" by the interruption of Lucia, who asks "Willie" to go to the store
and thus thrusts her back into reality. Finally, in our minds as well as in
her own, O'Connor "kills off" Miss Willerton by making her a completely
foolish figure. Our laughter, elicited by O'Connor's relentless attack, is
the killing blow. Thus from the deathblow she gives to Miss Willerton's
idea of art and the artist and on the basis of our dismissal of Miss Willerton as a character not to be taken seriously, we see Flannery O'Connor
deconstructing in order to construct. If we look carefully, we may see
O'Connor's acute awareness of limitation, restraint, and possibility in the
female artist's situation, perhaps especially in the South.

If O'Connor had been asked whether this story was concerned with the
specific problems of the woman writer, she would very likely have ridiculed
such an idea. She was certainly not a feminist, and she would never have
claimed that the difficulties of the female writer differ significantly from
those of the male writer. After all, O'Connor wrote her disclaimer to "A"
in 1956: "On the subject of the feminist business, I just never think, that is
never think of qualities which are specifically feminine or masculine. I suppose I divide people into two classes: the Irksome and the Non-Irksome

without regard to sex. Yes and there are the Medium Irksome and the Rare Irksome" (*HB* 176). Her letters show no indication that O'Connor felt restricted as an artist because she was a woman. Her insightful and instructive comments about the writing process are usually stated in the most authoritative and objective terms, at least when she is writing to young or inexperienced writers who have sought her advice and opinions. As a writer schooled in the New Criticism and thereby greatly influenced by notions of the objective, impersonal artist found in the work of T. S. Eliot and others, O'Connor would have decried any apparently self-indulgent or self-serving analysis of writing difficulties. She believed that writing talent is a gift of God and that it must be developed with discipline and responsibility. Indeed, her letters reiterate the necessity for the writer to struggle and to do without, almost in the manner of priestly self-denial, in the process of creation; she wrote to "A" in 1956: "There is a great deal that has to either be given up or be taken away from you if you are going to succeed in writing a body of work," and added, in an unusual personal revelation, "There seem to be other conditions in life that demand celibacy besides the priesthood" (*HB* 176). Moreover, the stringency of her opinions and the authority with which she writes seem to place O'Connor in that "priesthood of critics" established by Eliot (Scott, *Gender of Modernism* 12). Eliot, in his qualified admiration of Djuna Barnes and Marianne Moore—the two female writers to whom he gives any critical attention—concentrates on those elements in their work that are in keeping with the "tradition" of the canonical writers, ignoring aspects of their work—especially that of Barnes—not easily assimilated into the "tradition" that was "European, white, and male" (Scott, *Gender of Modernism* 140). O'Connor's statements about writing, in her essays and letters, are not tentative and offer little of the experimentation with idea and the flexibility of approach that we associate with Virginia Woolf or other female critics. Writing, for O'Connor, involves struggle and difficulty, which can be overcome only through self-denial and discipline. In 1957, again in a letter to "A," who as a writer herself was apparently in need of a good bit of caution and corrective, O'Connor wrote, "In my whole time of writing the only parts that have come easy for me were Enoch Emery and Hulga; the rest has been pushing a stone uphill with my nose" (*HB* 241); she concluded the letter with this often quoted statement, "all writing is painful and . . . if it is not painful then it is not worth doing" (242). And in 1960, in yet another long letter to "A" on writerly concerns, O'Connor authoritatively stated, "You do not write the best you can for the sake of art but for the sake of returning your talent increased to the invisible God to use or not use as he sees fit" (*HB* 419). In this last statement, of course, O'Connor separates herself from Joyce and the fin-de-siècle idea of autonomous art as an article of faith and replaces it with the conservative Christian view of art espoused by Eliot's later poetry and criticism.

In her letters in *The Habit of Being* and in her essays or lectures first published as *Mystery and Manners,* Flannery O'Connor writes (or speaks) with absolute conviction on two subjects: writing and faith. To be sure, in the case of the authoritative letter and lecture or essay, she is usually addressing an audience of "seekers," whether writers, critics, or the spiritually hungry, and such conclusiveness and certainty might be expected. A teacher, after all, may lose effectiveness by admitting uncertainty or doubt about the subject matter. The possibility is very real, however, that those who have read a great deal of O'Connor's nonfiction will be at the least a bit discomfited by her self-assurance and even suspect her of covering her own doubt with dogmatism. Indeed, as we read the letters, we may notice that after laughing at O'Connor's anecdotes and after underscoring certain of her memorable and pithy statements about life and faith, we recognize the absence of something we are accustomed to finding in our own letters, namely the evidence of our common human questions, doubts, and uncertainties. We may eventually realize that the admirable firmness with which the twenty-five-year-old O'Connor stands up to John Selby, her editor at Holt Rinehart, asserting that *Wise Blood* is not intended to be a conventional novel, is only a harbinger of the firmness and authority to come. Although we may continue marking and remarking those pithy admonitions, we may want assurance that Flannery O'Connor is flesh and blood like the rest of us and that, at least from time to time, she experienced uncertainty and doubt about her faith and her talent. Rarely, however, does such an admission occur in the letters. Thus when, in a 1962 letter to Father McCown, O'Connor requests that the priest pray that God will send her some more stories, we may feel curiously gratified by her candor: "I've been writing for sixteen years and I have the sense of having exhausted my original potentiality and being now in need of the kind of grace that deepens perception, a new shot of life or something" (*HB* 468). That unusual admission stands in sharp contrast to O'Connor's characteristic objectivity and toughness, especially concerning matters of writing and faith. I believe that the beginnings of that objectivity and toughness, at least with respect to her writing, are evident in "The Crop."

As one might expect in an early story, "The Crop" is sketchy in certain details. Critics generally assume that Miss Willerton lives in a boarding-house, though there is no statement in the text to that effect. Furthermore, O'Connor lets us infer that the forty-four-year-old spinster has no full-time employment and that her "writing" is the means of wish fulfillment for a person who has never really entered life. We are easily led into these assumptions, I believe, because the condition of the "redundant woman" is so familiar; after all, the foolish old maid who is emotionally and sexually deprived is traditionally the brunt of jokes. She is therefore an easy target for O'Connor. Additional comedy is provided in this case, however, when O'Connor at the outset of the story demonstrates Miss Willerton's apparent uselessness: "Miss Willerton always crumbed the table. It was her particular household accomplishment and she did it with great thoroughness" (*CS* 33). These opening sentences anticipate a motif that underlies this story and much of O'Connor's later fiction—an implicit reaction against, perhaps even contempt for, those domestic and social duties usually associated with the "feminine" and womanly, especially in the traditional South. Indeed, a bit later Miss Willerton, in contemplating the niceties of style, remembers a talk she has given to the United Daughters of the Colonies in which she discussed "'phonetic art'" (*CS* 35). In this passage O'Connor clearly has great fun with Miss Willerton's preoccupation with the *sound* of her writing, for she had hardly arrived at her subject (the sharecropper Lot Motun and his dog) when she was pleased to be able to strike the two "Lot's" in one paragraph because such repetition is displeasing to the ear. Before the assembled ladies Miss Willerton is obviously more taken with the *sound* of her voice uttering its writerly platitudes than she has been seized by the will to write. In her view, style—or, as Miss Willerton defines it, "tonal quality" (CS 35)—is the essence of writing. Although in her own story she finds the opening sentence, "Lot Motun called his dog," to be "biting and sharp" (CS 35), she cannot proceed because of her ignorance of what sharecroppers actually do. Might they not be "reasonably . . . expected to roll over in the mud" (CS 35)? Indeed, she has read in clandestine fashion about such things in a book so shocking that when Lucia found it in Miss Willerton's bureau, she concluded that Garner had put it there as a joke. When Lucia tells Miss Willerton that she felt it necessary to burn the book, Miss Willerton "was sure it could be none other's than hers but she hesitated in claiming the distinction. She had ordered it from the publisher because she didn't want to ask for it at the library. It had cost her $3.75 with the postage and she had not finished the last four chapters. At least, she had got enough from it, though, to be able to say that Lot Motun might reasonably roll over in the mud with his dog" (CS 36). Her knowledge of the world and hence her subject matter will have to come from her secret reading in material that is considered unladylike, to say the least. Garner may read this book or have it in his possession, but Miss Willerton may not. And given her exclusion as a woman from the corridors of power (perhaps a double exclusion when we consider that she is also a spinster), where is her subject matter to come from? Interestingly enough, Lucia came upon the forbidden book while performing her domestic duty of cleaning, and as a female conditioned by the patriarchy, she denies Miss Willerton's possession of it. (She, too, would have had to sneak a look at the book, of course, to be able to say, "It was awful. . . . I burned it.") Evidently, such "awful" material, the raw facts of life, is the privilege and province of the male; to the female writer, therefore, are relegated whatever "crumbs" she can secretly collect of that awful real life and matters of "style," harmless enough and certainly appropriate feminine concerns. Perhaps not surprisingly, Miss Willerton's story concerns a male protagonist, although she recognizes that "there had to be a woman" (36), correctly assuming that the "real world," the world of "social problems," centers around men. Miss Willerton will provide the requisite femme fatale, recognizing, of course, that "that type of woman" will have to be killed off: "Now she would plan her action. There had to be a woman, of course. Perhaps Lot could kill her. That type of woman always started trouble. She might even goad him on to kill her because of her wantonness and then he would be pursued by his conscience maybe" (*CS* 36). The components of this plot are revealing. The story that Miss Willerton, in spite of her propriety, will tell is the archetypal one of a man goaded into killing a woman because she is sexually promiscuous. Eve-like, "that type of woman" inevitably instigates trouble; the male is only doing his duty and *perhaps* might be "pursued by his conscience." There-fore, in God-like fashion, Miss Willerton considers the creation of her own Garden of Eden, in which, in proper order, the man exists with his dog and then is joined by the woman, who will lead the man to sin, specifically murder. Our creator feels that it will be easy to give the man "principles," though combining principles with "all the love interest there'd have to be" (36) would doubtless be difficult. Seemingly delighting in these fictional problems, Miss Willerton recognizes that she will have to create "passion-ate scenes," and though she likes to "plan" them, "when she came to write them, she always began to feel peculiar and to wonder what the family would say when they read them" (36). We are reminded here, of course, of Virginia Woolf's "Angel in the House," the powerful conditioning that hovers over the shoulder of all women writers urging them to cut out, to censor, to avoid offending. Woolf cautions the woman writer that she will never be free to create until she has killed the "Angel in the House" and the notion that her work must please ("Professions for Women" 59–60).

The sentences that immediately follow Miss Willerton's concern for her family's reaction to her scenes of passion seem to suggest that Miss Willer-ton does not, in fact, live in a boardinghouse but that Garner, Bertha, and Lucia are members of her family. She wonders what they will say when they read these passionate passages: "Garner would snap his fingers and wink at her at every opportunity; Bertha would think she was terrible; and Lucia would say in that silly voice of hers, 'What have you been keeping from us, Willie? What have you been keeping from us?' and titter like she always did. But Miss Willerton couldn't think about that now; she had to plan her characters" (736–37).

Just what are the relationships among the characters in "The Crop"? Was the young O'Connor simply less than painstaking in providing expository material to explain Miss Willerton's situation? Or was Miss Willerton's situation simply not clear in O'Connor's own mind? Such an apparent contradiction is common enough among young writers, although we might have expected Paul Engle or other readers of O'Connor's thesis to have discerned the problem. Fragments and drafts of this story in the O'Connor Collection at Georgia College do not suggest changes in setting or any real elaboration of Miss Willerton's situation. In several fragments, Miss Willerton is "Miss Medger," has been a writer since the age of ten, and "instantly begins imagining an acceptance from *Harper's* whenever her thoughts become impure" (Dunn and Driggers 7). Thus, regardless of her failure to provide details of setting or background, O'Connor seems to have had problems of the writer's use of "impure" subject matter on her mind from the beginning of her work on the story. Moreover, one fragment suggests that acceptance of her story by a reputable magazine would go a long way toward nullifying Miss Medger's impure thoughts.

That O'Connor herself had misgivings about the response to her fiction on the part of her own family and her community is not surprising. In Milledgeville, stories abound to the effect that the local gentry were appalled by the contents of *Wise Blood,* that O'Connor's own relatives could not imagine where she had gotten her ideas (as one reportedly put it, "Mary Flannery always associated with *her own kind*"), and that some of her relatives wanted her to produce another *Gone with the Wind* (a fact confirmed by O'Connor's comments in *The Habit of Being* and echoed in "The Enduring Chill"). Sometimes in the letters O'Connor expressed her own misgivings humorously, at other times, seriously. Even late in her career, for example, she was concerned with the local reaction to "The Partridge Festival," not a sexually explicit story but one based on a shooting spree that actually took place in Milledgeville. She wrote Cecil Dawkins in 1960 that she had finished the story ("that farce") and added that although she had "made it less objectionable from the local standpoint," her mother "still didn't want [her] to publish it where it would be read around [Milledgeville]" (*HB* 404–5). O'Connor seems relieved to report that the story was accepted for the first issue of a new Catholic magazine, which would seem to guarantee that then largely Protestant Milledgeville would not have had access to it. Thus the dramatization of Miss Willerton's concern over her "family's" reaction to her depiction of scenes of passion suggests O'Connor's own concern as well as that of women writers for centuries. In this century, feminist writers and critics—from Virginia Woolf to Adrienne Rich, Sandra Gilbert, Susan Gubar, Carolyn Heilbrun, and Louise Westling—have not ceased to remind us of this constraint of subject matter and the audacity of women writers in defying such constraint. In *Sacred Groves and Ravaged Gardens: The Fiction of Eudora Welty, Carson McCullers, and Flannery O'Connor*, Westling addresses the special dilemma of the white female southern writer, focusing on the courage required when any southern woman decides to write. As Westling and others easily demonstrate, the ideal of southern womanhood, with its emphasis on "acting pretty" and supporting the white patriarchal power structure by refusing to utter a discouraging word (or a smart or an unpretty one), would seem to have precluded a woman's choice of the writer's life: "How could a person brought up to be soft and yielding, warm and self-sacrificing, dare to intrude herself upon the public mind? How could she presume?" (54).

Moreover, intruding herself upon the public mind is only the first step. If the woman writer is to succeed in pursuing her own vision and thereby establish control of her text, she must be as free as possible from societal (including familial) pressure to "act pretty." In "A Good Man Is Hard to Find," the concern of the grandmother with maintaining the appearance of a lady and her desperate attempt to assure herself and the Misfit, who is amazingly polite, even chivalrous, to his victims, that he is a good man who comes from good people are obviously O'Connor's fierce attacks on such superficial notions of goodness and worth. Commentators on southern culture such as W. J. Cash and Anne Firor Scott have underscored the powerful antebellum image of the "soft, submissive, perfect [white] woman" (Scott 21), an image that maintained its hold well into the twentieth century and is clearly embedded in the grandmother's consciousness, preoccupied as she is with ladylike appearance and with Tara-like plantations containing secret vaults. There is every indication, of course, that in her characterization of many of her female characters, Flannery O'Connor was rebelling against that silly image. Although she would undoubtedly be horrified at such a comparison, O'Connor might well be allied with Margaret Mitchell in her refusal to allow her female protagonists to follow the script for acceptable behavior. The popular Scarlett O'Hara, passionate and headstrong, may seem worlds apart from the grandmother, Joy/Hulga Hopewell, Lucynell Crater, Sally Poker Sash, or Ruby Turpin, but all of these characters reflect their authors' subversion of the ideal of the docile, submissive "lady," whose motto "Pretty is as pretty does" was put to many of us who grew up as females in the twentieth-century South. The female child protagonists in both "A Temple of the Holy Ghost" and "A Circle in the Fire" enact the anger and rebellion many of us experienced as adolescents in a region in which "doing pretty" and *pleasing* our mothers and young men counted above nearly everything. Moreover, in countering the ideal of the pretty, sweet, docile female, O'Connor is in a significant way freeing herself, perhaps in the only way her situation allowed.

Many southern writers have left home, both literally and imaginatively, to be free. Lucinda MacKethan observes that the actual act of writing is often tantamount to a woman's separating herself from the familiar and the secure. In discussing the works of Catherine Hammond and Harriet Jacobs, nineteenth-century southern writers, MacKethan asserts that "language led [Hammond and Jacobs] away from the patriarch's home, toward themselves," obviously implying that such women writers could not get to themselves without such a distancing and adding that "we can view the act of writing as an act of separation, an act of leaving home" (MacKethan

37). The implications of these last metaphors—for a woman, writing as separation, leaving home—are serious when we consider that Flannery O'Connor's literal time away from home was severely curtailed because of illness. We might even conclude that O'Connor never really left home at all, for the primary relationship of her life was that with her mother.

Like Emily Dickinson, O'Connor remained a daughter in her parent's house. Barbara Mossberg writes that Dickinson "never progressed beyond her primary identity as a daughter functioning in reference to her parents: she never left home" (10). O'Connor clearly intended to leave home and had begun the process of forming strong friendships in Iowa, New York, and Connecticut when illness necessitated a permanent return to Milledgeville and her mother's household. From this point on, her old friendships were maintained and new ones formed primarily through correspondence. The only child, the only daughter, O'Connor may indeed have found serenity and identity only through the solitary activity of writing, a way of "leaving home" and separating herself when literal mobility and independence became impossible. O'Connor's room on the first floor of the farmhouse at Andalusia was certainly her own, and we sense that books and writing (fiction, essays, letters) gave her Woolf's requisite five hundred pounds and a measure of freedom. That O'Connor was actually separated from her mother only briefly for the remainder of her life is crucial to our understanding of her fiction.

Like Emily Dickinson, O'Connor clearly rejected her mother's values. Mossberg describes Dickinson as rejecting the masculine or patriarchal ideal of femininity and motherhood embodied in her mother; she notes that Dickinson's mother is "largely absent from her chronicles of her intellectual and spiritual life" (43) but that when the mother does appear, "it is with gentle humor as [Dickinson] records and makes fun of her mother's use of clichés: *cold as ice, like a bird, turn over a new leaf*" as she "[asserts] her independence and disapproval of her mother's limited mental and moral conventionality, especially regarding expectations for women which the other tries to enforce" (43). *The Habit of Being* is filled, of course, with O'Connor's own humorous depictions of Regina O'Connor, complete with conversational exchanges. In these letters Regina emerges as the practical businesswoman absorbed in the affairs of life on the farm and removed from the realm of literature and ideas that occupied her daughter, though O'Connor's comical stories about her mother contribute in large part to the success of the letters. It is as though Flannery O'Connor is often the straight man for the humor Regina provides; O'Connor's "gentle humor" (and when we compare the tone of these anecdotes to the fierce humor of the stories, indeed it is gentle) seems to be her way of distancing herself from her mother's undeniable obstinacy and domination. Although the relationship between Flannery and Regina O'Connor cannot and should not be oversimplified, replete as it is with both great affection and rebellion on the daughter's part (the only version of the relationship on record), the evidence is plain that O'Connor did use both her fiction and her letters as a means of breaking away from the parent's values, of separating herself— of "leaving home" in the only way she could.

In the most profound sense, however, Flannery O'Connor never left her Father's house: although we have reason to believe that O'Connor did experience moments of questioning and resistance, especially in her early years, she remained a devout Catholic, indeed a compelling apologist for the faith, until her death. And because the patriarchal church imposes its own set of constraints, many of which have to do with the subordination and denial of the flesh, O'Connor would seem not to have found the freedom Virginia Woolf and others advocate for the woman writer. After all, O'Connor was an apologist for a church that forbade its parishioners to read certain books because of their sexual and moral content. (We are, ironically, here reminded of Lucia's comment to Miss Willerton on the discovery of that unacceptable book in her bureau: "'It was awful. . . . I burned it. . . . I was sure it couldn't be yours'" [36]. Here Lucia, not the church, seems to function as the censoring agent, motivated by society's expectations of ladylike propriety.) One could well argue, perhaps, that O'Connor never felt a lack of the freedom Woolf and others suggest is essential for the woman writer; her letters and essays testify to an individual apparently secure in her beliefs. To those readers and friends who would suggest that her imaginative freedom is restrained by the Catholic Church, O'Connor would undoubtedly say, as she did in the essay "The Church and the Fiction Writer" (published in the Catholic magazine *America* in 1957), "When people have told me that because I am a Catholic, I cannot be an artist, I have had to reply, ruefully, that because I am a Catholic, I cannot afford to be less than an artist" (*MM* 146) and "It is when the individual's faith is weak, not when it is strong, that he will be afraid of an honest fictional representation of life; and when there is a tendency to compartmentalize the spiritual and make it resident in a certain type of life only, the supernatural is apt to be lost" (*MM* 151).

To the Catholic audience of this essay, O'Connor argues that the church demands her utmost in the use of her talent and that when the spiritual becomes separate from the flesh in what she, on another occasion, terms "the Pious Style," the supernatural may be lost. Though she appears to be making a case for the necessary freedom of the Catholic artist, O'Connor in this same essay argues in favor of the church's policy of censorship:

The business of protecting souls from dangerous literature belongs properly to the Church. All fiction, even when it satisfies the requirements of art, will not turn out to be suitable for everyone's consumption, and if in some instance the Church sees fit to forbid the faithful to read a work without permission, the author, if he is a Catholic, will be thankful that the Church is willing to perform this service for him. It means that he can limit himself to the demands of art. (*MM* 149)

Clearly O'Connor is walking a fine line here, arguing on the one hand that the Catholic writer must describe "truthfully what he sees from where he is" (*MM* 150), that only those of weak faith will be fearful of "an honest fictional representation of life" (*MM* 151), and, on the other hand, that the church provides a real service for the Catholic writer (and, of course, any Catholic reader) by determining which works of literature are fit for her "consumption." O'Connor argues, furthermore, that the writer should be grateful for such a service! Although one of O'Connor's aims in this essay is to admonish Catholic readers about their lack of the "fundamental equipment" necessary for reading some kinds of literature (*MM* 151), we are awed, if not dismayed, by her confident support of the church's power to censor and her willingness to allow the church (an institution governed, we are to assume, by individuals who do possess the "fundamental equipment" necessary for sophisticated reading) to restrain the artist's freedom to explore, at least inasmuch as freedom to read what she pleases is essential to that freedom of exploration. O'Connor, incidentally, was thirty-two years old when "The Church and the Fiction Writer" was published. We may stand in awe of her youthful authority; we may be appalled by it.

In our consideration of O'Connor's own attitude toward artistic freedom, we should not forget Miss Willerton. "The Crop" contains no overt religious theme. Furthermore, the conclusions of "The Church and the Fiction Writer" come some ten years after O'Connor's thesis stories, suggesting that her commitment as a Christian writer was not established at the time of her graduate study. Miss Willerton's problems as a writer, exaggerated and frivolous as they may appear, are not resolved by the church's doctrine, the intervention of the supernatural, or the humbling of the protagonist as she recognizes her mortal frailty. Thus in a sense this story provides an unusual glimpse of O'Connor in that it outlines in comic fashion only the dilemma of the female artist, specifically with regard to her subject matter; O'Connor does not imply a solution, though she suggests that Miss Willerton's inability to understand either what she reads or what she experiences is a major stumbling block. The limitations of her sensibility appear related to her limited experience and to an idealization of writers that derives from that limited experience. Of course, the question is, What comes first, limited sensibility or limited experience? I suspect that O'Connor herself saw Miss Willerton largely in terms of an innately limited sensibility, perhaps an impenetrable obtuseness. That view is consonant with the writings of the "mature" O'Connor, who as a Christian writer holds that our limited, mortal natures are our downfall. Joy/Hulga in "Good Country People," Asbury in "The Enduring Chill," and Thomas in "The Comforts of Home" are surely Miss Willerton's mortal relatives. To see these and other O'Connor characters as of the family of sinners is to read O'Connor as she has been read by many very discerning critics, who often relate the theme of human frailty in the master's thesis stories to the emphasis on original sin in the work of the more mature writer.

To read Miss Willerton's limitations as at least partly the result of her status as unmarried woman in a society that devalues and even ridicules the unmarried female is also possible. The story certainly testifies to the marginal experience of this unmarried woman, and it also demonstrates O'Connor's own internalizing of the scorn directed at such a marginal and ultimately "useless" existence. Yet—after the laughter subsides—serious questions about woman as writer remain, and it is Flannery O'Connor who has raised these questions. I believe that, in creating Miss Willerton, O'Connor at least unconsciously acknowledges her own limitation of experience and therefore her own likely difficulties as an aspiring woman writer. Women writers, of course, have until very recently had severe problems with subject matter because they have been denied access to the corridors of power—the realms of politics, world affairs, and education, for example—and because their work usually was concerned with the domestic, it was often dismissed as trivial. Even Miss Willerton recognizes the problem when, near the end of the story, she contemplates the women in the grocery store and their limited lives:

Silly that a grocery should depress one—nothing in it but trifling domestic doings—women buying beans—riding children in those grocery go-carts—higgling about an eighth of a pound more or less of squash—what did they get out of it? Miss Willerton wondered. Where was there any chance for self-expression, for creation, for art? All around her it was the same—sidewalks full of people scurrying about with their hands full of little packages and their minds full of little packages—that woman there with the child on the leash, pulling him, jerking him, dragging him away from a window with a jack-o-lantern in it; she would probably be pulling and jerking him the rest of her life. And there was another, dropping a shopping bag all over the street, and another wiping a child's nose, and up the street an old woman was coming with three grandchildren jumping all over her, and behind them was a couple walking too close for refinement. (*CS* 40–41)

While O'Connor is obviously having fun here with Miss Willerton's superiority and condescension to the lives of ordinary women (note that the "people" in the street are mostly female, or so Miss Willerton perceives the scene), she also acknowledges, even in caricature, the problems for the woman writer described by Woolf and others earlier in the century. We might say that O'Connor is poking fun at Miss Willerton's assimilation of the ideas of feminists like Virginia Woolf, while indirectly acknowledging, in the thematic emphasis of the total story, the truth of those ideas. Although critics such as John May, Carter Martin, and Frederick Asals suggest that "The Crop" is, in May's words, "a thoroughly delightful spoof of the pitfalls of the creative writer" (May *The Pruning Word* 29), none of these critics treats the story as a depiction of the distinct dilemma of the writer who is female.

O'Connor grew up in a largely matriarchal, protective society. As accounts of her early years in Savannah attest, her childhood was spent largely in the company of female relatives; even though she attended parochial school and associated primarily with children from Irish Catholic families in Savannah, O'Connor's mother carefully supervised her playmates. According to one apocryphal report, Mrs. O'Connor kept a list of approved playmates and on at least one occasion sent a child home who was not on that list. Although the young O'Connor enjoyed a very close and loving relationship with her father, his employment difficulties and, later, his illness and premature death ensured that Regina O'Connor would be the dominant adult in her daughter's adolescence. Furthermore, the Cline house in Milledgeville, where O'Connor spent her high school and college years, was, after the father's death, essentially a female household, consisting of Flannery, her mother, and several aunts; and Peabody Laboratory School was female, to say nothing of Georgia State College for Women, from which O'Connor graduated in 1945. Surely O'Connor, well apprised of the expectations for white women in her society, was acutely aware of the courage that would be necessary for any woman who determined to be a writer. Louise Westling, Lucinda MacKethan, and others have specifically applied the conclusions of Sandra Gilbert and Susan Gubar to the southern locale in describing the sheer gall required of a woman who genuinely wishes to be a writer, that is, a woman who wishes to control her own text. The respectable southern white woman is

controlled by a script that calls for her submission to the ideal of southern womanhood, an ideal that does not include the freedom to think for
herself, to imagine other worlds, to set about inscribing those worlds.
Flannery O'Connor absorbed that milieu and grappled with it in "The
Crop," a story that can be read, to say the least, as subversive of niceness
and propriety. And in this instance, she subverts the conventional without
recourse to the teachings of the church. We may need to be reminded, also,
that this story was written at the same time that she was working on *Wise
Blood,* a fact that O'Connor believed accounted for the weakness of "The
Crop." To be sure, *Wise Blood,* with its male protagonist and obviously
Christian themes, would seem a far cry from the concerns of "The Crop,"
yet the drafts of *Wise Blood* suggest that O'Connor was intensely involved
in matters of femaleness as she worked on the novel as well.

In "The Crop," then, O'Connor is defining for herself what a woman
writer is by delineating what she is not or cannot be. This effete, fin-
icky woman, who cannot face reality—warts and all—is no artist. We are
amused by the apparent fastidiousness of a "writer" who has yet to write
the first scene of passion (there is no indication that she has actually *written*
anything beyond the first three sentences), and we may suspect that her
hesitation has a great deal to do with her own inability to deal with the
realities of the flesh. On her trip to the store, for example, Miss Willerton
makes note of the couple walking "too close for refinement," and, earlier,
the account of childbirth in her fantasy demonstrates real naïveté and is
clearly intended to point up her foolishness. Willie, who has become the
character in her own story, awakens with what she describes as "a soft,
green pain with purple lights running through it," and "her head rolled
from side to side and there were droning shapes grinding boulders in it"
(39). The pain of childbirth, apparently something like a bad headache, is
increasingly mingled with the "drone," which turns out to be the sound of
raindrops, a fact that Willie recognizes just as she is delivered of a daughter.
Miss Willerton's aversion to the reality of the physical is clearly demonstrated in the end of the story when she is confronted by her characters
in the flesh (fat ankles, mottled skin, stooped shoulders, and all) and can

only be repelled: "'Ugh,' she shuddered" (41). If we continue to read this story somewhat autobiographically—or at least as O'Connor the youthful writer facing her own situation—we may conclude that Miss Willerton's simultaneous attraction to and repulsion from matters of the physical in some measure reflects O'Connor's own conflict.

Although she wants to write of a relationship between the sexes, certainly a great part of the essence of real life, Miss Willerton is unable to, for several reasons. First, she fears writing about passion; second, she becomes so much a part of her own plot that it amounts to little more than a very idealized wish fulfillment; and finally, when she encounters in the grocery story the very characters she has created, she is repelled by them. "The Crop" can therefore be read as (albeit playful) self-mockery, serving to objectify many of the uncertainties O'Connor herself felt in her decision to be a writer. In this connection, we may find that Miss Willerton's nickname, Willie (sometimes in the drafts spelled "Willy"), not only mocks Miss Willerton's lack of will but also suggests those androgynous names which many aspiring women writers throughout history and especially in the nineteenth century adopted to hide their femaleness from male publishers' discriminating eyes. Interestingly enough, in one of the drafts of "The Crop," O'Connor allows her character, here named Miss Medger, to consider using a pseudonym:

This novel was a terrific thing. She really didn't know, if it got published, what her friends would say to her. They were all in it. What she had decided to do was use a pen name. Medger was not a good name for a novelist—particularly Edith wasn't, which was her first name. What she really thought about doing was to use a man's name [*sic*] Hilary & Ralph were her two favorite names—she didn't know whether she would use Ralph Hilary or Hilery [*sic*] Ralph. The first was more normal sounding but the more she thought about it, the more she really thought the other would be better. (15a, 2)

Here the writer's concern seems to be with her friends' opinions of what she will write; she will not reveal that she is the author of "Swept from the Heart" (15a, 3), a title certainly suggestive of inappropriate subject matter

for a woman author in the 1940s. At least two of O'Connor's own under-
graduate efforts were signed with pseudonyms (the silly female names
of "Jane Shorebanks" and "Gertrude Beachlock," as found in folders 4b
and 4c in the O'Connor Collection), indicating, at the least, the author's
early name consciousness. Moreover, Sally Fitzgerald notes that in 1942
O'Connor dropped the first name "Mary" on her college written work
(*CW* 1239), and her work in the *Corinthian,* the college literary magazine,
was signed "M. F. O'Connor," acts that certainly suggest her intention to
resist the feminizing and softening associated with the southern tradition
of double names for girls. Despite its euphonious lilt, "Mary Flannery"
is hardly a name that would connote strength and authority or lend itself
to a book jacket. I believe that in giving herself a new name, O'Connor
was in a certain measure creating a new self, her own text, and claiming
her own territory, one apart from the scripted one for dutiful southern
daughters. And in typical O'Connor fashion, she is not above mocking her
own action in "Good Country People," in which Joy changes her name to
Hulga to spite her mother. Significantly, just as Mrs. Hopewell agonizes
that Joy is a "poor stout girl in her thirties who [has] never danced a step
or had any *normal* good times" (*CS* 274), Mrs. Hopewell thinks that Joy
has deliberately chosen "the ugliest name in any language" (274); indeed,
whenever she thinks of the name, "she thought of the broad black hull of a
battleship" (274). The name, therefore, is clearly associated in Mrs. Hopewell's mind with her daughter's rebellion against "normal" good times.
Joy/Hulga is obviously aware of her rebellion; she views the name Hulga
"as the name of her highest creative act" (275) and is gratified that the
change of name has prevented her mother from turning "her dust into Joy"
(275). In accordance with the less-than-pleasing, less-than-feminine sound
of the name, Joy/Hulga dresses "in a six-year-old skirt and a yellow sweat
shirt with a faded cowboy embossed on it," and, much to Mrs. Hopewell's
chagrin, she appears amused by her own get-up. From Mrs. Hopewell's
point of view, each year Joy/Hulga "grew less like other people and more
like herself—bloated, rude, and squint-eyed" (276).

"Good Country People," which has as its center the archetypal comedy of seduction, is as close as Flannery O'Connor ever comes to treating sexual passion directly; it is surely the most moving (and most nearly positive) treatment of passion to be found in her published fiction. Furthermore, much of the success of that treatment depends on O'Connor's harshly satirical portrait of southern womanhood. It is as though by this time she has determined that the flesh—including matters of passion—that both attracted and repelled Miss Willerton can best be dealt with in relentless satire and the blackest of humor.

Clearly, Joy/Hulga's rebellion is primarily against her own mother and all that she stands for. Glynese and Carramae, Mrs. Freeman's two "normal" daughters, become "Glycerin" and "Carramel" to Joy/Hulga, who is obviously weary with her mother's use of these girls to point up Joy/Hulga's failure to have "normal" good times, though she is also perversely fascinated with Mrs. Freeman's morning reports of her daughters' activities. For Joy/Hulga, rebellion against the scripted behavior for "normal" females has several sources: her sense of physical unattractiveness as the result of the wooden leg, her feeling that her mother has not really confronted her physical deformity (she is not "normal"), and her belief that her own superior intellect elevates her above others' conventional beliefs and expectations. Furthermore, we suspect that the development of the intellect and her pride in it may be compensatory for all that she has suffered as the result of her deformity. Thus when the Bible salesman appears to be interested in her, she exhibits ambivalent feelings. She is secretly pleased at the prospect of this date, perhaps flattered by the attention she is receiving, and simultaneously contemptuous of Manley Pointer's narrow mind and limited outlook. She plans to seduce him (thus maintaining control of the script and again mocking traditional expectations of appropriate behavior for a lady), exulting in the fact that, afterward, she will have to contend with his Christian remorse. Of course, Joy/Hulga receives her comeuppance. The passionate feelings she experiences for the first time in her life lead her to lose control and to be willing to reveal to Manley Pointer that most fragile and intimate part of herself, the "secret" of her wooden leg's connection.

The Bible salesman's name certainly suggests his sexuality and at least one way that the encounter with him is to be significant to Joy/Hulga: the reminder that she is flesh and that she is capable of losing control. Through the fact of her femaleness, then, Joy/Hulga is opened to the fact of her creatureliness and the possibility for change, a recognition essential to O'Connor's Christian emphasis on the need for conversion. Without denying O'Connor's conscious intention as a Catholic writer, Louise Westling asserts that O'Connor often uses female characters whose autonomy is "continually punished by masculine assaults" (172) and that, especially in the "complex and troubling presentation of mothers and daughters in the farm stories," she "has inadvertently presented a poignant and often excruciating picture of the problems these women have in living together, of female self-loathing, powerlessness, and justified fear of masculine attack" (174). Thus, even as we grant O'Connor her theological point, we may find also a social one: writing from her own knowledge and experience of mannered southern society, O'Connor is greatly concerned with questions of female power and control. I am convinced that these questions were very much part of her evolving conception of herself as a writer and that, in certain early works such as "The Crop" and *Wise Blood,* especially in the drafts of that novel, she grappled with these questions. The mature O'Connor's answers to those questions of power and control, of course, will not be palatable to every reader. For example, just as those who are social conservatives may not like O'Connor's subversion of southern "manners"—or the means of that subversion in her use of the horrible and outrageous—those who are unbelievers or feminists (or both) may be repelled by the Christian emphasis on the fact of our flawed, fallen natures.

Although the need to establish her own textual territory apart from the expectations of appropriate female behavior, or questions of female power and control, are crucial in our reading of O'Connor's fiction, she intended her mature fiction to reflect the Christian emphasis on humanity's fallen nature, the need for belief. But are these concerns contradictory? Is it possible for a writer to seek authority and control over her own text, creating in O'Connor's case a deliberately harsh and punishing realm where ugliness seems a matter of course, and, simultaneously, to seek to demonstrate within that fiction the foolishness of just such attempts at attaining power and control? Does O'Connor not repeatedly demonstrate that those who separate themselves from Hawthorne's "magnetic chain of humanity," desiring desperately to be in control, risk damnation for their arrogant and often manipulative behavior? Joy/Hulga, Asbury, Mrs. McIntyre, Ruby Turpin, Julian, the grandmother, Mrs. Cope, Sheppard—these and many other O'Connor characters run such a risk. The conflict between O'Connor's own situation as a southern white woman who, though she wanted to leave home to write and thereby create her own territory apart from conventional social expectation, could not leave home, and her strong belief that her art must be used in the service of her faith is, I believe, responsible for much of the shape and content of her fiction. In fact, O'Connor's large and startling figures are to some extent the measure of the tension within the artist who sought to control her text as a means of asserting her power, of moving away from the nice and the pretty, all the while, of course, dramatizing, in her fictional territory, the limits of such power. Unlike Miss Willerton, O'Connor will not shudder when she looks at the mottled skin and fat ankles of people in the real world; instead, she will incorporate those details and much more that is ungainly, unexpected—even grotesque—in her fiction. And she will thereby establish for her readers the terms of the ongoing debate: What kind of author is telling these tales? What kind of Christian?

Apocalypse of Self, Resurrection of the Double: Flannery O'Connor's *The Violent Bear It Away*

Suzanne Morrow Paulson

Flannery O'Connor's *The Violent Bear It Away* seems to resist the glimpse of the author's "sacred consciousness" that she promised the reader.[1] An odyssey toward madness rather than salvation, the novel begins with the death of Mason Tarwater and ends with a grotesque "resurrection" as old Tarwater's will takes over the psyche of his young nephew, Francis. This "resurrection" of Mason's evangelical self in fact signifies the boy's psychological death: "Nothing seemed alive about the boy but his eyes" (*CW* 477). Are those eyes traditional signifiers (windows of the soul)? Or are they post-Freudian (castration displaced upward)?

Some traditionalists tend to see *The Violent Bear It Away* as a failure, missing the artfully interwoven but crippling interrelationships of the three main characters: Mason, Rayber, and Francis. A psychological reading centered on doubling phenomena seems pertinent to this, her second novel, which "turns" on events surrounding Rayber, the psychologist—not that this intensely complex and carefully wrought novel can be finally or easily explained or that we ought to equate the author's views with those of Rayber. But certainly we ought to heed O'Connor's statements in her letters: "I really have quite a respect for Freud when he isn't made into a philosopher" (*HB* 491).[2] We may acknowledge her belief in the "sacred" and still understand that she does not primarily aim to be a philosopher in her novels. She does aim to understand human nature and modern life.

Although she is a religious writer, O'Connor accepts Freudian theory and understands Freudian symbols in her attempt to come to grips with modern times and secular thinkers. Her letters reveal a keen interest in the "doubling" tradition (which includes such writers as Poe, Dostoevsky, Conrad, and Nabokov) — a modern tradition of using "eyes" in the Freudian way. And John T. Irwin's 1975 study argues that understanding the tradition of the double figure as it relates to Freudian thought rewards the critic desiring a complete understanding of Faulkner, the southern writer O'Connor admired most. O'Connor purposefully drew her characters to render what she calls the "many wills conflicting in one man."[3] Because few critics attend to this aspect of her intention, I will approach *The Violent Bear It Away* through Freud and the psychology of the divided self to suggest new possibilities for all her works.[4]

Throughout this novel, O'Connor suggests that old Tarwater cannot transcend the physical self and the bonds of egoistic and narcissistic desires. Pathological, Mason creates Jesus in his own image. Otto Rank's Freudian interpretation of doubling is apropos; in *The Double: A Psychoanalytic Study* Rank sees the double figure as "a projected wish fulfillment — and as a reflection of the subject's narcissism" (30). Jesus is for Mason a manifest double representing his own salvation. Mason declares his transcendence through Jesus, while O'Connor paints his physicality with a vividness that negates any such possibility. She draws the would-be prophet in the "bleeding stinking mad shadow of Jesus" (465), a symbol for entrapment and not salvation: "red ropes appear in his face" (335–36) with the death stroke. Even his corpse is trapped, unable to fall because his belly is caught under the breakfast table. O'Connor further defines Mason with imagery of the caged, erotic self: a "bull-like old man," with "silver protruding eyes that looked like two fish straining to get out of a net" (335).

Mason, portrayed as a primitive, unholy, false prophet-father, significantly builds a religion without woman, and any woman in the novel, any fleshly "goddess," represents sin as well as death. By focusing on the father and excluding worship of the holy mother, O'Connor separates Tarwater's religion from Catholicism — but beyond that she also suggests his severe ontological insecurity, his fear of death.[5] As Joseph Campbell notes in *A*

Hero with a Thousand Faces, the rejection of woman represents the desire to deny one's origin in the womb and to become the omphalos, that is, to be alive without knowledge of death (129). Any acknowledgment of woman necessitates an acknowledgment of the body and its functions — that men cannot give birth and that women cannot give birth alone. Moreover, physical generation produces the son who perpetuates the Oedipal tragedy.

Mason's narcissistic project is to make good his own "rescue" from the "womb-tomb" by repressing his own physicality, by affirming instead his spirituality, and by appointing himself the prophet-creator of a "procreative double," Francis, who will carry out his "calling." Mason gives birth to Francis through the rite of baptism and then orders Francis to baptize Rayber's son, Bishop, a dimwit, if old age or death prevents the crazed uncle from performing this sacrament in his lifetime. Francis carries out the order to baptize Bishop as though the old man were a ghost at his side. Using baptism to extend his boundaries of self like a wall around young Tarwater, Mason simultaneously performs an act of regeneration and murder — to be repeated later when Francis baptizes/murders Bishop.

Francis, then, becomes Mason's "immortal self." O'Connor informs us that Mason "was a one-notion man" (354), and this is irony at its best when we consider the old man's psychic fragmentation. Mason is not one, but two — or several — especially as he relates pathologically to Francis, who functions as both son and wife, offering hope for the future as a procreative double and serving as the necessary partner who staves off the loneliness of a solitary existence. Francis provides Mason with a sense of existing, but the great-uncle can tolerate his grandnephew only as a double, not as an independent human being.

The fury of Mason's efforts to save himself through the creation of a prophet-self and a procreative double intensifies each time he encounters the unwanted double, Rayber — the nephew Mason most vehemently denies. O'Connor, though, draws a parallel between them by making both men evangelical zealots. Rayber's skepticism and Mason's religious fervor grow out of a narcissistic drive to bolster a weak and deprived sense of self—a fearful self unable to develop meaningful relationships with others.

Mason, feeling threatened by Rayber, denies his nephew's very existence and asserts that he is "Nothing. He's full of nothing" (366). His sense of emptiness within serves as the precursor of *his* schizophrenia. He denies the vacuum he feels within his own self by projection—sometimes feeling Rayber's presence as "Nothing," and other times, like Rayber, suffering from a pathological sense of being penetrated by a threatening "Other." The boundaries of Mason's self waver, sometimes projecting another self outward when he instructs Francis to follow the calling, sometimes experiencing a psychic split within when he accepts orders from the Jesus-voice, and sometimes fearing an intrusion by a completely foreign self when he encounters Rayber. Although we "know that within the territory of ourselves there can be only our footprints" (43)—to borrow a phrase from R. D. Laing's *The Divided Self*—Mason feels that Rayber has been "creeping into his soul by the back door" (331). Mason feels not only that Rayber can get into his mind but also that by so doing he will be made into "a piece of information inside his head" (339).

Rayber's fears follow the belief in primitive cultures that death results from reproductions of the self in a mirror, photograph, or reflection. Tarwater acts "like he had been killed in his very soul" (345) when Rayber publishes his article on Mason's pathological state. His sense of an inner void makes him vulnerable to such fears as those that cause obsessive drives toward self-preservation—or extension of self to encompass the immortal double.

Mason, then, relates to others in clear-cut ways (love or hate exclusively). By examining Francis and Rayber from his perspective, we better fathom his psyche. A similar approach to Rayber proves worthwhile because both Mason and Rayber try to generate a procreative double, Francis. Rayber, though, demonstrates a complexity of motivation that Mason lacks: he suffers from a troubled conscience, a sense of guilt, and a profound ambivalence in his relationships to others—simultaneously fearing and seeking Francis, coveting and abhorring Bishop. To understand Rayber's character and his effect on Francis, we must first examine his similarities to Mason—especially those revealed by the Lucette incident. Moreover, understanding how Rayber differs from Mason and accounting for Bishop's and Francis's influence will clarify the threesome at the heart of this novel.

Rayber—no less a prophet than Mason but a prophet of death rather than resurrection—tells Francis that men don't "rise again" (399), wishing to "save" him from the notion of resurrection, from the "mad Jesus." Likewise, Rayber wishes to "save" the Carmody girl. He feels "some mysterious connection" (414) between himself and Lucette, comparing her case to his own "seduction" (408) by Mason. Doubling here transmogrifies to exploitation of another: Lucette by her parents, himself by his uncle, Francis by his great-uncle. Of course, irony colors our perception of Rayber's outrage as O'Connor likens Rayber to Mason. Rayber commits the same crime of exploitation by doubling when he attempts to remake Francis.

In fact, Rayber's "fanatical country preacher" side (438) mimes Mason and reveals the narcissistic nature of his endeavors to create a procreative double out of Francis. Much like Mason, Rayber's "uncontrollable fury" (393) and "fantastic anger" (394) peak when Francis resists his efforts at "reconstruction." Rayber condemns Mason's "foolish violence" (377), and yet this accuser is nearly capable of drowning a child. Hypocrisy and narcissism dominate Rayber's personality. He preaches to Mason about "the real world where there's no saviour but yourself" (379) and then advocates the prophet of self to Francis even more fervently because his own identity is at stake.

It is soon clear that not only Rayber's efforts at "reconstruction" but also Mason's muddied baptismal waters threaten the freedom of Francis, who weakly perceives the devil-prophet within them both. Before his return to Rayber, Francis is haunted by images of his past—memories that conflate various versions of his uncle "as if the schoolteacher, like the devil, could take on any look that suited him" (365). Moreover, Francis perceives the resemblance between Mason and Rayber whenever he ponders Rayber's eyes: "He saw them as dark gray, shadowed with knowledge, and the knowledge moved like tree reflections in a pond where far below the surface shadows a snake may glide and disappear" (365). These shadows of the old man's bulging, fish eyes (both fish and snakes glide in water) represent sexual sublimation. The snake is hardly visible.

Like Mason, Rayber eliminates the female element from his life and sublimates his misogyny, which stems from incestuous wishes as well as a fear of the "womb-tomb." Guilt results, and he seeks the mother to make amends by marrying Bernice Bishop, a woman twice his age who could produce but half a child. He then finds it necessary to get "rid of his wife" (400). Bishop becomes the wife for Rayber, as Francis did for Mason. The relationship of Rayber and Bishop parallels an illicit marriage between "two bachelors whose habits were so smoothly connected that they no longer needed to take notice of each other" (400). They function, that is, as a "couple," although not of the usual mixed gender. This same-sex relationship destroys the autonomy of both Rayber and Bishop.

Rayber's psychic problem becomes clear only when we better understand his relationship to Bishop. Rayber sometimes feels "a love for the child so outrageous that he would be left shocked and depressed for days, and trembling for his sanity" (401). Algene Balliff's review suggests that latent wishes for homosexual incest cause Rayber's divided self. He notes how both Francis and Rayber fear penetration by Mason's "seeds" and how Rayber wishes to avenge his early "seduction" by Mason (360). Rayber's ambivalent relationship to Bishop began with an ambivalent relationship to Mason. Rayber remarks that he feels a "morbid surge of a love that terrified him" when he thinks of "a stick or a stone, the line of a shadow, the absurd old man's walk of a starling crossing the sidewalk" (401). He also feels a "longing to have the old man's eyes—insane, fish-colored—" (401). The stick, the stone, the line, the fish, and the eyes suggest phallic symbols to a wide variety of analytical persuasions from Freud to Lacan. How does Rayber control his "longing"? O'Connor answers that question directly: "He slept in a narrow iron bed, spoke little, and cultivated the dullest of friends." In short, he lives a half-life of sublimated, incestuous homosexuality "to have any dignity at all" (402). Moreover, the author tells us that Rayber's "outrageous love" for Bishop is also "irrational and abnormal" (401).

Bishop, then, might be defined as Rayber's *seelenspiegel,* or double as mirror revealing "the imperfections of his inmost mind and soul," as Ralph Tymms puts it in another context (*Doubles* 83). Rayber keenly feels himself fragmented and deformed, even confusing his own maimed ear with Bishop's: "Absently Rayber put his hand on the little boy's ear . . . his fingers tingling as if they touched the sensitive scar of some old wound" (424) — that is, Rayber's wound from Mason's shotgun. Even when comforting his only son, the father's narcissism intrudes. Francis observes that the idiot child "might have been a deformed part of [Rayber] that had been accidentally revealed" (390). Bishop's presence stokes the fire that drives Rayber to make of Francis a narcissistic reflection of his own thoughts, thus achieving a sense of wholeness and extending himself in time by establishing a procreative double.

Gradually, the reader notices that the inability of human personality to establish a full relationship of communication and love — acceptance of the "other" as a person and not merely as a double — results in a setting devoid of sound. Rayber, Bishop, and Francis all share the same affliction — deafness — during the course of this novel. Rayber is deaf by Mason's gun, Bishop by an act of God, and "the boy [Francis] for all the interest he showed might have been the one who was deaf. Silent, he viewed everything with the same noncommittal eye" (398).

Others have noted the thematic importance of silence in this novel, but no one has realized that a probable source is Freud's study on repetition — a study that discusses the basis for "the uncanny effect of silence." Freud explains that our sense of experiencing an event as "uncanny" has to do with the return of the repressed.

Silence and deafness, then, signify the return of infantile memories felt as the presence of Mason — an intruding double representing "silent seeds" of madness within Rayber and Francis. Both the nephew and the grandnephew of Mason fear that these "seeds" may open "one at a time" (478) in their blood. Rayber wants to exorcise Francis's "morbid impulse" to baptize his son—that impulse which he considers a manifestation of the Mason within Francis.

Francis therefore represents to Rayber the affliction of having Mason as the devil double within. When Francis enters his house, Rayber feels the presence of Mason: "Rayber had never, even when old Tarwater had lived under his roof, been so conscious of the old man's presence" (398). Paradoxically, it is the Mason in Francis that Rayber fears and his own double in Francis that he seeks. The boy represents both a promise for immortality as a procreative double and a threat to Rayber's own sanity as a symbol for Mason. Rayber struggles to save himself by saving Francis: "The eyes [Francis's] were the eyes of the crazy student father, the personality was the old man's, and somewhere between the two, Rayber's own image was struggling to survive" (402).

The fact that Francis also represents a fragment of Rayber's guilt intensifies the schoolteacher's struggle: Rayber sees "some horror of his dreams take shape before him" (386) in the form of Francis because the boy's "eyes were not his own. They were the student's eyes, singed with guilt" (392). Who is the one most singed with guilt? Rayber feels guilty because he served as a sort of pimp for his sister, failed to pursue custody of Francis, attempted to murder Bishop, and sublimated his own homosexual urges.

How can Rayber claim the power to save Francis when he himself is so riddled with guilt? He bases his claim to strength on the false premise that he has exorcised himself of the old man, something he cannot substantiate. After his assertion of freedom ("I've resisted him"), O'Connor undercuts that claim: "He felt a madness on him to talk about the old man" (436).

Everyone in this novel wants to destroy or escape from the father figure. Nobody wants to *be* the responsible father. Rayber's only genuine opportunity to be the father and the savior is missed. O'Connor relentlessly depicts the isolation of each individual, the unwillingness to make sacrifices for others and to be self-giving.

When at long last Francis is receptive, Rayber is unable to transcend the barriers of his own narcissism and fails to offer Francis the helping hand he so desperately needs. Rayber follows Francis through the midnight streets but rejects him when he finally finds him outside the tabernacle—although "the sight of Rayber seemed to afford [Francis] relief amounting to rescue" (415). Rayber's wooden response to Francis's need tells us that there is no rescue, no resurrection, no salvation—only collision of warring selves and disintegration. Every double with an open heart meets his shadow with a closed heart. Rayber realizes this the next day when he again approaches Francis—too late; he faces "the glint of a metal door sealed against an intruder" (417).

Rayber's despair reaches its apex when he, too, begins to hear "the voice of a stranger" (407) within. Finally rejecting Francis as double because Mason possesses the boy, Rayber creates his own inner double as a final, desperate compensation. Rayber faces the hopelessness of Tarwater's schizoid self with a schism of his own psyche into "a violent and a rational self" (417), an inner and outer voice. The schoolteacher's story ends with Bishop's drowning—severing the all-too-tenuous threads of his psyche. Without Bishop, Rayber cannot live with his own guilt.

Being lost themselves, both Rayber and Mason direct the explosive force of their actions toward Francis. Their struggle to survive decimates their nephew. Whereas the patterns of doubling that Rayber and Mason typify are for the most part other-dependent, Francis tries to fortify his psychic energies independently. He must build the integrity of his own inner self while defending that self against intrusion by those who would remake him. To preserve his identity, he constantly battles against Mason and Rayber. Finally, Francis cannot develop his own personality because other ruthless personalities crash the soundless barrier of his consciousness. Tracing Francis's enormous struggle to expel Rayber and Mason—especially Mason's compulsion to baptize Bishop—will reveal that this novel ends by depicting a shattered form of Francis's psyche, a form that seems to absorb the identity of his two uncles and thus is lost.

Early in this novel, O'Connor establishes a relationship of doubling between Francis and the old man's corpse. The boy's visage is skeletal and ancient as he goes about the "bidnis" of burying his uncle. That he is double for a corpse foreshadows his psychological death—his ultimate possession by his great-uncle: "His cheekbones protruded, narrow and thin like the arms of a cross, and the hollows under them had an ancient look as if the child's skeleton beneath were as old as the world" (360). Mason's corpse forms an alien double within Francis. Laing describes a similar sense of alien personality traits "embedded as pieces of shrapnel in the body" (105). The "corpse" later pursues Francis in the form of Bishop.

Francis struggles to exorcise the father-corpse to save himself. Mason as double within (and in Bishop as double without) acts as the primary force that overwhelms O'Connor's protagonist, who tries to overcome the father and the facts of death not by creating an immortal self in the form of a procreative double like Rayber and Mason but by making of himself a god. For one thing, he clings to the idea of being an orphan born in a wreck because this makes him unique. He strives to attain epic proportions and hopes to transcend the anonymous crowd. As a result, he believes he evades the usual male-female conception. He rejects the father much in the same way that Mason and Rayber deny the mother and for the same reasons.

Indeed, the circumstances of Francis's birth as he is extracted from his mother's dead body seem miraculous, while paradoxically reinforcing the impression that he was doomed from the start. When Rayber tells Francis, "You have a father," he responds by feeling "some unspeakable outrage" (407). Having a father exposes his physicality and his mortality, thus undermining his claims to special conception. Being born from the "womb of a whore" is a perverse parody of the virgin birth of Christ; Francis acts "as if he were declaring a royal birth" (407).[6]

Similarly, escaping school is equated with escape from mortality. It was "the surest sign of his election" to study the prophets "who escaped death" (340). He accepts his great-uncle's religion when it includes "strange beasts with giant wings of fire" (334), but he rejects it when there is "no fire in his uncle's eyes and [when] he spoke only of the sweat and stink of the cross, of being born to die" (334). After Mason's death, when Francis expects "to hear a voice from on high," he hears instead the sounds of "a hen scratching beneath him" (337)—unintelligible sounds that point to his solitariness. The upper, fantasized world of the numinous universe comes crashing down when the voice of the despairing imagination rejects the uncommunicative chicken grubbing in the ground. Francis creates instead its own shadow-voice. He straddles two realities—a fantasized, private inner landscape and the all-too-real, external, public "other"—until he slips and falls into the mad world of his old uncle.

Francis attempts to act when all those around him are attempting to make him act for them. The essence of his struggle poignantly emerges as he looks into the fountain pool at his wavering reflection "trying to form itself" (432)—the barriers of self, unsteady and unclear. O'Connor grounds Francis's inability to establish a secure identity in his compulsion to baptize Bishop. This compulsion, of course, was implanted by Mason.

Upon the death of old Tarwater, Francis hopes to be reborn and to build a new self. There seems to be hope for a new start early in the novel when Francis approaches the womb of the city, saying: "I'm just now waking up" (363), but he then mistakes the city lights for the burning shack. This rebirth is "earmarked" by death as surely as Rayber was "earmarked" by Mason. The Mason *within* lives, and the city ahead represents death as surely as the shack behind. The journey to the city appears to be an escape from Mason, but nonetheless, he is everywhere along the way. Meeks, the nameless auto-carrier driver, and the rapist are objective, "double-by-duplication" character fragments of Mason—creations O'Connor meant to further define the relationship between Francis and Mason.[7]

In other words, Francis journeys to his uncle's house and along the way meets the salesman, Meeks, who represents the preaching and teaching side of Mason—not to mention the voice of the community promoting societal mandates to attend school and participate in the community. His words fall on the sleeping boy as his great-uncle's ignored sermons often fell when the boy was busy dreaming out the window. Like Tarwater, Meeks plans to teach the boy something whether he is receptive or not. He preaches the merits of love and work while disclaiming: "I'm not going to be a preacher to you" (380). Then on his way home, Francis serves the auto-carrier driver as he served Mason in that he needs the boy to hang on to consciousness so as not to crash, much as Mason needed Francis to give him a sense of existing. Both relationships are purely narcissistic. Finally, near Powderhead Francis encounters the man in the lavender shirt. When they first meet, O'Connor tells us that the boy saw "something familiar to him" (469), perhaps suggesting both Rayber and Mason, as well as their latent homosexuality that finds expression in this incident. Francis burns the place of the rape just as he burned Mason's shack. The rapist takes Francis's hat just as Mason and Rayber both attempted to appropriate a fragment of his self.[8]

Thus Francis struggles to expel both the will of the old man and that of his uncle. When Francis returns to Rayber, he observes: "His uncle's face was so familiar to him that he might have seen it every day of his life" (386), perhaps even in the mirror. He brags that he burned the old man just as Rayber would have done it. And in the end, he completes the job Rayber started when he attempted to drown his own son.[9]

To resist becoming the double of Rayber, Francis keeps his distance from the schoolteacher, maintains his isolation, and protects himself from his uncle's penetrating eyes, ironically becoming more and more the Mason who isolated himself at Powderhead. Francis also becomes more and more like Mason in that he fears penetration by Rayber, worriedly asserting: "I'm free . . . outside your head. I ain't in it" (400).

Francis cannot escape becoming a character fragment of both Rayber and Mason. When Rayber takes the boy to Cherokee Lodge hoping to win him over, Francis envisions the lake as a baptismal site. Then at the lodge, Rayber's face appears in Francis's mirror. The confused boy notices his own "weakness working itself up from his knees [and forcing] . . . a tremor in his jaw" (434), like the tremors that typify Rayber.

Bishop additionally threatens Francis. The reader wonders whether Francis makes a captive of Bishop, or Bishop captures Francis? Although Rayber concludes "that it was Bishop who had . . . made the capture" (452), the interactions of these cousins go beyond a mere power struggle. The first description of Bishop bears a striking resemblance to that of Francis:

Bishop: His eyes were slightly sunken beneath his forehead and his cheekbones were lower than they should have been. He stood there, dim and ancient, like a child who had been a child for centuries. (388)

Francis: His cheekbones protruded, narrow and thin, like the arms of a cross, and the hollows under them had an ancient look as if the child's skeleton beneath were old as the world. (360)

Bishop's "ancient look" haunts Francis as a symbol for the old man's will, which he fears yet compulsively obeys. The old man finally gets into everybody. His resemblance to Bishop unnerves both Francis and Rayber. At the lodge, it becomes evident just how much Mason has penetrated Francis when the boy writes "in an old man's meticulous hand" (425). After Francis murders Bishop, the disturbed boy again sees the old man's bulging, "fish-colored" (461) eyes. He seeks a sense of true self by murdering the person who represents his devil self, and in that very act he becomes a confirmed slave to Mason.

Francis's progress toward madness can be most clearly traced in his relationship to the strange voice that Francis hears when he digs his great-uncle's grave at the start of this novel—a "voice" announcing the coming of Francis's psychic split. The crack of the anguished self manufactures its own balm to soothe its sense of isolation, but the balm allows the two selves to slide apart. The creation of "another" voice marks the concluding stages of madness well documented in the literature on doubling.[10]

In Part 3, O'Connor manages surreal effects when she renders Francis's struggle to repress his "momentous failure" (457) by asserting that he has been "tried in the fire of his refusal, with all the old man's fancies burnt out of him" (464). The language and imagery of his denial contradict his claim: if he were truly rid of the old man's thoughts (often expressed by infernal imagery), he would not be speaking in terms of "fire of his refusal" or "fancies burnt out of him." The inner voice transmogrifies from friend or "the wise voice that sustained him" (429) to "adversary" (475). Francis burns his alter ego, clarifying the extent of his failure to exorcise Mason: he devastates his other self with fire, Mason's element.

Culminating in the image of the "crater opening inside him" (476), the apocalyptic imagery in the last pages of this novel implies the final and complete resurrection of Mason in the form of the devil-double within Francis. The significance of the seemingly apocalyptic world does not register beyond each isolated, individual psyche. The Negro Buford senses only "a burning in the atmosphere" (477). He observes but is not singed. O'Connor here affirms man's ultimate isolation and the reality that there is no ground without a grave somewhere nearby.

And where in this novel is that ground sacred? The complex patterns of doubling form an iron mesh that traps Francis. In spite of O'Connor's belief in personal responsibility, this novel acknowledges the forces of psychological determinism.[11] This is not to say that Francis lacked the freedom to struggle against the forces that undid him. O'Connor declares in her letters: "You might make a case of sorts for Tarwater being determined since his great uncle has expressly trained him to be a prophet . . . but actually neither of them [Rayber or Francis] exhibits a lack of free will . . . an absence of conflict . . . they spend all their time fighting within themselves, drive against drive" (*HB* 488).

By emphasizing the divided self here, I do not finally wish to undermine the importance of other approaches to O'Connor's work. Theology and philosophy ought to play a role in any analysis of her art. And yet her primary aim in this particular novel is to explore the suffering and psychology of a child and those who shaped that child. This suffering was perhaps partly caused by living in the modern world devoid of true faith, but more important, the suffering in this case was caused by parental abuse.

That O'Connor so clearly represents the psychological realities and the inner landscapes of her characters bespeaks her intense compassion for them. Often, she objected to those who viewed her characters as if through "a glass-bottomed boat" (*HB* 376). The author is demanding here that her reader experience sympathetically what her characters experience. We ought to feel sympathy not only for Francis but also for Mason. It is in this sense that she declares she is "right behind him [Mason] 100 percent."[12] Her assertion (*HB* 536) that Mason speaks the truth does not necessarily imply that his *actions* are divinely inspired. The irony that obtains when an evil character speaks the "truth" because an author wishes to emphasize a point is common enough in modern literature. We should not let O'Connor's statements about Mason mislead us into assuming, as Martha Stephens does, that the author approves of Mason's basic character (108).

Another statement of this sort about another evil character in a neglected story, "The Partridge Festival," clarifies O'Connor's position: "I am all for Singleton in this, devil though I rightly consider him to be" (*HB* 443). O'Connor suggests that acknowledging man's capacity for deviltry and accepting it as human, not alien, enables a person to "face his own psychic realities" (*HB* 382), exactly Freud's goal during therapy.

O'Connor studies will always be an arena for debate, given her paradoxical religious stand and yet her interest in Freudian psychology—her pious assertion that she is "against [Freud] tooth and toenail" and yet her willingness "to admit certain uses for [Freud]" (*HB* 110). This underlying conflict is expressed again and again in her letters and manuscripts. For example, she says that we ought to "love everything and specifically Christ" (*HB* 484) but admits to feeling a "lack of love for the race of man" (*HB* 335).

How can anyone claim to solve the dilemma of what O'Connor intended?[13] As the pain of living with disease gave way to the pain of facing death, O'Connor's work and her attitude toward it underwent constant revision. Where we ought to expect her work to yield most fully and easily to religious interpretation—that is, in a novel rife with biblical references and one that even quotes the Bible in the title—she proves most resistant. What we can finally assert is that the value of *The Violent Bear It Away* depends on its insights into human nature and what it reveals about the psychology of the divided self. Her other works offer a rich store of possibilities for further analysis in this vein.

Notes

1. In "Novelist and Believer" O'Connor affirms that the "sacred consciousness" of the author "will inevitably suggest that image of ultimate reality as it can be glimpsed in . . . the human situation" (*MM* 158).

2. Although O'Connor may have said that "a Freudian could read this novel and explain it all on the basis of Freud" (*IIB* 343) with tongue in cheek—and she certainly would not approve of the reductive notion that God is wish fulfillment— still she was familiar with Freud's work and probably attracted to his focus on narcissism and self-awareness.

3. O'Connor's preface to *Wise Blood* here quoted seems to contradict what she says in *Mystery and Manners:* "[In Francis's] compulsion to be a prophet . . . there is the mystery of God's will . . . not a compulsion in the clinical sense. [And then she hedges.] However, this is a complicated subject and requires to be elucidated by someone with more learning than I have" (116). Many have been misled by the earlier part of this quote. The fact is that O'Connor exhibits a definite interest in Freud, even acknowledging that for her first novel, *Wise Blood,* "the Oedipus business comes nearer home" (*MM* 68) than other sources. Needless to say, I disagree with earlier critics (cf. Martha Stephens's *Question of Flannery O'Connor*) that see her as a writer of "nothing . . . except pure religious passion" (131).

4. Most of the critics dealing with O'Connor's "double" figures lack a psycho-analytic perspective (Kahane and Rosenfield are exceptions): see Donald Gregory, "Enoch Emery: Ironic Doubling in *Wise Blood*"; Claire Rosenfield, "The Shadow Within: The Conscious and Unconscious Use of the Double"; Albert Sonnenfeld, "Flannery O'Connor: The Catholic Writer as Baptist"; and Marion Montgomery, "Cloaks and Hats and Doubling in Poe and Flannery O'Connor." In "Comic Vibrations and Self-Construction in Grotesque Literature," Claire Kahane points out that Enoch Emory mirrors Hazel Motes and relates doubling phenomena to the uncanny in the manner of Freud. An early review in *Commentary*, October 1960, by Algene Balliff, considers Tarwater's "double" traditionally, conceiving of the boy as half-angel, half-devil, thus neglecting psychological doubles, although Balliff's insights regarding Rayber's split seem sound.

5. I am indebted to Professor Chester G. Anderson's lectures on double fictions (April 1975, the University of Minnesota, Minneapolis).

6. See Otto Rank, *The Myth of the Birth of the Hero,* for an analysis of how

the virgin and holy births are connected in myth and pseudo-history as well as in childhood fantasies.

7. Ralph Tymms points out that "an essential distinction is to be made between the double-by-duplication and the double-by-division, though these distinct psychological approaches constantly mingle" (16).

8. The manuscripts collected at the Ina Dillard Russell Library in Milledgeville reveal O'Connor's ongoing interest in homosexuality. In one early draft of *Wise Blood,* Hazel seems to be trying to convince Leora Watts, a prostitute, that he is sexually experienced:

> "No," he said, "you are not the first. I was ten years old," he said, "and it wasn't a girl. It was a boy named Ford Tester."
>
> "You're making that up," she said. . . . Her eyes were dark and mocking, and he tried to see down into them.
>
> "There's nothing under them," he said. "There was nothing under this boy's either."
>
> "Them what?" she muttered. "You needn't liken me to any filthy kid you jerked off."
>
> "His eyes were clogged up," he said. "They looked like puss."

In another example, a scoutmaster tries to interest one of his scouts in sex: "Johnson went forward quickly as if he had been hit on the legs from behind and when he was in reach the master caught him by the shoulder and propelled him with one push into the dark far end of the loft. Then he strode after him and disappeared. B. K. could hear their voices but not the words. He could make out Johnson's hat and his shoulder with the master scout's fingers clutched around it. The hand moved back and forth suddenly as if the shoulder were a broken ear. It was thrusting in and out, then he heard Johnson whine, 'Lemme be, I ain't going to do it'" (Folders 168c–168f). The master scout in other versions of this incident is called the Misfit. Rayber's behavior in "The Barber" also should be seen in this context. The story starts with a barber asking Rayber, "You a nigger-lover?" in relation to the election of Darmon, a liberal. Rayber then notices the black helper, George, and wonders "what George's leanings were. He was a trim-looking boy" (*CS* 16).

9. Robert Rogers sees the case in which one character completes what another started as a special case of doubling.

10. E. T. A. Hoffmann, Georg Büchner, and Fyodor Dostoevsky exploit the idea of the "figment" voice in their doubling fictions about madness.

11. In "Psychological Determinism and Freedom in Flannery O'Connor," Nancy B. Barcus offers some insights on this issue and on Freudian elements in this novel, explaining that Rayber "has homosexual urges toward his idiot child, who somehow reminds him of the old man" (30).

12. Hicks, "A Writer at Home," 22.

13. For a discussion of character fragments, condensation, decomposition, and the "composite mind of the author," as related to the author's intention, see Rogers, 67.

"The Artificial Nigger": A Dialogical Narrative

Mary Neff Shaw

If for no other reason than Flannery O'Connor's assertion that "'The Artificial Nigger' is my favorite and probably the best thing I'll ever write" (*HB* 209), critics continue to debate over this narrative, one of the most controversial of O'Connor's short stories. Central to this debate is the tension between O'Connor's intention to dramatize Mr. Head's redemption through grace and her determination to maintain fidelity to the dramatic unities of character and action. Readers ponder whether the ending, "criticized widely as implausibly absurd" (Strickland 458), remains faithful to the integrity of the characters—whether, as O'Connor contends, "Mr. Head's redemption is all laid out inside the story" (*HB* 350). O'Connor acknowledges her difficulty in writing this narrative and even appears to qualify the attainment of her religious intention: "I was two or three months writing 'The Artificial Nigger' —which is a story in which there is an *apparent* action of grace" (*HB* 160; emphasis added); I had "a lot of trouble with the end" (*HB* 78). The tension created by O'Connor's dual commitments manifests itself primarily in the incongruous voice of the narrator, a voice often rich in poetic imagery and parodic irony and one that, in the fictional theory of Mikhail Bakhtin, vacillates between omniscient and limited perspectives. Curiously, however, this confusing voice is present only in the opening and concluding sections of the final version; all manuscript drafts include a coherent, unquestionably authoritative narrator.

Why did O'Connor have to rewrite this story, especially the beginning and ending, "a good many times" (*HB* 78)? What differences do the changes in the early drafts and final manuscript make in this narrative? Is there a connection between O'Connor's dual intentions and these changes? Bakhtin's insights on the dialogical nature of fictional narratives throw some new light on O'Connor's revisions to "The Artificial Nigger." The dialogical approach permits the reader to separate the multiple voices embedded in the seemingly authoritative voice of the narrator; to view a complexity in the plot unexplained by traditional analyses; and to understand how the changes in the final manuscript transform "The Artificial Nigger" from a monological narrative controlled by an authoritative narrative voice to a dialogic story permeated with multiple, autonomous speaking voices. Struggling to maintain her authority, the narrator parodies the authenticity of the protagonist, Mr. Head. Conversely, intent on escaping the mocking assault of the narrator, the protagonist forays into the narrator's territory so that a struggle between the narrator and the protagonist takes place in the "real *present* of the creative process," in a dramatization of "life poised *on the threshold*" (*Problems* 63).

The problematic issue concerning whether the assertions of the narrator and of the protagonist, Mr. Head, should be understood emphatically or ironically, especially at the conclusion of "The Artificial Nigger," remains central to critical scholarship. Assuming the narrator's voice to be authoritative and accurate (Gentry *Religion* 85–86; Brinkmeyer 81), some scholars finally determine Mr. Head to be filled with "pride and self-love" (Nisly 54), "moral earnestness" (Strickland 453), and divine "mercy" (Cheatham 475). Others, who observe a clash between the perspectives of the narrator and protagonist (Rubin "Company" 131), acknowledge an "ironic narrator" and see Mr. Head as "the victim of the author's treacherous irony" (Ludwin 12). Of these, Brinkmeyer and Gentry consider the story dialogically, but neither views the utterances of Mr. Head and Nelson as examples of dialogical narration by means of which "rebellious characters fight for what they sense is the truth" (Gentry *Religion* 8). Indeed, the characters, in Gentry's words, "never freed themselves from the narrator" (87; see also Brinkmeyer 81). I would argue, however, that the protagonist initially rivals and eventually plunders the narrator's authoritarianism, an action that does not "lead him into error," as Gentry argues (82), but into "freedom"[1] and redemption. Moreover, contrary to Brinkmeyer's assertion that this story contains little dialogue (83), "The Artificial Nigger" is rich in "that special type of novelistic dialogue that realizes itself within the boundaries of constructions that externally resemble monologue" (*Dialogic Imagination* 320). This "novelistic dialogue" enables Mr. Head finally to escape the authoritarian control of the narrator and offers us some guidelines for distinguishing between the narrator's and characters' emphatic and ironic statements.

In contrast to monologic narratives, which are "illuminated by a single authorial consciousness" (*Problems* 67), dialogic narratives acknowledge consciousnesses that escape the narrator's authority. Restricted only by the author's "limits of artistic design" (64), these consciousnesses experience an "autonomy unsuppressed by the *author's* single authoritative voice" (*Problems* 67).[2] Mikhail Bakhtin notes that in dialogized fiction, "even in those places where the author's voice seems at first glance to be unitary and consistent, direct and unmediatedly intentional, beneath that smooth single-languaged surface we can nevertheless uncover . . . a plurality of consciousnesses, with equal rights and each with its own world" (*Dialogic Imagination* 315). O'Connor's dilemma, then, is dramatizing Mr. Head's redemption within her "limits of artistic design," or, in her own words, assuring that in "The Artificial Nigger" her "moral sense . . . coincide[s] with [her] dramatic sense" (*MM* 76).

All the manuscript drafts of "The Artificial Nigger" are monologic narratives; only the published story is a dialogic narrative. In the drafts the coherent, authoritative voice of the narrator unquestionably reigns, and the realistic tone, reflecting stark actuality, resounds throughout the narrative.[3] For example, in the unpublished manuscripts, the omniscient narrator accurately describes the moonlight, which literally brightens all it shines on: "Moon light [*sic*] slanted into the room and over Nelson's pallet, brightening one side of a slopjar that stood in the middle of the floor, and then it reached across-lit [*sic*] up the alarm clock."[4]

But in the opening and concluding passages of the published version, the dialogical technique is manifested in the "double voicing" established between the narrator and Mr. Head and in the distorted temporal context created by the moonlight: "Mr. Head awakened to discover that the room was full of moonlight. . . . It rolled forward and cast a dignifying light on everything. The straight chair against the wall looked stiff and attentive as if it were waiting an order and Mr. Head's trousers, hanging to the back of it, had an almost noble air, like the garment some great man had just flung to his servant" (249). In the published versions of "The Artificial Nigger," this "double voicing" is produced by third-person narration, hybridization, and contextualized framing, terms that I shall define later. The incoherent narrative voice in this final version is actually not one narrative voice but two, two consciousnesses engaged in a struggle mirroring O'Connor's own internal commitment to both her dramatic and moral senses. Implanted within the consciousnesses of the narrator and the protagonist, Mr. Head, this narrative voice engages in heteroglossia, a term Bakhtin employs to refer to discourse that serves two speakers and expresses two intentions, the "direct intention of the character who is speaking, and the refracted intention of the author" (*Dialogic Imagination* 325). Hence Mr. Head forfeits at times his first-person point of view for a third-person narrative perspective. Because of this shift, he is able to penetrate the narrator's seemingly autonomous character "zone," a territory Bakhtin identifies as "the field of action for a character's voice" (*Dialogic Imagination* 316), and to fulfill O'Connor's "refracted intention" by validating his own redemption. Rivaling the narrator's authority, this third-person narrative voice forces the narrator to engage in a "double-voiced" dialogue not simply "about the character and action" but "with the character and action," according to Bakhtin.[5] Such a dialogue appears to comply with O'Connor's dramatic design; as she maintained, fiction should speak "with character and action, not about character and action" (*MM* 76). Moreover, the primary function of this third-person narrative voice is, in Bakhtin's words, "to destroy the framework" of the narrator's words about the protagonist. Thus, by assuming the third-person narrative consciousness, Mr. Head fulfills O'Connor's dual intentions—to declare himself redeemed through grace in a manner that does not discredit his personal integrity or make the conclusion of this narrative dramatically culpable. Conversely, to regain the authority jeopardized by this intrusion and to vindicate what he perceives to be O'Connor's violation of the dramatic unities, the narrator strives to undercut the perception, morals, and belief of Mr. Head.

Third-person narration, which Ann Banfield has called "represented speech and thought," holds identifiable trademarks.[6] Providing both immediacy and authenticity, this voice generates contemporaneity," Bakhtin's term for a "simultaneity of times—past, present or future" (*Dialogic Imagination* 426). It permits the reader to see through Mr. Head's immediate perception, his NOW, but is not locked into an "absolute" past or future time as is the perception of the narrator (*Dialogic Imagination* 426).[7] To identify the multiple voices in this narrative more expediently, I will use the following abbreviations:[8] RT (Represented Thought of Mr. Head) and NS (Narrator's Sentence, direct from the author and possessing the capacity to make judgments of the characters).

Hybridization, another form of double voicing, employs words, phrases, and clauses to incorporate two voices into the same syntactical unit. These hybrids, injecting the RT into the NS and vice versa, include the sometimes hyperbolic phrases of the RT, which do not agree with the stylistics and axiology of the NS and which at times may clash with the reader's attitude, and the parodic phrases of the NS, which seek to undercut the ethical and spiritual credibility of Mr. Head. The tension between these voices ensures "the primacy of context over the text" (*Dialogic Imagination* 428) and eliminates the possibility of viewing finished characters or a single, monological perspective.

Dialogic interaction occurs not only in the merging of consciousnesses but also in the framing of consciousnesses. According to Bakhtin, the "context embracing another's word is responsible for its dialogizing background, whose influence . . . may bring about fundamental changes even in another's utterance" (*Dialogic Imagination* 340). By extending the time-space parameters of the setting in "The Artificial Nigger," the "effects of context" (*Dialogic Imagination* 340) created by the moonlight in the opening and concluding passages of the final version relax the dramatic restrictions imposed not only on the setting but also on Mr. Head, whose authentic voice may then assume a speaking consciousness commensurate with his surroundings of fantasy and mystery.

Throughout the introductory paragraphs of the final version, the NS and RT aggressively battle to establish and maintain their control and lay the groundwork for their complex dialogic exchange in the final passages of the narrative. In these paragraphs, the NS, intent on stifling the RT's credibility, relentlessly tramples the RT's perception as well as the RT's moral character.[9] Although critics generally attribute all of the sentences in the first paragraph to the narrator,[10] a dialogic reading indicates that in this paragraph the narrator's voice becomes incongruent, rent by heteroglossia effected by the emerging RT through whose singular perception the room assumes fantastical qualities. In the opening sentence of this paragraph, the NS establishes an indicative tone with temporal bounds similar to that found in manuscript drafts: "Mr. Head awakened to discover that the room was full of moonlight" (249). In the second sentence, however, which is a hybrid, the voice shifts from the emphatic declaration of the NS—"He sat up and stared at the floor boards"—to the emerging perception of the RT, the consciousness that controls the rest of the paragraph.

In these remaining, richly imagistic sentences, the moonlight enables the RT to extend his own perception. Employing the moonlight as "contextualized framing," the RT imbues the room with an ethereal quality and casts a "dignifying light on everything": the boards of the floor appear to be "the color of silver," the pillow ticking "might have been brocade," the chair "looked stiff and attentive as if it were waiting an order," Mr. Head's trousers "had an almost noble air, like the garment some great man had just flung to his servant," and the "grave"-faced moon "gazed across the room and out the window" (249). The dialogical interchange between this context of fantasy and the RT loosens the time-space limitations imposed by the dramatic unities so that the discourse and actions of the RT in this passage and in the penultimate paragraph can extend beyond finite rationale and monologic dramatic conventions without jeopardizing the RT's integrity.

Although the reader may ponder whether the comments of the NS in the second paragraph of the published story should be read emphatically, like the comments made by the NS at the beginning of the first paragraph, or whether the NS, whose voice dominates the two subsequent paragraphs, actually parodies the tenor of Mr. Head's insights as an "exposé to destroy" Mr. Head's "character" (*Dialogic Imagination* 364), in the third paragraph of the published narrative, the comments of the NS are clearly exaggerated to reveal parody. Here the NS ridicules not only Mr. Head's "physical reactions," but also his "moral" responses. The declaration of the NS that Mr. Head's physical and moral "reactions . . . guided by his will and strong character . . . could be *seen plainly* in his features, a long tube-like face with a long rounded open jaw and a long depressed nose" (249; emphasis added) rests on an unsound, superficially qualified correlation. Although in these initial paragraphs the reader is not yet privy to Mr. Head's moral reactions, the fact that Mr. Head "was not dependent on any mechanical means [as the alarm on a clock] to awaken him" hardly reflects a "will and strong character." Moreover, to discredit the "effects of context," the NS declares the moonlight to be "miraculous" (249). Unlike the subjective, authentic perception of the RT, however, which has been freed from the temporal by this framing, the perception of the NS, whose dramatic boundaries remain distanced from his surroundings, is not loosened by this "miraculous" moonlight. Therefore, within this context, the declarations of the NS that Mr. Head's eyes assume a "look of composure and of ancient wisdom" like the gaze of Dante or Raphael are ridiculous. These opening passages lay the groundwork for our understanding of the final paragraphs of the story.

Only in the final version is the statue scene placed within the context of a "great mystery" (269), a dialogic framing essential for the revelation of the RT in the penultimate paragraph. According to O'Connor, such revelation through the particular is necessary to all "good fiction": "You need to go through the concrete situation to some experience of mystery" (*HB* 520). Devoid of this mysterious context, the manuscript drafts permit the NS to give only tentative sanction to the conciliatory effect of the "painted plaster figure" (MS 158: 30): "Neither Mr. Head nor Nelson ever knew how they were actually reconciled and neither suspected that it was the plaster negro that did it. Mr. Head thought later that it was the mercy of God and Nelson didn't like to think about it" (MS 158:29). Cast within the framework of mystery in the final version, however, this plaster figure somehow becomes a means of reconciliation, bringing the two "together in their common defeat," for they "could both feel it dissolving their differences like an action of mercy" (269). Neither understands, although each feels the effect of this humble "artificial nigger," intended, according to O'Connor, to suggest "the redemptive quality of the Negro's suffering for us all" (*HB* 35). Thus the reunion of the grandfather and grandson is somehow achieved through the "tragedy" of "nigger statuary" (*HB* 101), a "terrible symbol of what the South has done to itself" (*HB* 140).

In the manuscript drafts and in the published story, Nelson and Mr. Head return home immediately after their experience with the statue. In subsequent passages appended only to the published narrative, however, the RT describes the moonlit surroundings as Mr. Head and Nelson disembark from the train. Through the perception of the RT, the moon again assumes mysterious qualities that evoke the ethereal: "Restored to its full splendor, [the moon] sprang from a cloud and flooded the clearing with light. As they stepped off, the sage grass was shivering gently in shades of silver and the clinkers under their feet glittered with a fresh black light. The treetops, fencing the junction like the protecting walls of a garden, were darker than the sky which was hung with gigantic white clouds illuminated like lanterns" (269). Freeing the RT from temporal limitations, this mysterious framing context privileges the RT, which is inherently vested with the "contemporaneity" of an ever-present "NOW." In these circumstances the RT, examining the "mystery of [Mr. Head's] existence," judges Mr. Head and determines that he is redeemed by grace.

The RT's implementation of the "confessional self-utterance" (*Problems* 55–56) to understand the "truth" of this mystery accords with Bakhtin's conception of the fundamental mission of a fictional character in dialogism: "Clarifying the events to himself," the speaking person must discover "the *sum total of his consciousness and self-consciousness*" (*Problems* 48), or the "truth" of his "own consciousness" (*Problems* 55). This truth is vested in the "authentic" dialogue of the RT (*Problems* 63), not the representative dialogue of the NS, a crucial distinction to Bakhtin, for "in the mouth of another person [like the NS] a word or a definition identical in content would take on another meaning and tone, and would no longer be the truth" (*Problems* 55). The "truth about a man in the mouths of others," such as the NS, is "a *secondhand truth* . . . a *lie* degrading and deadening him" (*Problems* 59).

Only in the final version does O'Connor append the dialogical penultimate paragraph to the statue scene. In monologic narration, the deduction in this paragraph would have been embodied in the NS's consciousness; however, in dialogic narration, the revolution emanates from the RT's privileged perspective that bears the unquestioned "truth" of his own consciousness and extends beyond the restrictions imposed by the dramatic unities. As the confessor in this passage, Mr. Head echoes many of the ideas that O'Connor considers essential to grace:[11]

Mr. Head stood very still and felt the action of mercy touch him again, but this time he knew that there were no words in the world that could name it. He understood that it grew out of agony, which is not denied to any man and which is given in strange ways to children. He understood it was all a man could carry into death to give his Maker, and he suddenly burned with shame that he had so little of it to take with him. He stood appalled, judging himself with the thoroughness of God, while the action of mercy covered his pride like a flame and consumed it. He had never thought himself a great sinner before but he saw now that his true depravity had been hidden from him lest it cause him despair. He realized that he was forgiven for sins from the beginning of time, when he had conceived in his own heart the sin of Adam, until the present, when he had denied poor Nelson. He saw that no sin was too monstrous for him to claim as his own, and since God loved in proportion as he forgave, he felt ready at that instant to enter Paradise. (269–70)

Other than two hybrids injected by the NS, this entire passage is controlled by the RT, who engages in dialogue with both the NS and the reader. The first hybrid occurs in the initial clause of the first sentence when the NS states an indicative fact: "Mr. Head stood very still." This clause is immediately enjoined by the RT, who declares that he "felt the action of mercy touch him again, but this time he knew that there were no words in the world that could name it."[12] In this paragraph Mr. Head appears to experience both sorrow and contrition: "Appalled," Mr. Head "saw now . . . his true depravity" and acknowledged himself "a great sinner." Suddenly piercing the monologue of the RT, the voice of the NS mocks the RT's spiritual comprehension and parodically accuses him of deifying himself by "judging himself with the thoroughness of God." Regaining control in the final clause of this hybrid, the RT, empowered with "contemporaneity" and released from temporal bounds, silences the accusation of the NS by confessing that he "saw" his pride, recognized himself as "a great sinner," "realized that he was forgiven," knew that "God loved in proportion as he forgave," and now "felt ready . . . to enter Paradise"—to be redeemed. Thus, by breaking away from the grasp of the NS and plundering the "zone" of the NS, the RT realizes his "internal freedom" and "indeterminacy" and becomes "a fully valid 'thou,'" that is, an "autonomous *I*" (63), a role that, in Bakhtin's view, constitutes his "essence" (*Problems* 68).

Unlike monologism, which transforms the "consciousnesses of the characters into objects," dialogism permits an "active dialogic penetration into the unfinalizable depths of man" (*Problems* 68). Perhaps O'Connor is referring to these "depths" when she says, "There is a good deal more to it ['The Artificial Nigger'] than I understand myself" (*HB* 140). Although O'Connor dramatizes her belief in redemption by means of what Bakhtin refers to as a "concrete event made up of organized human orientations and voices" (*Problems* 93), her dramatization of this belief "does not extend beyond the limits of the dialogue and is not finalized" (*Problems* 99). As O'Connor points out, great fiction does not present the "Instant Answer" but may "[leave] us, like Job, with a renewed sense of mystery" (*MM* 184) or entrust us with a "new vision." In O'Connor's words, "Mr. Head is changed by his experience even though he remains Mr. Head; . . . he bears his same physical contours and peculiarities but they are all ordered to a new vision" (*HB* 275).

Returning to a temporal setting centered on these "peculiarities" belonging to Mr. Head and reinstating the coherent, authoritative voice of the narrator, the last paragraph of the story allows the reader to appreciate, from his grandson's perspective, Mr. Head's redemption: "Nelson, composing his expression under the shadow of his hat brim, watched him with a mixture of fatigue and suspicion, and as the train glided past them and disappeared like a frightened serpent into the woods, he muttered, 'I'm glad I've went once, but I'll never go back again!'" (270). Although Mr. Head has achieved his goal for Nelson, who agrees "never [to] go back" to the city, Nelson still holds his grandfather accountable for the consequences of his actions. According to the NS, instead of trusting Mr. Head, whom he earlier considered "indispensable" (257), Nelson now views his grandfather with "suspicion." Moreover, the concluding sentence of this paragraph may offer yet another reminder of Mr. Head's essential identity. The reader may wonder, in fact, if the "frightened serpent" that disappears "into the woods" is actually Mr. Head, who, by returning to the country, where prejudice prevails, figuratively goes back to the "woods," where he may again languish in prideful self-satisfaction.

In "The Artificial Nigger" O'Connor presents, in Bakhtin's terms, "an unclosed whole of life itself" (*Problems* 63), a snippet of Mr. Head's journey of life as he develops a measure of spiritual maturity. Such a journey follows an uneven road, moving from vanity to spiritual sensibility. Dialogism provides the "artistic design" vital to O'Connor's dramatization of this journey. Serving as an essential critical cipher for comprehending "The Artificial Nigger," dialogism allows the reader simultaneously to attribute the plurality of consciousnesses that seethe beneath the seemingly smooth surface of the story and to appreciate the rich complexity of its plot structure. Only in the published story, in which O'Connor ruptures the narrator's authority, alters the realistic opening paragraphs, and appends several paragraphs to the concluding section so that both the introductory and concluding passages are enclosed in a frame of mystery, is "The Artificial Nigger" transposed from a monologic to a dialogic narrative. Only then are O'Connor's religious and dramatic intents concomitantly achieved. Such an achievement, however, might have surprised even O'Connor, who might not have anticipated or consciously discerned that by meeting these dual commitments she would suspend her narrator's authority and deny her narrator's omniscience.

Notes

A version of this essay originally appeared in the *Flannery O'Connor Bulletin*, 1991. Reprinted by permission of the *Flannery O'Connor Bulletin*.

1. Gentry notes that unlike "most of O'Connor's protagonists, [Mr. Head does not] achieve freedom by turning away from the narrator's strictures" (*Religion* 82).

2. "A character's discourse is created by the author, but created in such a way that it can develop to the full its inner logic and independence. . . . As a result it does not fall out of the author's design, but only out of the monologic authorial field of vision" (*Problems* 65).

3. A comment by the narrator, later identified as NS, that appears only in the final version simultaneously directs the reader's attention to this realistic description and implicitly distinguishes its opposite, a context imbued with a mysterious aura: "The sun shed a dull dry light on the narrow street; *everything looked like exactly what it was*" (264; emphasis added).

4. In addition to the germ of "The Artificial Nigger" contained in the draft of *The Violent Bear It Away*, the O'Connor Collection includes four manuscripts of "The Artificial Nigger": a typescript carbon of thirty-one pages; a single-page typescript of the opening and a single-page script of the ending, which, when one considers the condition of the paper, may come from the same manuscript; and four pages of consecutive typescript that progress from Mr. Head's betrayal of Nelson to the account of the boarding of the train to return home.

5. More specifically, Bakhtin notes that the third-person voice allows the author

to engage in a "practical *transmission* of information," rather than simply to serve as a "*means* of representation" (*Dialogic Imagination* 340).

6. Employing untagged quotations from the character, this third-person narration shifts the verb tenses to the preterite, employs the conditional verb to function in a nonconditional, indicative role, and uses the third-person pronoun to refer to the speaker (Banfield 66). Banfield, in turn, adapts "represented speech and thought" from Otto Jaspersen. For a history of the evolution of the concept of *style indirect libre,* see Banfield 227 n14.

7. In *Unspeakable Sentences,* Ann Banfield notes the "atemporal" nature of this perspective, which "makes present . . . what is either absent or past" (268).

8. Christine Brooke-Rose employs these abbreviations for her paradigm.

9. Gentry states, "The narrator's pronouncements generally reinforce and extend what seems to be going on in Mr. Head's psyche" (*Religion* 82).

10. Some critics, such as Fiondella, have noted, however, the "clash between an omniscient viewpoint . . . and the contents of the narrative sentences" (121).

11. Acknowledging that in this confession she has "practically gone from the Garden of Eden to the Gates of Paradise" (*HB* 78), O'Connor elaborates in her letters on many of the elements mentioned in this passage. For instance, she notes the necessity of turning from the "terrible radical human pride" that "causes death" (*HB* 307) and points out the reciprocal nature of love: "Our salvation is worked out on earth according as we love one another" (*HB* 102).

12. According to O'Connor, this mercy or grace is "given" by God (*HB* 345) and "not denied to any man"; it uses "as its medium the imperfect, purely human, and even hypocritical" (*HB* 389), such as Mr. Head's betrayal of Nelson. To O'Connor, although "grace changes us and the change is painful" (*HB* 307), penance "follows sorrow" (*HB* 354).

Exhortation in *Wise Blood*: Rhetorical Theory as an Approach to Flannery O'Connor

Laura B. Kennelly

The impatience, often outright annoyance, shown by early critics of *Wise Blood* furnishes a clue to its rhetorical genre.[1] The clue lies in the respondents' emotionality. Flannery O'Connor seems to have struck a nerve, and I believe she has done so because she has written an exhortative novel. I use the term "exhortation" here in the sense introduced by Edwin Black in his pioneering 1965 study of modern adaptations of classical rhetorical techniques, *Rhetorical Criticism: A Study in Method* (138). First I wish to explain Black's concept of exhortative discourse and then look at *Wise Blood* as an exhortative communication whose genesis may be found in O'Connor's own alien or prophetic interpretation of life.

Black describes an "exhortative discourse" as one that falls outside the traditional neo-Aristotelian types, which use emotion as an adjunct in appeals to reason, justice, and so forth. In exhortation, emotion does not "bias the judgment of the auditors" and thereby affect their decision; instead, emotion creates a belief. As Black theorizes, in "this genre, a strong emotional experience does not follow the acceptance of a belief, or even accompany it; it precedes it. Emotion can be said to produce the belief, instead of the reverse" (138). Others who have noted this use of emotion, according to Black, include social psychologist Leon Festinger, who labels it "cognitive dissonance," and William James, who described the process as one that created "mental rearrangements."[2] These "mental rearrangements" are created not by appeals to reason, or to self-interest, or even to altruism, but by dramatic evocation of emotional experience. The work sweeps the reader into feeling, sensation, and perhaps empathy, thus producing an imaginative jolt that may cause a change in belief. Here we see impassioned pleas and calls to action in the tradition of Jonathan Edwards's "Sinners in the Hands of an Angry God" or William Lloyd Garrison's speeches against slavery. Here, too, I believe, we may find *Wise Blood*.

According to Black, exhortative discourse has three distinguishable features: it promotes an intense conviction and "alien" view; it depends on an extensive use of emotion to inspire belief; and it relies on a clear, easily understood literary style that uses the copula and concrete description. Although many works display some of these features, an exhortative work deliberately uses them to move the reader to adopt a new viewpoint—one the author believes is vitally important.

It is important to understand that an exhortation's first characteristic, its alien quality, is linked to its intent to produce a "radical conversion" and its "power to promote intense conviction." As Black explains,

It will be alien because its ideas and the values on which they are founded will be initially radical to its uncommitted auditors. The exhorter strives to convey an entirely different way of viewing the world and of reacting, in thought and in feeling, to it. What before was an ordinary convention of behavior to be considered, if at all, with cordial apathy, is now to be an object of intense reprobation. And what before was an extremist notion of a lunatic fringe is now to be an imperative guide to conduct and a cosmic epiphany. (142)

Certainly O'Connor's own account of her intentions, seen most clearly in her letters to fellow artists, strongly suggests that she believed her view to be alien and that she consciously wrote in what Black labels an "alien tongue" to seize the attention of her readers.[3] As she explained to John Hawkes in 1959, she feared that secular society lacked an awareness of the holy, an awareness that permeated everything she attempted:

I don't think you should write something as long as a novel around anything that is not of the gravest concern to you and everybody else and for me this is always the conflict between an attraction for the Holy and the disbelief in it that we breathe in with the air of the times. It's hard to believe always but more so in the world we live in now. There are some of us who have to pay for our faith every step of the way and who have to work out dramatically what it would be like without it and if being without it would be ultimately possible or not. I can't allow any of my characters, in a novel anyway, to stop in some halfway position. . . . Haze is saved by virtue of having wise blood; it's too wise for him ultimately to deny Christ.[4] (*HB* 349–50)

In O'Connor's case, then, "alien" means that she felt estranged from secular society. She cited with approval a 1955 critic who commented "that the best of my work sounded like the Old Testament would sound if it were being written today—in as much (partly) as the character's relation is directly with God rather than with other people" (*HB* 111).

As was true of the Old Testament prophets, she was inspired by an intense conviction, but her novelistic imagination prohibited her from consciously shouting out a message. A 1956 letter makes this point clear:

I believe that the writer's moral sense must coincide with his dramatic sense and this means that moral judgment has to be implicit in the act of vision. . . . It is popular to believe that in order to see clearly one must believe nothing. This may work well enough if you are observing cells under a microscope. It will not work if you are writing fiction. For the fiction writer, to believe nothing is to see nothing. I don't write to bring anybody a message, as you know yourself that this is not the purpose of the novelist; but the message I find in the life I see is a moral message. (*HB* 147)

This letter reveals a drive, if not to send a message, at least to share her moral vision with those she thought needed it.

Although O'Connor's extensive correspondence indicates that she realized her audience was varied, she seems to have had a special interest in reaching those she sometimes called "wingless chickens" in her letters. In 1950, she wrote to a friend: "The Brothers Rinehart and I have parted company to our mutual satisfaction and I have a contract with Harcourt,

Brace, but I am largely worried about wingless chickens. I feel this is the time for me to fulfill myself by stepping in and saving the chicken but I don't know exactly how since I am not bold. I only know I believe in the *complete* chicken" (*HB* 21). Her reference becomes clear in another letter, written five years later, when she complains about a bad review: "The notice in the *New Yorker* was not only moronic, it was unsigned. It was a case in which it is easy to see that the moral sense has been bred out of certain sections of the population, like the wings have been bred off certain chickens to produce more white meat on them. This is a generation of wingless chickens, which I suppose is what Nietzsche meant when he said God was dead" (90). Together the two letters suggest that a desire to save the "morally handicapped" impelled O'Connor and reveal her disgust at the notion that critical objectivity depends on absence of ethical beliefs. O'Connor took up the challenge of dramatizing for the secular world "an entirely different way of viewing the world and of responding to it"—a challenge Black believes inheres in an "alien vision."

The second distinguishing characteristic of an exhortation is that its "primary persuasive force" (Black 142) rests with emotional appeal. Situations and descriptions that trigger emotional responses permeate *Wise Blood*. By describing with relentless honesty Hazel's appearance and actions, O'Connor moves the reader first to pity, then despise, again pity, and finally, perhaps, to admire him.

We first meet Hazel on his way to the big city. When he arrives he seems pitiable as he desperately seeks support, even chasing a man who supposedly blinded himself as testimony to his faith in Jesus. Failing to find an answer with the fake blind man, Hazel tries to save himself by becoming a street preacher, grabbing strangers, collecting crowds, and shouting, "Show me where this new jesus is . . . and I'll set him up in the Church Without Christ and then you'll see the truth. . . . Give me this new jesus, somebody, so we'll all be saved by the sight of him!" (*CW* 80). Not only is Hazel frustrated in his search for a "new jesus," he seems to suffer from a very modern sense of *angst* when he preaches in one sermon that there is only "one truth and that is that there's no truth. . . . No truth behind all truths is what I and this church preach. Where you come from is gone, where you thought you were going to never was there, and where you are is no good unless you can get away from it. Where is there a place for you to be? No place."

"Nothing outside you can give you any place. . . ."

"Where in your time and in your body has Jesus redeemed you? . . . Show me where because I don't see the place." (*CW* 93)

Substitute "peace" for "place" in this passage and the anxiety of the spiritually dispossessed Hazel becomes even more poignant. The reader, initially, seems to be asked only to pity Hazel and perhaps to laugh at his foolish theological excesses.

Pity, however, is a dangerous emotion to feel for an O'Connor character because the author often uses it to trap the reader into a maudlin empathy, based on condescension, which she then destroys by having the pitied character do something horrible. To continue with the example of Hazel, initially he seems to be a relatively ineffectual hick for whom we feel sorry. As his trials continue, we share Hazel's indignation over the mercenary Hoover Shoat's coaching of Solace Layfield to imitate Hazel's oratory. The reader's sympathy quickly turns to revulsion, however, when Hazel hunts down Layfield, makes him strip, hits him with his Essex, and then deliberately runs it back and forth over his body. Hazel shows no sympathy when he gets out of the car to see whether he has killed the false preacher:

The man didn't look so much like Haze, lying on the ground on his face without his hat or suit on. A lot of blood was coming out of him and forming a puddle around his head. . . . Haze poked his toe in his side and he wheezed for a second and then was quiet. "Two things I can't stand," Haze said, " —a man that ain't true and one that mocks what is. You shouldn't ever have tampered with me if you didn't want what you got." (*CW* 115)

Now any pity for Hazel is offset by disgust at the single-minded violence with which he dispatches his enemies.

But O'Connor is not through with the reader's emotions yet. After

Hazel realizes that he himself is not true and that he has been mocking what is, he turns his judgment on himself, destroying his own eyes because they are his chief enemies. In contrast to his landlady, Mrs. Flood, who dogs him like a fury in his blindness, Hazel shows an admirable dignity in his calm, systematic search for the Jesus he has finally accepted. We know that Hazel ultimately succeeds in his quest because O'Connor grants us a vision through Mrs. Flood's eyes of the dead Hazel moving "farther and farther into the darkness until he was the pin point of light" (*CW* 131–32). That light, as I will explain more fully below (in context with the copula), seems to represent the light of God.

By forcing the reader to change feelings about Hazel several times, O'Connor also asks the reader to question common assumptions about who is to be pitied—the fool for Christ or the spiritually vacant?

We may also feel pity for Enoch Emory, the rural lad who tries to be-friend Hazel, but it is fleeting because Enoch's wise blood seems to protect him. Enoch wants Hazel to take care of him because, as he says, with his "face seamed and wet and a purple-pink color," his Daddy threw him out and he "ain't but eighteen year old . . . and [he] . . . don't know nobody, nobody here'll have nothing to do with nobody else" (*CW* 32). Enoch amuses us primarily because he acts unaided by his brain, trusting in his wise blood: "Sometimes he didn't think, he only wondered; then before long he would find himself doing this or that, like a bird finds itself build-ing a nest when it hasn't actually been planning to" (*CW* 73). We last see Enoch wearing a gorilla suit, happy at last as a powerful beast, but sur-prised because he still cannot make friends—now they run away screaming. Here our pity might well be turned to envy of those who are as easily pleased as Enoch.

On first reading *Wise Blood,* one may experience a predominance of unpleasant emotional effects, but comic effects become more readily ap-parent after one recovers from the shock of initial exposure to Mr. Hazel Motes and his friends. O'Connor's sharp, satirical eye is especially good at mocking contemporary priorities. In one of the funniest scenes exhibiting this mockery, the intensely practical Mrs. Flood confronts Hazel with the manifest insanity of wrapping barbed wire around his chest. She says, "It's not natural," and when Hazel replies that it is, she shifts her attack, saying, "Well, it's not normal. It's like one of them gory stories, it's something that people have quit doing—like boiling in oil or being a saint or walling up cats. . . . There's no reason for it. People have quit doing it" (*CW* 127). The scene closes with Mrs. Flood using what O'Connor describes as the "voice of High Sarcasm," reminding Hazel, "It's easier to bleed than sweat, Mr. Motes." Here we have a truly odd couple—a materialist and a mystic.

Other jabs at secular views appear throughout *Wise Blood*. We have Sabbath Lily Hawks parroting the advice she has received from newspaper columnist Mary Brittle: "A religious experience can be a beautiful addition to living if you put it in the proper prespective [*sic*] and do not let it warf [*sic*] you. Read some books on Ethical Culture" (*CW* 67). In one sentence O'Connor has satirically demolished newspaper advice, proofreading, situation ethics, and religion-as-social-patina. Another jest at the expense of pop religion may be seen in the genial religious tolerance Onnie Jay Holy preaches: "In the first place, friends, you can rely on it that it's nothing foreign connected with it. You don't have to believe nothing you don't understand and approve of. If you don't understand it, it ain't true and that's all there is to it. No jokers in the deck, friends" (*CW* 86). Hazel, of course, disagrees saying, "Blasphemy is the way to the truth . . . and there's no other way whether you understand it or not!" But Onnie Jay Holy will not be silenced and concludes that in his church "You can sit at home and interpit your own Bible however you feel in your heart it ought to be interpited . . . just the way Jesus would have done it" (*CW* 86–87). Hazel, who believes in dogma—albeit his own bizarre one—will have none of this wishy-washy stuff and denounces Holy to the crowd.[5] Indifference such as Onnie Jay's disguised as tolerance receives short shrift in *Wise Blood*.

In *Wise Blood*, O'Connor seems to appeal primarily to the reader's feelings. Eventually one may question the nature of Hazel's belief ("What could be worth dying for?") or Enoch's faith ("What do I treasure?"), aware of a subtly altered perspective; but the initial reaction is more likely to be close to that of the 1952 reviewer in the *New Republic* who felt only "pity, yes, sympathy, aversion, fear—all the emotions the insane call out" when considering O'Connor's fictional world (see note 1).

Because O'Connor was not especially interested in style per se, it seems unlikely that she deliberately set out to write in a particular rhetorical genre, but she did include stylistic elements that correspond to Black's third criterion for exhortative discourse. For O'Connor, form was inseparable from function, thus her desire to communicate clearly may have instinctively directed her to an exhortative style. "I have . . . led you astray by talking of technique as if it were something that could be separated from the rest of the story," she once wrote, "[because] it works best when it is unconscious" (*HB* 171). Deliberately or not, however, O'Connor consistently used the copula and precisely realistic description—the primary stylistic features with which Black characterizes an exhortation.

Exhortation, as Black points out, must be realistic because it must be easily understood, easily, immediately felt: "The concrete description, more readily grasped than abstractions would be, offers no hindrances to the understanding and, at the same time, serves to stimulate emotionally charged responses" (144). O'Connor's early critics generally agreed that *Wise Blood*'s style was realistic. As John Simons observed in *Commonweal* (1952), the novel is "written in a taut, dry, economical, and objective prose" (66, 297). Unusual actions occur, but they are physically possible ones. When, for example, Haze sneaks into Asa Hawks's room to see whether he is really blind (Hawks is a preacher, but Hazel doubts his authenticity), O'Connor supplies enough detail to place the reader in the scene:

He drove back to the house and let himself in but instead of going upstairs to his room, he stood in the hall, looking at the blind man's door. He went over to it and put his ear to the keyhole and heard the sound of snoring; he turned the knob gently but the door didn't move.

For the first time, the idea of picking the lock occurred to him. He felt in his pockets for an instrument and came on a small piece of wire that he sometimes used for a toothpick. There was only a dim light in the hall but it was enough for him to work by and he knelt down at the keyhole and inserted the wire into it carefully, trying not to make a noise.

After a while when he had tried the wire five or six different ways, there was a slight click in the lock. He stood up, trembling, and opened the door. His breath came short and his heart was palpitating as if he had run all the way here from a great distance. He stood just inside the room until his eyes got accustomed to the darkness and then he moved slowly over to the iron bed and stood there. Hawks was lying across it. His head was hanging over the edge. Haze squatted down by him and struck a match close to his face and he opened his eyes. The two sets of eyes looked at each other as long as the match lasted; Haze's expression seemed to open onto a deeper blankness and reflect something and then close again. (92)

O'Connor's description places us inside Haze as he trembles at the door, panting, his heart racing. We move across the floor with him to the sleeping body of Hawks, and his shock is ours when the "blind" man looks at him. O'Connor's meticulous rendering here, typical of the whole of *Wise Blood,* underscores Haze's desperation and despair when his worst suspicions about Hawks prove true.

The corporal reality of people in *Wise Blood* matches the verisimilitude of their actions. Haze is depicted, for example, obliquely but meticulously through the medium of a *doppelgänger.* While preaching, Motes immediately recognizes his twin: "He was so struck with how gaunt and thin he looked in the illusion that he stopped preaching. He had never pictured himself that way before. The man he saw was hollow-chested and carried his neck thrust forward and his arms down by his side; he stood there as if he were waiting for some signal he was afraid he might not catch" (91). O'Connor also draws minor figures with care. Sabbath Lily, for one, has a "pinched homely little face with bright green eyes and a grin" (92). Mrs. Wally Bee Hitchcock, the southern "lady" Haze meets on a train, is "a fat woman with pink collars and cuffs and pear-shaped legs that slanted off the train seat and didn't reach the floor" (9). These people seem real because O'Connor's ironic eye shapes, but does not destroy, her characters' authenticity.

Setting frequently signals the mood of an episode, but O'Connor's world breathes grimy reality, not fantasy. When Hazel, stepping off the train, first glimpses Taulkinham, the big city, he sees "signs and lights. PEANUTS, WESTERN UNION, AJAX, TAXI, HOTEL, CANDY. Most of them were electric and moved up and down or blinked frantically" (*CW* 15). He finally wanders into a men's toilet where he goes

into a narrow room lined on one side with wash-basins and on the other with a row of wooden stalls. The walls of this room had once been a bright cheerful yellow but now they were more nearly green and were decorated with handwriting and with various detailed drawings of the parts of the body of both men and women. Some of the stalls had doors on them and on one of the doors, written with what must have been a crayon, was the large word, WELCOME, followed by three exclamation points and something that looked like a snake. Haze entered this one. (*CW* 15)

Haze, who moved to Taulkinham to overcome his country upbringing's emphasis on Jesus and sin, must certainly believe he has come to the right place.

The copula, the second technique Black cites as characteristic of exhortation, also figures in O'Connor's rhetorical strategy in *Wise Blood*. First, it contributes to an important aspect of Hazel Motes's sermons. In his orations, like those of Black's exhorter, Hazel describes reality as he sees it rather than as he thinks it ought to be. As Black explains, exhortative discourse must describe what is:

Since radical conversion, which is the end of exhortation, implies the acceptance of a belief as absolutely true, the exhorter commonly bases his appeal on what he claims to be realities. Where the theoretician may conclude that there ought to be a revolution, or war, or last judgment, or reform, the exhorter, clad in the mantle of prophecy, proclaims that there *will* be. The exhorter aims, not so much at the inculcation of a belief in the moral superiority of certain modes of behavior, as at a belief that the world *is* a certain way. His concern is only incidentally with the rectitude of his proposals; he is more directly concerned with realities. Therefore his language is characterized by the use of the copula instead of the moral imperative. (143–44)

Haze, true to Black's analysis of an exhortative speaker, never says people should believe in the new jesus or that they should be clean. Instead, as the following passage from one of his sermons illustrates, he says they *are* clean or that the time of the new jesus *is* here:

"Sweet Jesus Christ Crucified," he said. "I want to tell you people something. Maybe you think you're not clean because you don't believe. Well you are clean, let me tell you that. Every one of you people are clean, and let me tell you why if you think it's because of Jesus Christ Crucified you're wrong. I don't say he wasn't crucified but I say it wasn't for you. Listenhere, I'm a preacher myself and I preach the truth. . . . Don't I have eyes in my head? Am I a blind man? Listenhere," he called, "I'm going to preach a new church. . . . It won't cost you nothing to join my church. It's not started yet but it's going to be." (*CW* 30–31)

Ironically, *Wise Blood* shows that the answers to Haze's rhetorical questions are, "Yes, you have eyes in your head" and "Yes, you are blind." Hazel, however, is presenting what he believes to be the truth about the world as it is, not as it ought to be.

This brings us to a second use of the copula in *Wise Blood*—as a pervasive metaphor, yoking key ideas. Richard Weaver's *Ethics of Rhetoric* (1948), a book O'Connor had in her library, explains the impact when ideas are joined grammatically—a common use of the copula:[6]

Because a sentence form exists in most if not all languages, there is some ground to suppose that it reflects a necessary operation of the mind, and this means not simply of the mind as psychologically constituted but also as logically constrained.

It is evident that when the mind frames a sentence, it performs the basic intellectual operation of analysis and re-synthesis. In this complete operation the mind is taking two or more classes and uniting them. . . . The unity itself, built up through many such associations, comes to have an existence all its own. . . . It is the repeated congruence in experience or in the imagination of such classes as "sun-heat" . . . which establishes the pattern, but our point is that the pattern once established can become disciplinary in itself and compel us to look for meaning within the formal unity it imposes. . . . Accordingly, although sentences are supposed to grow out of meaning, we can have sentences before meanings are apparent, and this is indeed the central point of our rhetoric of grammar. When we thus grasp the scope of the pattern before we interpret the meaning of the components, we are being affected by grammatical system. (117–18)

Weaver points out that joining two entities creates a new "thing in itself," something whose meaning may be known before the author's whole message is understood. An exhortation, as a whole, acts in a similar way on the audience, causing feeling, subconscious knowing, before conscious thought. It is in her use of visual imagery and visual experience that I suggest O'Connor's second use of the copula is closest to that described by Weaver. Metaphorically, the copula links the concept of Haze's vision and its unreliability throughout the novel. Time and again, Haze learns that his sight has deceived him.

As *Wise Blood* begins, Haze's visual errors are frequent. In the first chapter he mistakenly believes he recognizes the train's porter and makes a fool of himself with an assumed familiarity which is quickly rebuffed. In the second chapter he misses the right train because he had "been looking the other way" (*CW* 15). When he arrives in the city he is not sure whether he is visiting a whore or a lady and mistakes a sexually precocious teenager for a little girl. Chapter 3 finds him accepting a fake blind man as truly blind and crossing against the light because, as he tells the policeman in a comic scene, he "didn't see [the light]" (*CW* 24). Similar misidentifications continue as Haze tries to make his way in the urban environment of Taulkinham. At one point, about one-third of the way into the novel, Haze senses an idea similar to Weaver's that partial recognition of meaning may precede global understanding when he thinks about the strange things he has been seeing: "He had the feeling that everything he saw was a broken-off piece of some giant blank thing that he had forgotten had happened to him" (*CW* 42). Indeed, Haze recognizes that his sight is confused, but he does not yet recognize that his eye is diseased.

It is not until Chapter 11, however, that Haze's reliance on vision really begins to crack and he begins to doubt the truth of his central metaphor for life—namely, that what he sees is what *is,* and that since he cannot see Jesus, He does not exist for him. True to his oppositional nature, Haze betrays his doubt by hysterical insistence that he is right: "'I don't want nothing but the truth!' he shouted, 'and what you see is the truth and I've seen it!'" (*CW* 107). This speech signals the beginning of the end of Haze's trust in sight. In Chapter 13 he blinds himself, and in Chapter 14, the last one, he dies. Although O'Connor indicates by the light that Mrs. Flood "sees" in Hazel's eyes that the preacher is finally moving toward truth, his craziness, by worldly standards at least, seems to prove Black's observation that to "become convinced that our experiences have no validity, that the things we see and feel have no justification in fact, would be to undermine our sanity" (145). Unlike O'Connor's readers, who can comfortably reject the author's exhortative stance and the world drawn in Taulkinham, Haze is trapped there; each time his vision betrays him, he moves closer to total madness until finally, ironically, his "madness" saves him.

The idea of vision's inherent deceitfulness metaphorically dramatized in *Wise Blood* seems to have been used by O'Connor for several reasons. One is that it enables her to finish the novel. It was not until after reading *Oedipus* that she decided Haze should blind himself.[7] After that decision and after accepting some changes suggested by Caroline Gordon (as O'Connor explained in letters written between June 1951, when Harcourt took the book, and February 1952, when she sent back the page proofs to the publisher), she had to rework *Wise Blood.* Another reason that sight was important to O'Connor was her conviction that the eye, central to the spirit, had roots tracing pathways to the heart. As she wrote in "The Church and the Fiction Writer,"

For the writer of fiction, everything has its testing point in the eye, an organ which eventually involves the whole personality and as much of the world as can be got into it. . . . In any case, for the Catholic they [the roots of the eye] stretch far and away into those depths of mystery which the modern world is divided about— part of it trying to eliminate mystery while another part tries to rediscover it in disciplines less personally demanding than religion.[8] (*MM* 144–45)

It is also possible that O'Connor had in mind the biblical passage about the eye as the lamp of the body: "The lamp of the body is the eye. If thy eye be sound, thy whole body will be full of light. But if thy eye be evil, thy whole body will be full of darkness. Therefore if the light that is in thee is darkness, how great is the darkness itself" (*New Catholic Edition*, Matthew 6:22–24). As the novel progresses, the pattern of Hazel's experiences establishes the paradigm "What Hazel sees is false because his sight *is* distorted."[9]

Thus O'Connor uses the copula in two significant ways: first, in Haze's exhortative approach to the world in his sermons, and second, as a metaphor connecting Haze's trust in empirical sight with falsity.

While in *Wise Blood* O'Connor chose to mirror the novel's content (an exhortation) in its hero (an exhorter), she shifted focus in later works, diffusing her exhortative intent. She achieved this, primarily, by using characters who were more ordinary and less obviously God-driven than Hazel, with the notable exception of those in *The Violent Bear It Away*. Possibly she did so because she realized that a larger audience, unfamiliar with southern life, easily discounted the experiences of men they felt imaginary. In a 1955 letter, she wrote that her audience's refusal to accept Haze hurt the novel: "The failure of the novel seems to be that he [Haze Motes] is not believable enough as a human being to make his blinding himself believable for the reasons that he did it. For the things that I want them to do, my characters apparently will have to seem twice as human as humans. Well, it's a problem not solved by the will; if I am able to do anything about it, it will simply be something given" (*HB* 116). O'Connor's observation that by rejecting her characters critics could also reject her vision fits neatly with Black's comments on the same point when he speaks of the necessity of verisimilitude in exhortative dramatization:

Exhortation may be suggestively compared to the drama in one respect, and the suggestion can serve as a final comment on the basic strategy of exhortation. The auditor of the drama presupposes throughout the play, *If this character were really alive and in this situation, he would act thus and so in fulfilling the conditions of his personality.* For the playwright and the actor to adhere to these conditions, or even to provide unexpected but plausible alternative behavior, is what we call verisimilitude. The auditor of exhortation presupposes, *If I feel this strong emotion, then a certain set of propositions must be true.* The exhorter asserts the antecedent. (146)

And when the protagonist is not believable, as O'Connor's early critics seemed to tell her, then the novel is subject to critical misinterpretation because either the readers cannot relate to the characters and thus be emotionally affected or because the novel's applicability to "real" experience is discounted. Either way, the writer's desire to transform the reader's existing beliefs is frustrated.

Although O'Connor's assumption that her characters' strangeness contributed to the early critical misinterpretation of *Wise Blood* seems correct, I believe that part of the trouble also stemmed from rejection of O'Connor's rhetorical mode. *Wise Blood*'s alien view, its unsettling, vivid insistence that readers react emotionally, surprised and confused reviewers accustomed to appeals to reason or to abstract, intellectualized concerns. O'Connor exhorted her audience to listen to the wise blood within, to feel, and then to think, because she believed that contemporary society faced a dangerous loss of spiritual awareness. If the saga of Hazel Motes and those around him could transmit a new way of seeing life, then perhaps O'Connor could also, ultimately, encourage a transformation of beliefs in her audience, beliefs that harmonize with the spiritual outlook she believed vital to "saving the wingless chickens." By identifying *Wise Blood* as an exhortative discourse, we can better understand its early reception—and, by implication, the early reception of other controversial works—and we can also better understand our own response to Mary Flannery O'Connor.

Notes

1. O'Connor's fiction often provokes a visceral response, but her first novel, *Wise Blood* (1952), especially confounded reviewers. Many reacted condescendingly, seeing her as a possibly religious, definitely regional, writer concerned with grotesque, "strange, predatory people" (*New Yorker*, 14 June 1952, p. 118), who bore little relationship to real life or to real problems. Isaac Rosenfeld's reaction in the *New Republic*, 7 July 1952, page 19, was typical. Admitting that he may have "drawn some faulty observations," he continued that O'Connor dwelled on "degeneration" in an "insane world, peopled by monsters and submen." He concluded that because Hazel Motes is "a poor, sick, ugly raving lunatic" he cannot be taken seriously. Other reviewers agreed, seeing "a book which has no real plot," consisting of the "private twitchings of several almost totally dislocated individuals" indulging in "grotesque variations of the same evangelical enterprise" (Lewis 150), or one which was a "kind of Southern Baptist version of *The Hound of Heaven*" (Simons 297) or the result "if Kafka had been set to writing the continuity for L'il Abner" (*Time*, 9 June 1952, p. 110). These critics and others declared O'Connor's work applicable only to the remote, morally unredeemed, and backward South, a location packed with resident crazies and tolerated eccentrics. There are, of course, helpful works that discuss O'Connor as a regional author, including Gentry's "The Eye vs. the Body," Schleifer's "Rural Gothic," Shinn's "Flannery O'Connor and the Violence of Grace," Duhamel's "The Novelist as Prophet," and Cheney's "Flannery O'Connor's Campaign for Her Country." Longer works that also examine early responses to O'Connor include May's *The Pruning Word,* Driskell and Brittain's *The Eternal Crossroads,* Friedman and Lawson's *The Added Dimension,* and Coles's *Flannery O'Connor's South.*

2. Cognitive dissonance, as Leon Festinger describes it, arises when a person feels or believes something that cannot be reconciled with his existing belief system. If these differences cannot be rationalized or reconciled, then the person becomes upset and unhappy. Because people instinctively seek a state of "consonance," or harmony between belief and action, the conflict created by cognitive dissonance may result in acceptance of a new belief to justify new feelings or it may cause rejection of the source of the upset. Either reaction restores psychological harmony.

3. W. F. Monroe refers to the result of this effort to get attention as one that makes us "squirm." He observes that O'Connor prefers to engage readers in "an experiential process, especially if it is a moving or unsettling one" (64).

4. Throughout her letters as well as in her numerous articles and lectures, O'Connor indicates her abiding interest in spiritual matters. For a discussion of religion in her letters see Ficken, Klug, and Coulthard.

5. Hazel's fierce conviction that some things can only be absolute seems to reflect O'Connor's own belief, dramatically stated at the famous dinner party with Mary McCarthy and other "Big Intellectuals" (her words). When someone said that the Holy Eucharist was a pretty good symbol, O'Connor, who had been silent all night, lashed out "in a very shaky voice, 'Well, if it's a symbol, to hell with it'" (*HB* 125).

6. O'Connor evidently valued Weaver's ideas because she wrote just before she died, "I once had a copy [of Weaver's book] but I gave it to somebody . . . and now I'm sorry I did" (*HB* 595).

7. Fitzgerald, "Introduction," xiii.

8. For further discussion of light and vision in Flannery O'Connor see Maida.

9. It is interesting that in another biblical passage a man called Hazael knows himself so poorly he doubts that "this dog" could be so ruthless (2 Kings 8:9–13).

Asceticism and the Imaginative Vision of Flannery O'Connor

Robert H. Brinkmeyer, Jr.

In her commentary on a letter that Flannery O'Connor wrote to Robert Lowell in 1958, Sally Fitzgerald writes that "Flannery seemed fated to asceticism. The one time she decided that she should contribute to the frolics at Yaddo, she tripped and broke her bottle on the way to the party" (*HB* 310). Behind Fitzgerald's comment is the unspoken reference to the more serious strike of fate that severely limited O'Connor's life—the onset in late 1950 of lupus, the incurable blood disorder that for all purposes confined O'Connor (with the exception of occasional trips) to a solitary life with her mother on a farm outside Milledgeville. Whatever rage and resentment O'Connor must at times have felt about her disease and its torments, she established a productive routine of work, rest, and recreation that allowed her creative energies to flourish. Certainly her Catholic faith helped O'Connor in her trials, as did, later in her life, her reading of Teilhard de Chardin, who in *The Divine Milieu* discussed the concept of "passive diminishments"—the idea that in the face of an incurable disease, as O'Connor wrote (31 March 1963) to Janet McKane, "the patient is passive in relation to the disease—he's done all he can to get rid of it and can't so he's passive and accepts it" (*HB* 512).

That O'Connor could apparently adapt herself so well to the pain and confinement of her disease (a presumption not unanimously accepted by O'Connor critics) no doubt also owes in part to the vocation she had chosen. After all, having to adjust one's life to getting around on crutches, for all the physical and psychological discomforts, certainly was quite different to someone who made her living by sitting in front of a typewriter than it would have been to somebody who was, say, a roofer. Indeed, O'Connor's understanding of the demands of the artistic vocation that called for an unbending commitment involving self-denial in effect meant she could embrace by choice the lifestyle to which she was fated by the disease. And there is little reason to believe that she developed her ideas on the ascetic life of the modern artist entirely in response to her confinement at Andalusia; she was without doubt already embracing these ideas before she became ill, as is clear in her work and social habits during her stay at Yaddo. In a 1959 letter to Cecil Dawkins, O'Connor commented on her stay at the artists' retreat and her essential difference from the other participants. After speaking of the parties, the sleeping around, the drugs and alcohol, O'Connor counseled Dawkins (who apparently was considering going to Yaddo) about how she got along there: "You survive in this atmosphere by minding your own business and by having plenty of your own business to mind; and by not being afraid to be different from the rest of them" (*HB* 364).

If O'Connor felt isolated by her withdrawn life at Yaddo (a situation certainly enhanced by her shyness, together with her southern and Catholic origins), her commitment to her vocation placed her amid a large company of modernist writers who ascribed—or at least said they did—to a similar regimen of self-denial for the sake of their art. Probably the most visible origin of the ascetic basis of literary modernism is Gustave Flaubert's famous 1852 letter to Louise Colet describing his trials with *Madame Bovary*. "I am leading an austere life, stripped of all external pleasure, and am sustained only by a kind of permanent frenzy, which sometimes makes me weep tears of impotence but never abates," Flaubert wrote. "I love my work with a love that is frenzied and perverted, as an ascetic loves the hair shirt that scratches his belly" (*Letters* 158). Before long a number of modernist writers were characterizing the artistic vocation in religious terms, seeing themselves as members of a literary priesthood of self-sacrificing writers with its own rituals, covenants, and disciplines. "Art has its own hagiography and its Book of Martyrs," Malcolm Cowley forthrightly declared (qtd. in Simpson 165), and Allen Tate described the modernist search for meaning and order as a choice between "Religion *or* Literature" (3).

Although O'Connor had no sympathy whatsoever for those modernist writers who went so far as to make religion their god—one thinks of the scathing portrayal of Asbury in "The Enduring Chill"—she nonetheless frequently spoke of her commitment to the literary vocation in terms similar to the religious rhetoric of the modernists. "There is no excuse for anyone to write fiction for public consumption unless he has been called to do so by the presence of a gift," she wrote in "The Nature and Aim of Fiction," and she added: "A gift of any kind is a considerable responsibility. It is a mystery in itself, something gratuitous and wholly undeserved, something whose real uses will probably be hidden from us. Usually the artist has to suffer certain deprivations in order to use his gift with integrity" (*MM* 81).

The deprivations of which O'Connor speaks here no doubt in part suggest the rigid discipline and routine by which the artist must live in following his or her calling. O'Connor, who never married, wrote of ascetic demands of the artist's life in a letter (22 September 1956) to "A": "There is a great deal that has to either be given up or taken away from you if you are going to succeed in writing a body of work. There seems to be other conditions in life that demand celibacy besides the priesthood" (*HB* 176). Throughout her career she held to an unbending work routine, for she knew the temptation of idleness, of not bearing the responsibility of the writer's gift. Certainly she had this temptation in mind when, in a letter (2 August 1955) to "A," she declared, "I myself am afflicted with time" (91); and again years later, in another letter (10 February 1962) to her friend, when she wrote that "time is very dangerous without a rigid routine. If you do the same thing every day at the same time for the length of time, you'll save yourself from many a sink. Routine is a condition of survival" (*HB* 465). Never a sentimentalist or apologist, O'Connor had no sympathy for those who complained about the rigorous life of the artist—"I always want to throw up when I hear people talk about 'The Loneliness of the Artist,'" she wrote (29 November 1956) to "A"—because she saw those people assuming that writing came about without struggle, discipline, or cost. For this sort of writer, writing was not a life's work but a pastime, or even worse, a catering to the desires of an audience.

O'Connor's words on the necessity of disciplined routine call to mind the strict regulations of cenobitic monasticism practiced by monks who live entirely regimented lives in isolated communities. As Geoffrey Galt Harpham observes in *The Ascetic Imperative in Culture and Criticism,* the cenobite lives by the routine performance of tasks, striving in a sense "to live a life without content, without events" so as "not to protect one's vital selfhood but to extinguish whatever spark of temptability lay within." "The cenobite is faultless rather than excellent," writes Harpham, "a subtracted rather than an achieved self, a pure disciple of what Durkheim called 'the negative self'" (28). The cenobite's striving for a negative self becomes for the modernist artist the effort to achieve "negative capability," the ability to extinguish everyday desires and passions so the unsullied mind can create a pure art. Thus for T. S. Eliot, extolling the virtues of the artist's impersonality, "the more perfect the artist, the more completely separate in him will be the man who suffers and the mind which creates; the more perfectly will the mind digest and transmute the passions which are its material" (7–8). Likewise, for Flannery O'Connor, who in "The Nature and Aim of Fiction" observes that "art is a virtue of practical intellect, and the practice of any virtue demands a certain asceticism and a very definite leaving-behind of the niggardly part of the ego. . . . No art is sunk in the self, but rather, in art the self becomes self-forgetful in order to meet the demands of the thing seen and the thing being made" (*MM* 81–82).

O'Connor's observation here reveals the tremendous influence of Jacques Maritain's Thomism upon her aesthetic thinking. As she admitted in a letter (20 April 1957) to "A," Maritain's *Art and Scholasticism* was the book she "cut her aesthetic teeth on" (*HB* 216); she was, moreover, a serious student of his other works, including *Creative Intuition in Art and Poetry* and *The Range of Reason,* the latter of which she reviewed for the diocesan paper the *Bulletin.* Maritain's aesthetics presented a profoundly ascetic view of the artist, drawing on the distinction in scholastic thinking between two activities of the practical intellect (the active intellect involved with getting something done; the speculative intellect involved with pure knowledge for its own sake): action and creation. Action concerns the use of our free will in our conduct and thus is the sphere of morality, with prudence as its chief virtue. Creation, in contrast, involves the production of an artifact and is thus the sphere of art, with its chief virtue being the unbending commitment to the rules of perfection that govern the work made. The creation of art involves submission to the laws of the artifact, a rewarding act of profound self-denial. Maritain writes:

> Hence the despotic and all-absorbing power of art, as also its astonishing power of soothing: it frees from every human care, it establishes the *artifex,* artist or artisan, in a world apart, cloistered, defined, and absolute, in which to devote all the strength and intelligence of his manhood to the service of the thing which he is making. This is true of every art; the ennui of living and willing ceases on the threshold of every studio or workshop. (*Art and Scholasticism* 6)

Eliot's, O'Connor's, and Maritain's observations all suggest a motion toward artistic control and perfection entailing the purification of a creative self from the taints of an everyday self or ego. In *Creative Intuition in Art and Poetry,* Maritain poses the "creative self" against the "self-centered ego," arguing that in artistic production the creative self must be entirely removed from everything but the artistic act. "This essential disinterestedness of the poetic act means that egoism is the natural enemy of poetic activity," Maritain writes, adding that "the artist as a man can be busy only with his craving for creation" (107). When egoism invades the sphere of art, Maritain argues, not only is the artistic activity crippled, but the ego, feeding wildly on the very act of artistic creation, grows without restraint (the metaphor is Maritain's). With the ego entirely in control, the artist no longer submits to the demands of the artifact but instead makes "him[self] into a hero, a priest, or a savior, offering himself in sacrifice no longer to his work but to the world and to his own glory" (108).

Egoism is not the only threat to the artist and artistic activity. As Maritain points out, ascetic submission to the rules of the artifact can be so total that the artist's moral life is subsumed into the all-consuming quest for art. The results are disastrous. "Baudelaire himself has warned us against the exclusive passion for art," Maritain writes, "which progressively destroys the human subject and finally—through an indirect repercussion, owing to material or subjective causality—destroys art itself: for once a man is through, his art is through also" (*Creative Intuition* 37). The very act of submission, therefore, provokes the destructive temptation to make the submission complete, an act that collapses the sphere of morality into that of art. The artist, Maritain writes, "is tempted, when he totally yields to his cherished demon, to develop, for the sake of his art, a peculiar morality and peculiar moral standards of his own, directed to the good of the work, not of his soul. Then he will endeavor to taste all the fruits and silts of the earth, and will make curiosity or recklessness in any new moral experiment or vampiric singularity his supreme moral virtue, in order to feed his art" (*Creative Intuition* 37). In so yielding, the artist undermines what Maritain identifies as "the human ambiance of the activity of art"—the relationships between thought and sensibility and between the sense and the intellect and the world.

Maritain's suggestion here that the ascetic dynamics of artistic creation itself engenders the most threatening temptation to the artist—that of complete control by the ego or of utter submission to the artifact—points to the complex interplay of temptation and resistance that Harpham finds embedded in asceticism. Harpham argues that ascetic self-denial is not merely a simple gesture of rejection of some aspect of the self (the body, its impulses and desires, for instance) but actually the invoking of a transgressive self so virtue may be achieved through its discipline and control by a judging self. Asceticism thus both denigrates and celebrates transgression because the transgressive self represents both error and the opportunity to master error. Describing ascetic dynamics on a broad level, Harpham writes that asceticism engages an issue by "articulat[ing] an opposition with which dialogue and dialectic can occur; but it leaves the issue unsettled by privileging both sides" (xv). Maintaining a dynamic opposition between antagonistic yet interdependent elements is thus the goal of asceticism, and it is achieved by resisting the temptation to collapse the opposition to embrace one extreme without the other. Harpham's explanation of asceticism provides a useful commentary on Maritain's aesthetics: in the artist's submission to the demands of art, neither the creative self nor the self-centered ego should utterly dominate; the artist must resist the temptation of both, holding them in dynamic opposition.

Maritain's ascetic aesthetics and Harpham's reading of asceticism provide a useful means for approaching O'Connor's aesthetics and, further, her imaginative life. In constructing a Thomist understanding of artistic creation, O'Connor was well aware of the temptations facing the artist that Maritain identified. As we have already seen in the discussion of O'Connor's work habits, she embraced a cenobitic strategy of disciplined routine in large part to control the unruly ego by attempting to steer clear of the temptation not to submit to the demands of art. But cenobitism breeds its own temptation: to believe through routine and mastery that a person can utterly free himself or herself from the transgressive ego and its impulses and desires. Such freedom, however, negates the human condition, implying as it does the assumption of God-like purity and power. As artist, O'Connor knew this temptation, expressed as the creative self's complete leaving behind of the ego. Practicing the virtue of the practical intellect to create art, she says in "The Nature and Aim of Fiction," "demands a certain asceticism, a very definite leaving-behind of the niggardly part of the ego." She adds that in this act of leave-taking "the writer has to judge himself with a stranger's eye and a stranger's severity. The prophet in him has to see the freak" (*MM* 81–82). But to achieve complete self-forgetfulness would mean the stranger's eye was all there was, that the prophet would see the freak only in others, not herself. Beset by such damning pride, the creative self would understand itself as a completely detached and inviolable supreme creator, similar to the artist of Stephen Dedalus's musings in *A Portrait of the Artist as a Young Man*, who, "like the God of the creation, remains within or behind or beyond his handiwork, invisible, refined out of existence, indifferent, paring his fingernails" (215).

To resist the cenobitic temptation, O'Connor embraced another ascetic strategy, that of eremitism. Eremitism, as Harpham points out, derives from "the heroic fanaticism of the early desert solitudes such as Anthony, who lived essentially alone in remote settings in Egypt or Syria, torturing themselves and confronting demons in improvisational, unregulated, and ecstatic warfare" (20). Unlike the cenobite, who sought to extinguish the transgressive self, the eremite embraced it, actively courting and battling with desire and temptation to define the self by mastering its transgressions. O'Connor embraced eremitism as an artist by striving not to remain utterly detached from her fiction, primarily by invoking in it a variety of her own transgressive voices—southerner, intellectual, woman, to name only several—that challenged the authoritativeness of a judging and creating self essentially Catholic in perspective. As did the eremite with his desires, she struggled to control and master these tempting internal voices, invoking them and then going to great extremes to silence them, in a sense engaging in violent self-laceration. Claire Kahane has argued that O'Connor's violent attacks on her characters, which she says jar them back from their attempts to live autonomously and into a realization of "the need for absolute submission to the power of Christ," represent the working out of O'Connor's infantile anxieties in which her superego attempts to punish her own demonic impulses ("Rage of Vision" 120). What Kahane fails to see is that the calling forth and punishing of transgressive voices itself represents resistance to the demand for complete submission to Christ that Kahane sees undergirding O'Connor's thought. The pressing temptation for O'Connor as eremetic artist is less the utter submission to the Thomist demands of art and more generally to Christ than the giving in to the transgressive voices her fiction calls forth, the allowing of her ego to dominate and so distort her artistic commitment. O'Connor's cenobitism, poised against her eremitism, helped her resist this trap.

In all of this, O'Connor is a fitting embodiment of Maritain's and Harpham's ascetic artist, one who in artistic creation poses two ascetic strategies against each other in an ongoing dynamic resisting resolution. This resistance, invoking the ego while denying it, keeps O'Connor from falling prey to the destructive temptation of either extreme so that she paradoxically creates a fiction of self-articulation that is at the same time a fiction of self-abandonment. Absolutely aware of the paradoxical situation, O'Connor described in a letter (9 December 1961) to "A" the ascetic dynamics involved in writing fiction: "Writing is a good example of self-abandonment. I never completely forget myself except when I am writing and I am never more completely myself than when I am writing. It is the same with Christian self-abandonment" (*HB* 458).

In suggesting the similarities between the self-abandonment of authorship and that of faith, O'Connor points to the ascetic dynamics that shape her Christian belief. Echoing Kierkegaard's observations in "The Gospel of Suffering," O'Connor believed that faith was not a certainty but a burden, a bearing of the cross that demanded ongoing struggle with doubt and unbelief. Time and again in her letters, she railed against those who rested easy in the security of their faith (she believed Catholics were particularly guilty of this), finding such believers repulsive because, as she wrote (16 July 1957) to Cecil Dawkins, "they don't really have a faith but a kind of false certainty. They operate by the slide rule and the Church for them is the poor man's insurance system. It's never hard for them to believe because actually they never think about it. Faith has to take in all other possibilities it can" (*HB* 231).

As O'Connor's final observation to Dawkins suggests, faith must be continuously pitted against challenges to it, probing and being probed by them and in the process being enlarged by this ongoing dialogic encounter. The true believer resists the temptation to collapse the binary of faith and unbelief, either by resting completely in an unchallengeable faith or by giving in to the doubt and questionings that accompany sincere faith. Such temptations and resistance to them lie behind her comment (30 May 1962) to Alfred Corn that Peter's prayer, "Lord, I believe. Help my unbelief," "is the most natural and most human and most agonizing prayer in the gospels, and I think it is the foundation prayer of faith" (*HB* 476). "Help my unbelief" of course suggests a call to alleviate the hauntings of doubt as one's faith matures; but it also suggests a call to augment these questionings because engaging the burden of doubt ultimately enriches and deepens faith. In a letter (20 July 1955) to "A," O'Connor described her own religious struggles in terms of this thickened understanding of faith. After characterizing herself as "a Catholic peculiarly possessed of the modern consciousness, that thing Jung described as unhistorical, solitary, and guilty," she added: "To possess this *within* the church is to bear a burden, the necessary burden for the conscious Catholic. It's to feel the contemporary situation at the ultimate level" (*HB* 90). As she suggests here, faith necessarily involves the resistance to it; faith thus does not ease one's burden but augments it because the comfort of faith is forever being challenged by the doubts of unbelief. Here again O'Connor echoes Kierkegaard, who in "The Gospel of Suffering" writes that "faith signifies precisely the deep, strong, blessed unrest which urges on the believer, so that he cannot find rest in this world, so the one who does find complete rest here, would also cease to be a believer" (4). "Don't expect faith to clear things up for you," O'Connor advised Louise Abbot (undated, 1959); faith, she added, gives only "enough certainty to be able to make your way, but it is making it in darkness." "When we get our spiritual house in order," she told Abbot, "we'll be dead" (*HB* 354).

Dead is precisely the condition in which a number of O'Connor's characters end up, most of them having been shocked out of their complacent everyday existence by some act of intense violence that propels them to a complete acceptance of Christ—an acceptance so overwhelming and pure that their spiritual houses are indeed in order, freed from any taint of doubt or unrest. As Frederick Asals has persuasively argued, this motion toward a totally unquestioning faith involves the "purification of the rebellious self" (*Flannery O'Connor* 221), "a cleansing of [the character's] most cherished illusions, or indeed of any loving self at all" (254). Asals rightly terms this motion of stripping away of the prideful self ascetic, and he argues that the intense pressure of this ascetic motion toward radical acts of self-denial drives O'Connor's fiction forward and best embodies the essential cast of her imagination. Asals locates the primary source of O'Connor's asceticism in the predominant religion of her homeland, southern fundamentalism, a faith that demands that its believers make the uncompromising choice of either accepting Christ (and thereby giving up the world to follow Him) or of denying Him (and thereby choosing the world and its sinfulness). The Misfit in "A Good Man Is Hard to Find" knows the fundamentalist imperative, saying of Christ and the choice that everyone must make in regard to Him: "If He did what He said, then it's nothing for you to do but throw away everything and follow Him, and if He didn't, then it's nothing for you to do but enjoy the few minutes you got left the best way you can—by killing somebody or burning down his house or doing some other meanness to him. No pleasure but meanness" (CS 132). In her deep sympathies with such thinking, O'Connor, says Asals, creates a deeply ascetic fiction in which the emphasis is "not on a bringing together, but on a splitting apart, not on harmony, but on sundering" (231).

There is no doubt that O'Connor deeply identified with southern fundamentalists. In her letters and essays, she frequently speaks of her admiration for and affinities with fundamentalist fanatics, particularly their intense and rigorous brand of faith. In "The Catholic Novelist in the Protestant South," she suggests that her "underground religious affinities" lie with "backwoods prophets and shouting fundamentalists" and that these feelings are shaping forces in her imaginative life. She says that when the southern Catholic writer descends within himself to find himself and his region (the pronouns are hers, and she includes herself in the discussion), he discovers there "a feeling of kinship [with the fundamentalists] strong enough to spur him to write" (MM 207).

As formative as fundamentalism most certainly was to O'Connor's thinking and imagination, however, one should not see its influence as reigning unchallenged and pure. As I have argued in The Art and Vision of Flannery O'Connor, the voice of the southern fundamentalist that was internalized by O'Connor was merely one—albeit a very forceful one—of many voices, or selves, vying for expression in her rich consciousness. O'Connor's fundamentalist voice is perhaps best understood as a transgressive self that, in a continuous ascetic interplay of resistance with her Catholicism, engages, pressures, and tempts her faith. This dynamic is the foundation of O'Connor's fiction, expressed most basically in the charged interaction between the Catholic author, fundamentalist narrator (an objectification of her own fundamentalist voice), and the stories that the narrator tells. By objectifying her fundamentalist voice in her narrator, O'Connor employs the ascetic strategy Harpham finds so productive: she pits against her Catholic faith and vision an opposing perspective, establishing a dynamic of temptation and resistance that never fully resolves itself. Enriching growth remains ongoing as long as the opposition holds, as long as resistance keeps the binary intact. The ascetic cast of O'Connor's imaginative life is thus best understood not in the simple gesture of self-purification, as Asals would have it, but in this ongoing dynamic of temptation and resistance that invokes the transgressive self while at the same time seeking to repress and control it.

In her letters and essays, O'Connor frequently characterizes her imaginative life in terms of ascetic oppositions. In a letter (15 September 1955) to Andrew Lytle, for instance, she depicts her creative sensibility as the interplay between her Catholic and southern identities: "To my way of thinking, the only thing that keeps me from being a regional writer is being a Catholic and the only thing that keeps me from being a Catholic writer (in the narrow sense) is being a Southerner" (*HB* 104). She enlarges on this healthy opposition in "Catholic Novelists in the Protestant South," pointing out the enriching gains for her art and vision that result from maintaining the interplay, from not giving in to the temptations to be merely a Catholic writer or merely a southern writer. She notes that "in a literature that tends naturally to extremes, as Southern literature does, we need something to protect us against the merely extreme, the merely personal, the merely grotesque, and here the Catholic, with his older tradition and his ability to resist the dissolution of belief, can make his contribution to Southern literature, but only if he realizes first that he has as much to learn from it as to give it." If his Catholicism keeps the southern Catholic writer from being merely extreme and violent, his southernness compels him to be "less timid as a novelist, more respectful of the concrete, more trustful of the blind imagination" (*MM* 208).

O'Connor characterizes the vision of the Catholic writer in broader terms in "Catholic Novelists and Their Readers," once again portraying imaginative life in terms of ascetic dynamics. She writes that Catholic writers possess two opposing sets of eyes—their own as individuals and the church's—and that they must somehow use both sets, closing neither. "It would be foolish to say there is no conflict between these two sets of eyes," O'Connor writes. "There is a conflict, and it is a conflict which we escape at our peril, one which cannot be settled beforehand by theory or fiat or faith. We think that faith entitles us to avoid it, when in fact, faith prompts us to begin it, and to continue it until, like Jacob, we are masked" (*MM* 180). To disrupt the interplay by seeing with only one set of eyes is to wreak disaster. For a Catholic writer to see merely with the eyes of the church results in "another addition to that large body of pious trash for which we have so long been famous." Writing only with one's own eyes, thus seeing things "as nearly as possible in the fashion of a camera," flattens the Catholic writer's vision, emptying it of its awareness of the Christian mysteries, what O'Connor likes to call "the added dimension." Only by working with both sets of eyes, by cultivating rather than obliterating the tension between them, could Catholic writers write—and see—with fullness. Underscoring the ascetic dynamics of this tension, she writes of the near impossibility of ever achieving a vision unfraught with conflict: "The tensions of being a Catholic novelist are probably never balanced for the writer until the Church becomes so much a part of his personality that he can forget about her—in the same sense that when he writes, he forgets about himself. This is the condition we aim for, but one which is seldom achieved in this life, particularly by novelists" (*MM* 181). Her comment here recalls her observation to Louise Abbot regarding the necessity of always struggling with one's faith, that "when we get our spiritual house in order, we'll be dead" (*HB* 354).

And so, returning to the Misfit, who embraces a rigid fundamentalist imperative demanding that a person make either a total commitment to Christ or a total commitment against Him, we can see that he has it wrong, at least by O'Connor's thinking. To her this stark either/or binary, compelling a choice that denied its opposite, was too rigid and reductive, an expression of the type of Manichaean thinking that utterly separated matter from spirit and that O'Connor set in opposition to her sacramentalism. In seeing the material world as evil, the Manichaeans, O'Connor wrote in "The Nature and Aim of Fiction," mistakenly "sought pure spirit and tried to approach the infinite directly without any mediation of matter" (*MM* 68). O'Connor believed otherwise, asserting that in approaching the ideal, artist and believer must remain firmly engaged with the world and the body, enduring *and* celebrating humanity's trials with an asceticism of temptation and resistance. Put another way, at the same time that a person makes commitments to Christ and art (following Maritain's strategies), he or she makes commitments to challenge and provoke these affirmations. Only in the resistance to utter submission does the artist and believer progress toward a more perfect vision and art. "I don't like the idea some people have that the novelist has this untouchable sensibility that ought to be left to its pleasure," O'Connor told C. Ross Mullins, Jr., in a 1963 interview in which she also pointed to the dangers of unchallenged faith. "What makes the sensibility good is wrestling with what is higher than itself and outside it. It ought to be a good bone-crunching battle. The sensibility will come out of it marked forever but a winner" (105). A winner, one must add, to be challenged again and again in a series of self-denials that lead a person toward wholeness. It is this series of conflicts, one always resisting resolution, that signifies the asceticism that shaped the faith, imagination, and art of Flannery O'Connor.

Flannery O'Connor and the Aesthetics of Torture

Patricia Yaeger

In *Killers of the Dream,* Lillian Smith describes a central trauma from her childhood. A white child who has been "living with a Negro family in a broken-down shack" comes to Smith's home, where the two girls become constant companions. But when her family discovers that the child is black—that she comes from African American parentage—the young Lillian Smith is overcome with ambivalence: "She crept closer and put her arms around me and I shrank away as if my body had been uncovered. I had not said a word . . . but she knew, and tears slowly rolled down her little white face" (38). To describe the effects of similar episodes on southern children, Smith compares the experience of being southern to the anguish created by a torture instrument that turns southern children into creatures wracked by social and psychic deformities:

I began to understand slowly at first but more clearly as the years passed, that the warped, distorted frame we have put around every Negro child from birth is around every white child also. Each is on a different side of the frame but each is pinioned there. And I knew that what cruelly shapes and cripples the personality of one is as cruelly shaping and crippling the personality of the other. . . . We may, as we acquire new knowledge, live through new experiences . . . yet we are stunted and warped and in our lifetime cannot grow straight again any more than can a tree, put in a steel-like twisting frame when young, grow tall and straight when the frame is torn away at maturity. (39)

The grotesque is a neglected trope in recent criticism of southern women's writing, but it is central to the southern experience. When a southerner writes in the mode of grotesque realism, the body is metaphorized in a way that expresses a character's or author's troubled relation to his or her social formation. In *My Mamma's Dead Squirrel: Lesbian Essays on Southern Culture*, Mab Segrest uses a grotesque tropology to dramatize a collusion between the white cult of feminine beauty and southern racism: "I have felt the destructive effects of personal race and class privilege first through [my mother's] life: her skin allergies that made her scratch her own white skin raw. The her in me feels the trap of that whiteness, the need to claw out. The times I have realized my own racism most, this image has come to mind: I am sitting in a white porcelain bathtub scraping my skin with Brillo pads; there is blood in rivulets in the tub" (167). The first attribute of the southern grotesque is its propensity to condense background information and push this information into the foreground of our imaginations. This means that the grotesque body is never what it seems; Segrest's bloody flesh is all too penetrable; turned inside out it reveals the social agon hidden beneath the happy surfaces of female charisma and cleanliness, as well as the work of domination that the white female body performs on behalf of "race and class privilege."

If the grotesque propels background information into the foreground, its operations do not stop there. Segrest's wounded white body, her Brillo pad wounds, demands that the "pure" white body discover its hybrid color, its blood, its complicity in the sufferings of African Americans. Terry Eagleton argues that the grotesque is "intrinsically double-faced, an immense semiotic switchboard through which codes are read backwards and messages scrambled into their antitheses" (145). In southern women's fictions, the grotesque foregrounds social codes that are embarrassing, damaging, invisible: codes the status quo recognizes but is interested in hiding. What the grotesque offers the southern woman writer is a wealth of bizarrely democratizing forms.

What does this suggest about our reading of Flannery O'Connor's fiction? Although grotesque bodies flood the pages of southern stories, there are great variations in its themes and forms. In *The Old Order* Katherine Anne Porter explores a world made from the energy of workers' bodies that does not replenish these bodies; she asks her literary grotesques—often the bodies of former slaves or white children—to depict the toll taken on workers of color, white women, and children when their labor is misspent. In contrast, Zora Neale Hurston, Eudora Welty, Ellen Gilchrist, and Alice Walker use the grotesque—respectively—to trouble a stratified black-white social spectrum, to explore connections between embodiment and powerlessness, to critique white southern bourgeois subjects defined through race or ethnic dominance, and to expose the pollution behavior implicit in southern racial ideologies. In each case the grotesque offers a way to move back and forth between history and the body; each of these authors uses her own somatography, her own style of writing-on-the-flesh, to propose subversive readings of regional politics. The grotesque is, then, an ill-mannered trope. When it intrudes into social contexts preoccupied with the canons of southern gentility, its rough energy shatters old norms. By focusing on the unruly orifices and openings in a character's body, or on the body's ecstatic doubleness and excess, southern women writers attack the conservatism of a southern ideology designed to close off the movement of social contradictions and to create in southern subjects an illusion of coherence and consistency.

Within this cultural context, the stories of Flannery O'Connor should offer intricate readings of a social system gone awry; after all, O'Connor uses the greatest proportion of grotesque personae per paragraph of any southern writer. For all her objections to northern critics' fascination with the grotesque, their obsession with the idiots, half-wits, deaf-mutes, sideshow freaks, one-armed bandits, unruly women, conmen, old children, and angry African Americans who populate her fiction, O'Connor's stories still manage to represent the pinnacle, the acme, the sine qua non of the grotesque as a southern literary experience. Her stories should be the very place, then, to carry out a politicized reading of the grotesque as southern form, to drive home the argument I'm longing to make: that southern literary bodies are grotesque because their authors know that bodies cannot be thought of separate from the racist and sexist institutions that surround them.

Having made this observation, I find myself numbed at the keyboard, or if not entirely numbed, then blank, battered, joyless, mute. O'Connor is both the funniest and the most intractable of southern women writers, the hardest to describe within the literary-political terms I have just announced. What hysterico-political messages are being recoded in O'Connor's fictions? Beyond theology, what sort of history-making does she represent? If, as Peter Stallybrass and Allon White have suggested, bodies cannot be thought of separate from their social formations (1–26), how do we insert O'Connor's broken bodies into the race and gender politics of southern history?

In "Black and White Together: Teaching the 'Beloved Community' in Today's Racially Divided Classrooms," Julius Lester describes the South that gave birth to the southern grotesque:

It is almost impossible to describe that world the civil rights movement destroyed, that world of my childhood and adolescence ruled by signs decreeing where I was and was not allowed to go, what door I had to enter at the bus station and train station, where I had to sit on the bus. How do I explain what it is to live with the absurd and pretend to its ordinariness without becoming insane? How do I explain that I cannot be sure that my sanity was not hopelessly compromised because I grew up in a world in which the insane was as ordinary as margarine? (30)

I want to suggest that Lester's description of a world where "the insane was as ordinary as margarine" can give us new insights into O'Connor's fictions. In her firmament the absurdities of ordinary southern life become terrifying, graspable, gargantuan. The problems O'Connor presents for the civilized critic may, in fact, persist because of her fiction's closeness to this everyday southern insanity; O'Connor's critics are rarely willing to match this insanity, to participate in a version of sadism that mirrors the ordinary cruelties of some southern lives. My intent in this essay is to come as close to matching this insanity as critical protocol will allow. I want to establish that a poetics of torture—a painful reenactment of a sadistic world whose sanity is "hopelessly compromised" by its race and class politics—becomes the foundation of O'Connor's best work.

At the center of this essay is the problem of the sleeping body and whether I want to wake this body up. For years I have been asleep when teaching and reading O'Connor's stories and novels. Last year, in the midst of a lecture on low style versus high style in *The Violent Bear It Away*, I woke up. Now I want to sleep again.

In the beginning of *Revolution in Poetic Language* Julia Kristeva argues that we make the texts we read somnambular, that "our philosophies of language . . . are nothing more than the thoughts of archivists, archaeologists, and necrophiliacs" (13). Instead of reading, we codify; we ignore the text as political-historical process and look instead for the truth of the subject by listening "to the narrative of a sleeping body—a body in repose, withdrawn from its socio-historical imbrication, removed from direct experience" (13). What happens when we read otherwise? What happens to O'Connor's stories when we wake up the personal and political terrors of her texts? To answer these questions, I will develop a phenomenology of pain in O'Connor's fiction, trace her literary sadism as an inchoate form of readerly torture, and then track the relationship between this phenomenology and O'Connor's moment in history. In so doing, I hope that fresh terms for reading O'Connor's fiction will emerge: terms that refuse O'Connor's Catholicism as the pivotal focus for her grotesques and substitute, instead, a new set of connections between O'Connor's psyche and her southernness.

Let's begin our pursuit of this readerly dementia with an analogy from Lewis Carroll. At the end of *Through the Looking Glass*, after completing the game of chess, Alice becomes a queen. As she sits down to celebrate, a leg of mutton is set before her, and Alice is struck with a new and grownup anxiety—how should she proceed? She has never had "to carve a joint before." The Red Queen sweetly guides her. " 'You look a little shy,' " she says to Alice. " 'Let me introduce you to that leg of mutton . . . Alice— Mutton: Mutton—Alice.' " The leg of mutton stands up to make its bow just as Alice, by now quite hungry, is ready to carve away. "'May I give you a slice?' she said . . . looking from one Queen to the other. 'Certainly not,' the Red Queen said very decidedly: 'it isn't etiquette to cut anyone you've been introduced to. Remove the joint!'" (209)

Like Alice, Flannery O'Connor is an author who always cuts the characters to whom she has been introduced. There are examples on every page:

She stared at the violent black streak bounding toward her as if she had no sense of distance, as if she could not decide at once what his intention was, and the bull had buried his head in her lap, like a wild tormented lover, before her expression changed. One of his horns sank until it pierced her heart and the other curved around her side and held her in an unbreakable grip. She continued to stare straight ahead but the entire scene in front of her had changed—the tree line was a dark wound in a world that was nothing but sky—and she had the look of a person whose sight has been suddenly restored but who finds the light unbearable. (*CS* 333)

We find an equally chilling moment in "A View of the Woods," when a grandfather murders his look-alike granddaughter, a diminutive child of nine:

He got hold of her throat. With a sudden surge of strength, he managed to roll over and reverse their positions so that he was looking down into the face that was his own but had dared to call itself Pitts. With his hands still tight around her neck, he lifted her head and brought it down once hard against the rock that happened to be under it. Then he brought it down twice more. Then looking into the face in which the eyes, slowly rolling back, appeared to pay him not the slightest attention, he said, "There's not an ounce of Pitts in me." (*CS* 355)

While O'Connor persistently cuts into her characters, her professional readers, for the most part, are like the Red Queen—they want to remove this cutting and carving of animate flesh from the critical contexts in which O'Connor's fiction is discussed.[1] To wake up the body of O'Connor's texts, we need to think thoughts about her characters that will challenge this languor. To understand O'Connor's lacerating grotesques—and the pleasure she asks us to feel in the pain her characters endure—I will argue for the invention of a southern "aesthetics of torture." This aesthetics needs to account for both the extraordinary display of cruelty and laceration in O'Connor's fictions and the repression of this laceration by the sleeping critic.

To create this nontheological context for understanding O'Connor, I want to move past Lewis Carroll's Alice and look at a second theater of cruelty: the body of that oddly limbless statue the Venus de Milo. With her truncated torso, she could be a character in any of O'Connor's stories. Let's imagine three scenarios for reacting to her form. First, we could examine the Venus as a statue now in the Louvre, originally conceived by a sculptor from Antioch on the Maeander about 150 b.c. The lines of the Venus are graceful, proportional; the composition imitates a fourth-century statue from Corinth.

This art-historical reading is none too inspiring; it makes the Venus into a sleeping body whose placid beauty offers a contemplative fetish removed from historical turmoil. To wake her from slumber, we could embroil the statue in struggle. What were the forces that drew the statue's maker back two centuries in search of a model? Does the Venus's tranquillity depict a world at ease with itself or a polity searching for past images of harmony and tranquillity because the present offers none?

This is a little more interesting, but it keeps what is most disturbing about the Venus's body in check: her absence of arms. Let's respond to this absence by thinking as primitively as we can, that is, by approaching the mutilated statue through our own psyches. Here we have two related choices. We can either look at her body empathically and identify with Venus as limbless victim—an identification that makes the statue compelling because it evokes pathos for the loss of her arms. Or we can react to her body from the viewpoint of the aggressor; we can identify with the Venus sadistically, via the person or agency who removed her arms. This sadistic identification brings us closer to the subjectivity of the torturer.

It is this punitive subjectivity, this delight in sadism, that gives O'Connor's stories their peculiar vivacity. Just as the Venus de Milo may disperse

pleasure because she is blankly in pain, because the statue stirs up aggressive material in the psyche that we try in our everyday lives to repress, so
O'Connor's fictions give pleasure because of their perverse dalliance with
sadistic agency.

In thinking so directly about sadism, we come closer to the southern
world Julius Lester describes, where terrible things happen, without rhyme
or reason, to real human bodies. In *Uncle Tom's Children*, Richard Wright
provides a searing portrait of these everyday scenes. "Big Boy Leaves
Home" depicts a grisly act of lynching; it forces us to enter a world where
African American bodies are mutilated at whim, where they dangle from
trees, writhing and burning:

"LES GIT SOURVINEERS!". . .

. . . .

"Everybody git back!". . . .

"Look, Hes gotta finger". . . .

"C'MON! GIT THE GALS BACK FROM THE FIRE!"

"He's got one of his ears, see?"

. . . .

There was a sudden quiet. Then [Big Boy] shrank violently as the wind carried,
like a flurry of snow, a widening spiral of white feathers into the night. The flames
leaped tall as the trees. The scream came again. Big Boy trembled and looked. The
mob was running down the slopes, leaving the fire clear. Then he saw a writhing
white mass cradled in yellow flame, and heard screams, one on top of the other,
each shriller and shorter than the last. The mob was quiet now, standing still, looking up the slopes at the writhing white mass gradually growing black, growing
black in a cradle of yellow flame. "'PO ON MO GAS!'" (48)

What is amazing about Wright's story is the way his lyrical diction (the
feathers like snow, the body cradled in flame) allows us to endure this
scene, to contemplate a sadism that goes beyond sanity. That is, Wright
cradles our bodies in soothing metaphors to lower our psyches into the
violence of southern history.

What is curious about O'Connor's fiction is that she also depicts a southern world driven by violence—but with a crucial difference: O'Connor not only omits the political context that drives Wright's fiction; she burns it away. She attacks her own characters and deliberately violates or eviscerates their political referents, the narrative coordinates that might help us make sense of her cruelty. Contemplating her fiction, we are left, then, with a primitive sadism that most critics convert into an old and comfortable theology. To begin to investigate the workings of this sadism in O'Connor's fiction (to cut her text in new ways) may seem difficult, stupefying, agonizing—precisely because O'Connor's stories duplicate so well, on an aesthetic plane, the psycho-linguistic patterns of physical torture.

In *The Body in Pain,* Elaine Scarry points out that in the torture chamber "the prisoner becomes a colossal body with no voice and the torturer a colossal voice . . . with no body" (57). Something similar happens to O'Connor's critics. Just as in torture the afflicted body of the victim is heightened in its abjection by the contaminating pressure of the torturer's voice, so O'Connor's critics, myself among them, have been obsequious in quoting and agreeing to O'Connor's point of view when they analyze her texts. In lecturing on O'Connor in the past, I have given O'Connor's own readings of her stories enormous credence (citing her essays with servility, using her religious maxims to anchor my secular readings of her prose), so that I have become (even as I grimace from my lectern) all body, while she becomes all voice. In a critical age noted for its insistence on a hermeneutics of suspicion, such slavishness seems exceptional. I will argue that this pattern of servility is programmed into the fiction and that while we are invited into O'Connor's texts as sadists, as torturers, as compadres in violence, we exit as masochists, as torture victims.

At this point you may wish to lodge a protest against this analogy and argue that writing and torture are incommensurable; physical torture is one thing and an "aesthetics" of torture quite another. In an aesthetics of torture pain becomes voyeuristic and metaphorical; the reader's experience of coercion can be only a shadow of the coercions experienced by those in the grip of military, judicial, or state apparatuses. To colonize this discourse of torture for literary criticism, to speak of textual masochism and actual torture in the same breath, is to participate in an act of dissemination that may be reprehensible—a spreading out and wearing thin of the only language we have to describe real human suffering and pain.

Yet in pursuing an aesthetics of torture in O'Connor, I am not arguing for the commensurability of these acts but merely for the wound of comparability. Lacking an adequate discourse to talk about literary violence, the description of O'Connor's writing as torture helps me to grasp something about O'Connor that—without the analogy—I would be unable to grasp. First, this hyperbole suggests not only the ways in which I am hurt by O'Connor's texts but also the ways in which I am attracted to the grandiose persona of the literary torturer, driven by my own version of critical sadism. In trying to challenge the rules of O'Connor criticism, I am looking for a new way of cutting what cuts me. I, too, want to become a colossal voice.

Second, the analogy helps illuminate a frightening dynamic we have already begun to explore. In *Killers of the Dream,* Lillian Smith describes the southern world of her childhood as a torture chamber in which "I was put in a rigid frame too intricate, too twisting" to be born (29). In preaching integration to a new generation of southerners, Smith finds a world of pain ("My mind feels as if it is full of barbed wire," a white student exclaims [54]). Smith begins to define southern ideology as a torture instrument that turns southern children into victims wracked by psychic deformities. What does it mean for O'Connor to parody this southern drama, with Smith's moral suasions left out? Why are her stories so packed with this intricate machinery of barbed wire and truncated bodies?

To answer, let me offer a few words on cutting and writing. Roland Barthes argues that a reader's pleasure always involves pain; that textual pleasure emanates from a cut or a seam—a space between styles or languages where the reader's formal complacency is defamiliarized: "The pleasure of reading . . . proceeds from certain breaks (or certain collisions) . . . the language is redistributed. *Now such redistribution is always achieved by cutting.* Two edges are created: an obedient, conformist, plagiarizing edge . . . and *another edge,* mobile, blank (ready to assume any con tours)" (*Pleasure*, 6). My favorite example comes from *Gone with the Wind*, where we discover that Scarlett O'Hara's face is fascinating not because it is conventionally beautiful but because it is split or divided between her mother's pleasant beauty and her father's grotesqueness, between "the delicate features of her mother, a Coast aristocrat of French descent, and the heavy ones of her florid Irish father." Barthes suggests that a crack-up or collision between two warring styles gives texts their energy, and Margaret Mitchell would seem to agree. Scarlett's "eyes were pale green without a touch of hazel, starred with bristly black lashes and slightly tilted at the ends. Above them, her thick black brows slanted upward, cutting a startling oblique line in her magnolia-white skin." It is the slash, the bristle, the cut in Scarlett's face that makes her character vivid and memorable (5).

O'Connor's fictions mobilize an even more explicit form of cutting and slashing. In "The Life You Save May Be Your Own" the image of the one-armed Mr. Shiftlet driving away after abandoning the sleeping Lucynell gives us an example of Barthes's cutting edge: "Very quickly he stepped on the gas and with his stump sticking out of the window he raced the galloping shower into Mobile" (156). O'Connor's stories not only arouse anxiety in the reader about bodily integrity and consistency, they also arouse a terror about what the body can do—and wants to do and sometimes does—to other bodies. "She heard the brake on the large tractor slip and, looking up, she saw it move forward, calculating its own path. . . . She felt her eyes and Mr. Shortley's eyes and the Negro's eyes come together in one look that froze them in collusion forever, and she had heard the little noise the Pole made as the tractor wheel broke his backbone" (234). Paragraphs after witnessing this collision, the property-owning employer of these men, Mrs. MacIntyre, loses her eyesight, her voice, and the use of her limbs. These are tragic events, but O'Connor has trained her reader to desire this "redistribution" of body and language from the beginning. Mrs. MacIntyre is not only complicitous in cutting and crushing her hired man, she becomes someone the reader wants to cut down to size.

"The Displaced Person" is filled with characters who cry out for narrative punishment. Mrs. Shortley, the unsavory wife of Mrs. MacIntyre's hired man, "stood on two tremendous legs, with the grand self-confidence of a mountain, and rose, up narrowing bulges of granite, to two icy blue points of light that pierced forward, surveying everything" (194). When she dies of a heart attack, overwhelmed with her own prophecy that "the children of wicked nation will be butchered. . . . Legs where arms should be, foot to face, ear in the palm of hand" (210), we feel more than satisfied: "Her huge body rolled back still against the seat and her eyes like blue-painted glass, seemed to contemplate for the first time the tremendous frontiers of her true country" (214). In O'Connor's prose, the cutting Barthes describes as linguistically pleasurable does not simply happen to a style or point of view—it happens to someone's body.

As these cuttings multiply, the story itself comes to resemble a huge torture chamber in which agonies proliferate, until someone loses a limb or an eye or a life, and we feel implicated in this loss because we have begun to desire it. And just as pain is inflicted in O'Connor's stories "in ever-intensifying ways" (mimicking the pain of the torture chamber in Scarry's *The Body in Pain* [28]) so this pain is also objectified or distanced. We are not asked to identify with or feel pathos or sorrow for her victims. Instead, we begin to feel that the hurts they receive are just because they are such unpleasant people.

At the same time, this tormenting of language and character can create in O'Connor's readers an oppressive uneasiness, an almost insatiable appetite to escape their own pseudo-sadism and try for a kinder dimension of experience. To inhabit O'Connor's ordinary spaces, to seek sites of comfort or familiarity (those narrative loci Barthes calls the repetitive or "plagiarizing edge") is a dangerous occupation. Here is O'Connor's portrait of that innocent moment when child meets baby-sitter: "The child stood glum and limp in the middle of the dark living room while his father pulled him into a plaid coat. His right arm was hung in the sleeve but the father buttoned the coat anyway and pushed him forward toward a pale spotted hand that stuck through the half-open door" (157). Elaine Scarry explains that one of the characteristics of torture is that everything in the environment contributes to pain. While ordinary rooms allow us to satisfy

bodily needs and to miniaturize the world, in the torture chamber everything but the prisoner "stands present as a weapon" (38–40). We find this
pain-giving duplicated in "The River." In a living room filled with stale
whiskey and "dead cigarette butts," the little boy's father comes over to
say good-bye. "Good-by," the little boy replies, and he jumps "as if he had
been shot" (158).

From the beginning of an O'Connor story the mimetic, plagiarizing
edge of the story—the space where we are supposed to feel comfortable—
is transposed into the cutting edge: another site for the body in pain. In
"The River" these comical, unkind scenes of horror continue. On the bus,
the baby-sitter's "mouth fell open to show a few long scattered teeth, some
gold and some darker than her face; she began to whistle and blow like
a musical skeleton" (160). Meanwhile, the little boy keeps adding things
to his body—her handkerchief, a story book—so that we sense his lack,
but these additions do him no good. When the sitter's children play with
him, he is attacked by their pig: "Another face, gray, wet and sour, was
pushing into his . . . rolling him over and pushing him up from behind
and then sending him forward, screaming through the yellow field, while
it bounded behind" (162).

O'Connor creates an almost unbearable tension about the vulnerability
of the body. There is barely space for Barthes's writerly cutting to begin,
since it has always, already, begun; there is no place the reader can feel safe,
except in identification with the narrator's sadism and in the frequent up-
heavals of laughter that punctuate the text's discomforts with such bizarre
gaiety.

But O'Connor does provide this zone of safety when she breaks from
vernacular to visionary speech, from low style to high. There is a point
in each of her stories where her sentences soar free of the gritty pain of
the body toward a high, singing, ethereal voice that tries to take us out of
this world. This "high style" intervenes in "The River" as baby-sitter and
boy make their way toward the baptismal site: "When they turned off the
highway onto a long red clay road winding between banks of honeysuckle,
he began to make wild leaps and pull forward on her hand as if he wanted

to dash off and snatch the sun which was rolling away ahead of them now" (163–64). Although many of O'Connor's critics find her visionary moments consonant with her interest in prophetic Christian writings, I link these moments not only with grace but also with another aspect of the aesthetics of torture.

In *Mystery and Manners,* O'Connor explains her stories' violence in terms of her supernatural intent: "I suppose the reasons for the use of so much violence in modern fiction will differ with each writer who uses it, but in my own stories I have found that violence is strangely capable of returning my characters to reality and preparing them to accept their moment of grace. Their heads are so hard that almost nothing else will do the work" (112). Ironically, O'Connor's "high style"—her oddly placed lyricism, her "sun-snatching"—is also complicitous in this violence. Her sonorous speech seems, at first, to provide an exit from the text as torture chamber. But this exit is devious. In O'Connor's most visionary and disembodied moments, pain enters in a new and vexing way. She opens a gap, a wound, an unbearable space of discomfort for the reader between the sadistic diction of dead cigarette butts and the numinous diction of spiritual excess, between the painful world of hungry white-trash children and their reincarnation as prophets standing in God's holy fire. This gap between the mundane and the spiritual, the low and high, the pornographic and the biblical, becomes another rack upon which the reader is stretched. Encompassing these disparities is painful; it is like being put upon a wheel of fire to be asked to encompass this distance in one moment of reading.

The fiercest example occurs in *The Violent Bear It Away,* when the narrator asks us to accept the drowning of a Down's syndrome child, dreadful, profane act though it is, as the sacred moment of his baptism. The primal bellow welling up in the text when Bishop's small body goes under I take to be not only the idiot Bishop's cry but also the idiot reader's cry of pain at the wound that suddenly opens between signified and signifier, at the impossibility of collapsing these opposites into narrative coherence. The pleasurable, primary sadism of the story's opening reverses itself, and we are trapped in the more difficult pleasures of the masochistic—caught between two different language systems, two different ontologies, two different sets of desire—that are incommensurable.

The reader's easiest recourse, her way out of this dissonance, is to confess, to obliterate this second dimension of torture, this new access of pain, by choosing one style over the other, by relinquishing the role of the sadistic reader who makes new cuttings in text or character for the role of the masochistic critic who submits to the idealized other in exchange for the illusion of self-unity. Typically, O'Connor's readers confess: they profess some momentary belief in the validity or aesthetic elegance or downright perversity or atheistic imponderability of O'Connor's prophetic point of view.

If we give up this masochism, if we refuse to interpret O'Connor's stories in her own voice and refuse the echo of the critical victim, we do not, of course, give up the process of painful reading but simply begin, in the midst of pain, to reinvoke our own sadism, to make new incisions in a text that both invites and refuses our tortures.

Alice makes a similar discovery in Wonderland:

She didn't see why the Red Queen should be the only one to give orders; so, as an experiment, she called out "Waiter! Bring back the pudding!" and there it was again in a moment, like a conjuring trick. It was so large that she couldn't help feeling a little shy with it, as she had been with the mutton; however, she conquered her shyness by a great effort, and cut a slice and handed it to the Red Queen.

"What impertinence!" said the Pudding. "I wonder how you'd like it, if I were to cut a slice out of you, you creature!" (209)

Once Alice has made this cut, the Red Queen is forced to become a new sort of critic; she ceases to defend against the carving of the pudding—and cuts back. " 'Make a remark,' the Red Queen says to Alice in a lacerating voice. 'It's ridiculous to leave all the conversation to the pudding!' " (209)

O'Connor's texts are hardly puddings, and yet the critical vocabulary we have developed to describe them is all too saccharine. To trace the aesthetics of torture which haunts both the reading and writing of her texts, I have taken my cue from Elaine Scarry, who suggests that torture involves three invariables. First, "pain is inflicted on a person in ever intensifying ways." Second, the pain that is amplified within the victim's body is also amplified by being objectified, "made visible to those outside the person's body." Third, this "objectified pain is denied as pain and read as power" (28). These three "invariables" also elucidate the emotional rhythms of O'Connor's stories—the dynamic in which pain is repeatedly denied as pain and remapped or reread as religious power or insight.

In response to these new incisions, what can we discover about the historical bases of O'Connor's textual tortures? We should start with O'Connor's connections to other southern women, for images of crippling and torture pervade southern women's writing:

> When I was growing up in the South it was expected by polite society that one be faithful to God and beauty. . . .
>
> We all understood the categories of beauty: there were, of course, the girls who were "absolutely beautiful," and then there were all the many girls who were described as being, each one of them, "Just as cute as she can be with a darling personality!" This was my category. . . . These were the girls who had charm . . . a crippling thing that entailed turning one's whole intelligence toward an effort to be pleasing to other people. (Dew 117, 121)

In her memoir of childhood Robb Forman Dew argues that young southern girls are disabled by a cult of female beauty. Dew recalls one shining morning when she was afraid to go to school because she could not find her eyelash curler. "Without curled eyelashes I would be remarkable . . . I would look grotesque" (122). Chaste and pale, terrified by the prospect of ugliness, Dew's white female body serves as an intensifying grid for southern racism and patriotism. ("The cultivation of all this beauty, and all the exhausting work of acquiring charm, was really about power; it was about recognition; it would ensure glory" [121].)

Although O'Connor bruises her characters to bring them to grace, she also uses these characters to disabuse us of the value of the southern cult of beauty. Her stories reveal a litany of ugly women—Sally Cope from "A Circle in the Fire," Joy/Hulga Hopewell from "Good Country People,"

Mary Grace from "Revelation"—who refuse to be socialized into pale southern beauties. Each of these characters tells a bitter story of gendered anger; their lives are filled with hateful emotions unacceptable to a southern lady.

In this context, it is tempting to rewrite O'Connor's tortured texts as angry feminist legends. Writing in a culture that refuses women their rage and intelligence, O'Connor uses both; like Mary Grace she throws the book at a southern world in which women are not allowed to be angry, ill-mannered, intelligent, or visionary. In cutting her characters, she usurps white male turf; she appropriates the cruel role of the patriarchal God of the Old Testament to foment her own cruelties. But we limit the terror of O'Connor's aggression if we stop here, if we simply read her stories as angry solutions to southern white women's plight as cultural victims. If the white female body can serve as an intensifying grid for the depravities of southern patriotism, it is because this body also becomes a reservoir for the worst compulsions of southern racism. "No I can't see James Baldwin in Georgia," O'Connor writes to Maryat Lee. "It would cause the greatest trouble and disturbance and disunion. In New York it would be nice to meet him; here it would not" (*HB* 329). Although her stories explore this disturbance and disunion, O'Connor was wary of the tempestuous racial politics of her time. Her letter to Maryat Lee was written in 1959, a time of extraordinary upheaval in the South. Three years earlier, when African Americans refused to ride segregated buses in Montgomery, their boycott ended in triumph when the Supreme Court ordered city officials to desegregate. But the South O'Connor inhabited in the 1950s and 1960s was still ruled by Jim Crow. In 1960 the Greensboro, North Carolina, lunch counter sit-ins ignited a widespread protest movement among black students that had no discernible impact on segregationists, while 1961 witnessed horrifying scenes of cruelty as black and white freedom riders were brutally attacked by white mobs. O'Connor lived in a region that thrilled to racist violence and danger. The white southerners of her era struggled to enforce sharp demarcations between genders, classes, and, most viciously, between races.

Although O'Connor satirizes race prejudice in her fictions, in public she would not take a stand: "I observe the tradition of the society I feed on— it's only fair," she insists in her letter to Maryat Lee. "Might as well expect a mule to fly as me to see James Baldwin in Georgia. I have read one of his stories and it was a good one" (*HB* 329). The white southern middle-class woman of the 1940s and 1950s inhabited a painful double position. Muted in relation to the dominant culture, she was also dominant in relation to a muted African American culture and thus occupied a status Rachel Blau DuPlessis calls "ambiguously nonhegemonic" (140); she inhabited an acute double consciousness, a double role. How does O'Connor deal with this doubleness in her fiction? I want to answer this question with an ab- breviated reading of O'Connor's most famous short story, "A Good Man Is Hard to Find." Curiously, O'Connor shares her victims' plight in this story: "It's the only one of mine that I can read aloud without laughing and its about the right length. But after I read it I feel as if I've been shot five times" (*HB*). Why is O'Connor tortured by her own fictions?

Among the people actually shot in this story is the grandmother, a well- bred southern lady: "The grandmother had on a navy blue straw sailor hat with a bunch of white violets on the brim. . . . Her collars and cuffs were white organdy trimmed with lace and at her neckline she had pinned a purple spray of cloth violets containing a sachet. In case of an accident, anyone seeing her dead on the highway would know at once that she was a lady" (118). Such complacency is a sure sign that an O'Connor character is about to be cut. The grandmother persuades her family to take a trip into the historic South, to drive deep into a plantation heaven uplifted by ornate Greek columns and happy slaves. On the way to cloud-cuckoo land, the family has an accident; they meet the Misfit, an escaped convict who takes them into the woods and shoots them, two by two. According to O'Connor, the dead bodies don't count in this story. Instead, she says, "You should be on the lookout for such things as the action of grace in the Grandmother's soul" (*MM* 112–13). Nevertheless, I would like to dwell on the dead bodies.

The bodies in "A Good Man Is Hard to Find" are typical O'Connor bodies. That is, they are grotesque, hybrid bodies contaminated with otherness. In *The Politics and Poetics of Transgression* Peter Stallybrass and Allon White suggest that there are two different working models of the grotesque. In the first, the grotesque simply represents the opposite of the classical body of the dominant culture: the southern classical body (for example, the pale, pristine body of the southern belle) is a body without untoward openings or orifices, a body high, distant, remote, beautifully frozen in time. But in their second model, the grotesque is not so much oppositional as it is an amalgam of opposites (44). We find an example in "Everything That Rises Must Converge," when a demure white lady in a large purple hat meets a brawling black giantess wearing the same apparel. As twins, these women become hyper-grotesque—their bodies are not only anomalous and excessive but formed through a process of the "hybridization or inmixing of binary opposites, particularly of high and low, such that there is a heterodox merging of elements usually perceived as incompatible," and, according to Stallybrass and White, "this latter version of the grotesque unsettles any fixed binaryism" (44). It is this version of the grotesque that gives us a politics—that is, a site for reading the trauma and crisis of high-low social relations.

Although fiction by most southern women uses the grotesque as a political surface to explore unequal distributions of political power, as an opportunity to image and envision the return of the oppressed, O'Connor is most interested in the grotesque as hybrid form: as an unstable forum in which the self comes apart. O'Connor uses the predicaments of her characters to ask, What happens when the values supporting southern bodies collapse under pressure? Her answer is that these values are so precariously constructed, so full of contradictory codes, that when they are disturbed or interrupted, the bodies they support fall apart.

Let's look at a few of these hybrid characters from "A Good Man Is Hard to Find." Before the accident, everything in this story is colorfully described but slightly off. We meet Bailey, the grandmother's son, "bent over the orange sports section" of his paper. When Bailey addresses his son, his jaw is "rigid as a horseshoe." His wife's face is "broad and innocent as cabbage"; her handkerchief, tied in "two points on the top like a rabbit's ears" (117), gives her a mute, beastly look. What O'Connor aims for in these descriptions is a very precise category confusion. Everything is in its improper place. The grandmother's valise looks like the head of a hippopotamus; when the family stops at Red Sammy Butts's barbecue for lunch, we see that Red Sammy's stomach hangs over his trousers "like a sack of meal swaying under his shirt" (121).

As I've suggested, our readerly response to these hybrid forms is sadistic—but safely so.[2] That is, part of our desire to cut into these characters has to do with their comical bodily excess. O'Connor's bodies seem to be able to regenerate themselves, to find spare parts among the meal sacks and cabbage patches of southern culture.

But our sadism may also strike a more serious note; we may also take pleasure at the prospect of dismantling these bodies because of their unappealing adherence to the worst southern norms. Most of the grandmother's stories change racial violence into euphemism. "'Oh look at the cute little pickaninny,'" she says, pointing to an African-American child "standing in the door of a shack. 'Wouldn't that make a picture, now?'" As they wave at the little boy, her granddaughter, June Star, is startled: "'He didn't have any britches on.'" Her grandmother reassures her by aestheticizing his poverty: "'He probably didn't have any. . . . Little niggers in the country don't have things like we do. If I could paint, I'd paint that picture'" (118).

The Misfit's role in the grandmother's story is a grand and distorted anagram of this very moment. This child is bottomless in a system where his parents' labor is designed to feed and clothe a dominant white culture. The Misfit parodies this dominance. His cruelty becomes an elaborate reversal in a cruel southern game: "'I'm sorry I don't have on a shirt before you ladies,' he said hunching his shoulders slightly. . . . 'We're just making do until we can get better. We borrowed these from some folks we met'" (129). Having killed "some folks we met" to amend his bottomlessness, the Misfit now kills some other folks to amend his shirtlessness and consolidate his position on top.

Oblivious to the grotesque implications of her story, the grandmother spends the hours before the accident entertaining the children with another story about the prodigious watermelon yearnings of African Americans. Her reduction of African American culture to the low, the appetitive, is continuous with her classificatory euphemisms later in the story when, faced with the Misfit's gun, she tries to define them both in terms of "high" culture: "'You wouldn't shoot a lady, would you? . . . I know you're a good man. You don't look a bit like you have common blood. I know you must come from nice people!'" (127).

In the story's conclusion, these bodies—and these values—lose their pliability. In "A Good Man Is Hard to Find" the feeling of menacing embodiment shifts to the landscape: "Behind them the line of woods gaped like a dark open mouth" (127). With this forbidding lyricism, our own roles as readers begin to shift. Instead of the condensed, hybrid body made out of the delightful detritus of southern culture, we are greeted by bodies that come apart—bodies menaced by a gargantuan symbolic apparatus localized in the southern landscape.

This part-body has a terrifying career in southern history. It resurrects the terrible scenes of mutilation and lynchings of African Americans that occurred with increasing frequency into the twentieth century; it also evokes the pre–Civil War bodies of slaves, who were not only attacked by white culture but defined as part-bodies, since each slave was counted as three-fifths of a nonslave body for the purposes of determining congressional representation.[3]

In O'Connor's stories, it is only as part-bodies that her characters recover some of their dignity. As Bailey contemplates his death at the Misfit's hands, "his eyes were as blue and as intense as the parrots in his shirt, and he remained perfectly still." Hand in hand, he goes with his son to "the dark edge" of the woods. Suddenly, he sounds like a real person: "'I'll be back in a minute, Mamma, wait on me'" (128). Some shots ring out, and then Bobby Lee, the Misfit's henchman, returns from the woods dragging a yellow shirt with bright blue parrots on it. The body disappears, and only its hybrid parts remain.

O'Connor represents a society that is incapable of supporting its bodies. Her bodies disintegrate, become part-bodies devoid of even the contradictory ideology that went into their making. Finally, O'Connor rejects the regenerative promise of the southern grotesque. Living in a society where she feels forced by her own social status not only to cut James Baldwin but to cut countless others from her own local history (she lived, ironically, in a house built by slaves in Baldwin County), she responds by blowing that history up; she enacts a violent response to southern violence.

This is not to argue that O'Connor writes as a militant radical, or even as a redeemed integrationist, but simply to suggest that, by turning the sadistic allure of her stories into a masochistic machinery that gobbles up her readers as well, she produces terrifying elegies for a system that lives but does not work. Finally, the frightening values that hold southern bodies together cannot even support the efflorescence and fertile confusion of the grotesque as southern hybrid form; these bodies splinter apart, and we are left in a bizarre southern landscape that has lost its social reference points and absorbed the torturer's role: "She could hear the wind move through the tree tops like a long satisfied insuck of breath" (129).

Let me conclude by suggesting that these parameters began to change for O'Connor in the early 1960s, during the height of civil rights activism. We do not ordinarily read her famous story "Everything That Rises Must Converge" in the light of the Montgomery bus boycott, but this is a story that depends on the changes in southern society wrought by Martin Luther King, the freedom riders, and thousands of other African American activists. In this story O'Connor's grotesques help us register the massive category confusions that arise and converge in the New South as segregationist principles start to break down. When the militant black woman wearing a grotesque purple hat seats herself in the front of the bus, close to a white woman wearing the same apparel, and this white woman, apparently filled with girlish innocence and unknowing, tries to humiliate the black woman by patronizing her little boy, a sense of white privilege starts to break down. It explodes as the black matron's fist swings out, brandishing a bulging pocketbook like a mighty pendulum, and knocks this image of southern gentility to her knees.

The story ends by deliberately derailing its own political bravado and drawing attention to Julian, the half-baked liberal son who comes to the painful realization that he loves his mother—and perhaps even shares her ridiculous prejudices. As he enters the spiritual world of "guilt and sorrow," O'Connor insists that this is not, after all, a story about race or dead bodies but about the pain and humility necessary to achieve Christian salvation (420). But I want to argue, instead, that O'Connor's Catholic obsessions—her acute self-consciousness about death, guilt, sin, physical pain, and the imperfect search for social perfection—become the consummate vehicle for her southern unease—her ambivalent pleasure at living in a region that makes its tortures aesthetic.

In her final stories O'Connor transfers the tortuous role that floats back and forth between narrator and landscape in her earlier fictions to African Americans. Her vengeful black characters remain fearsome, hyperbolic, and surreal. At the same time, in these final stories, it is white southern culture that O'Connor excoriates. Had she lived longer, would she have decided to put into practice the frightening political lessons of her ultimate grotesques?

Alice Walker suggests an answer when, recounting her visit to O'Connor's house in "The Voice of the Peacock," she finds O'Connor's relation to an upper-class southern ethic both admirable and frightening. At first, Walker admires O'Connor's rebellion; she imagines "O'Connor at a Southern social affair, looking very polite and being very bored, making mental notes of the absurdities of the evening. Being white she would automatically have been eligible for ladyhood, but I cannot believe she would ever really have joined" (46). At the same time, Walker finds O'Connor's world entirely repugnant. She describes the black caretakers who watch over Faulkner's and O'Connor's grand houses, while Walker's own sharecropper's shack, as well as Zora Neale Hurston's and Richard Wright's humble homes, have tumbled to the ground. "I know how damaging to my own psyche such injustice is. In an unjust society the soul of the sensitive person is in danger of deformity from just such weights as this. For a long time I will feel Faulkner's house, O'Connor's house, crushing me" (58). This crushing and cutting become the dominant motifs in O'Connor's fiction, as if to acknowledge the power of her world over other people's bodies. Finally, O'Connor turns this southern capacity for torture upon her characters and her readers alike, as if bearing secret witness to her own ambivalent participation in the making and unmaking of southern bodies in pain.

Notes

1. For a similar perspective and detailed indictment of O'Connor's religious critics, see Frederick Crews. For a selection of books and essays liberating themselves from this perspective, see Claire Katz, "Flannery O'Connor's Rage of Vision"; Claire Kahane, "The Maternal Legacy"; and Louise Westling, *Sacred Groves.*

2. If "grotesque realism images the human body as multiple, bulging, over- or under-sized, protuberant and incomplete," then the grotesque bodies in "A Good Man" remind us that this body in process—this "mobile and hybrid creature, disproportionate, exorbitant, outgrowing all limits"—is bizarrely malleable. See Stallybrass and White 9.

3. See C. Vann Woodward. Woodward suggests that even after the Civil War, "John C. Calhoun's schemes were highly useful. Thirty of the South's seats in the House came by virtue of a black population not permitted to vote, a number enhanced by a bonus of twelve because of the emancipation the South had failed to prevent. Under the old antebellum rule in which three-fifths of the slave population was counted toward the South's representation in Congress, eighteen House seats were produced. But with the Emancipation Proclamation and the passage of the Fourteenth Amendment, the black population was counted whole."

Works Cited

❖ ❖ ❖

Abrahams, William, ed. *Fifty Years of the American Short Story, from the O. Henry Awards 1919–1970*. New York: Doubleday, 1970.

Aldridge, John. *In Search of Heresy: American Literature in an Age of Conformity*. New York: McGraw-Hill, 1956.

Alighieri, Dante. *Inferno*, trans. Charles S. Singleton. Bollingen Series LXXX. Princeton: Princeton University Press, 1970.

Asals, Frederick. *Flannery O'Connor: The Imagination of Extremity*. Athens: U of Georgia P, 1982.

———. "Flannery Row." *Novel* 4 (1970): 92–96. Rpt. as "The Limits of Explanation." *Critical Essays on Flannery O'Connor*. Ed. Melvin J. Friedman and Beverly Lyon Clark. New York: G. K. Hall, 1985. 49–52.

Babinec, Lisa S. "Cyclical Patterns of Domination and Manipulation in Flannery O'Connor's Mother-Daughter Relationships." *Flannery O'Connor Bulletin* 19 (1990): 9–29.

Bacon, Jon Lance. *Flannery O'Connor and Cold War Culture*. New York: Cambridge UP, 1993.

Bakhtin, Mikhail. *The Dialogic Imagination: Four Essays*. 1975. Trans. Caryl Emerson and Michael Holquist. Ed. Michael Holquist. Austin: U of Texas P, 1981.

———. *Problems of Dostoevsky's Poetics*. Ed. and trans. Caryl Emerson. Minneapolis: U of Minnesota P, 1984.

———. *Rabelais and His World*. Trans. Hélène Iswolsky. Cambridge: MIT Press, 1968.

Balée, Susan. *Flannery O'Connor: Literary Prophet of the South*. New York: Chelsea House, 1995.

Balliff, Algene. Review of *The Violent Bear It Away*. *Commentary* 30.4 (October 1960): 358–62.

Banfield, Ann. *Unspeakable Sentences: Narration and Representation in the Language of Fiction*. Boston: Routledge, 1982.

Barcus, Nancy B. "Psychological Determinism and Freedom in Flannery O'Connor." *Cithara* 12.1 (1972): 26–33.

Barthes, Roland. *The Pleasure of the Text.* Trans. Richard Miller. New York: Hill and Wang, 1975.

———. *Writing Degree Zero.* 1953. Trans. Annette Lavers and Colin Smith. New York: Hill, 1968.

Bauer, Dale M. *Feminist Dialogics: A Theory of Failed Community.* Albany: State U of New York P, 1988.

Black, Edwin. *Rhetorical Criticism: A Study in Method.* Madison: U of Wisconsin P, 1978.

Bliven, Naomi. Review of *Everything That Rises Must Converge,* by Flannery O'Connor. *New Yorker,* 11 September 1965, 220–21.

Booth, Wayne C. "Freedom of Interpretation: Bakhtin and the Challenge of Feminist Criticism." *Critical Inquiry* 9.1 (1982): 45–76. Rpt. in *Bakhtin: Essays and Dialogues on His Work.* Ed. Gary Saul Morson. Chicago: U of Chicago P, 1986. 145–76.

Brinkmeyer, Robert H., Jr. *The Art and Vision of Flannery O'Connor.* Baton Rouge: Louisiana State UP, 1989.

Brooke-Rose, Christine. "Ill Logics of Irony." *New Essays on "The Red Badge of Courage."* Ed. Lee Clark Mitchell. Cambridge: Cambridge UP, 1986. 129–46.

Brooks, Cleanth. "Eudora Welty and the Southern Idiom." In *Eudora Welty.* Ed. Harold Bloom. New York: Chelsea House, 1986. 93–108.

Brown, Peter. *The Body and Society: Men, Women and Sexual Renunciation in Early Christianity.* New York: Columbia UP, 1988.

Burns, Stuart L. "*The Violent Bear It Away:* Apotheosis in Failure." *Sewanee Review* 76 (Spring 1968): 319–36.

Butters, Ronald R. "Dialect at Work: Eudora Welty's Artistic Purposes." *Mississippi Folklore Register* 16.2 (Fall 1982): 33–39.

Cain, William E. *The Crisis in Criticism: Theory, Literature, and Reform in English Studies.* Baltimore: Johns Hopkins UP, 1984.

Campbell, Joseph. *A Hero with a Thousand Faces.* New York: World, 1949.

Carroll, Lewis. *Through the Looking Glass.* New York: Columbia UP, 1984.

Cash, Jean W. "O'Connor on *The Violent Bear It Away:* An Unpublished Letter." *English Language Notes* 26.4 (1989): 67–71.

Cassuto, Leonard D. "The American Grotesque." Diss. Harvard U, 1989.

Cheatham, George. "Jesus, O'Connor's Artificial Nigger." *Studies in Short Fiction* 20 (1983): 475–79.

Cheney, Brainard. "Flannery O'Connor's Campaign for Her Country." *Sewanee Review* 72 (Autumn 1964): 555–58.

Chew, Martha. "Flannery O'Connor's Double-Edged Satire: The Idiot Daughter Versus the Lady Ph.D." *Southern Quarterly* 19.2 (1981): 17–25.

Coles, Robert. *Flannery O'Connor's South.* Baton Rouge: Louisiana State UP, 1980.

Coulthard, A. R. "The Christian Writer and the New South: or, Why Don't You Like Flannery O'Connor?" *Southern Humanities Review* 13 (1979): 79–83.

Cowley, Malcolm. *The Literary Situation.* New York: Viking, 1954.

Crews, Frederick. "The Power of Flannery O'Connor." *New York Review of Books,* 26 April 1990, 49–55.

Davidson, Donald. "A Prophet Went Forth." Review of *The Violent Bear It Away,* by Flannery O'Connor. *New York Times Book Review,* 28 February 1960, 4.

Desmond, John F. *Risen Sons: Flannery O'Connor's Vision of History.* Athens: U of Georgia P, 1987.

Dew, Robb Forman. "The Power of the Glory." *A World Unsuspected: Portraits of Southern Childhood.* Chapel Hill: U of North Carolina P, 1987. 117, 121.

di Renzo, Anthony. *American Gargoyles: Flannery O'Connor and the Medieval Grotesque.* Carbondale: Southern Illinois UP, 1993.

Driskell, Leon V., and Joan T. Brittain. *The Eternal Crossroads: The Art of Flannery O'Connor.* Lexington: UP of Kentucky, 1971.

Duhamel, P. Albert. "The Novelist as Prophet." *The Added Dimension: The Art and Mind of Flannery O'Connor.* New York: Fordham UP, 1977. 32–48.

Dunn, Robert, and Stephen Driggers, eds., with Sarah Gordon. *The Manuscripts of Flannery O'Connor at Georgia College.* Athens: U of Georgia P, 1989.

DuPlessis, Rachel Blau. "For the Etruscans." *The Future of Difference.* Ed. Hester Eisenstein and Alice Jardine. Boston: G. K. Hall, 1980. 128–56.

Eagleton, Terry. *Walter Benjamin, or Towards a Revolutionary Criticism.* London: Verso, 1981.

Eliade, Mircea. *Patterns in Comparative Religion.* Trans. Rosemary Sheed. New York: Sheed, 1958.

Eliot, T. S. "Tradition and the Individual Talent." *Selected Essays, 1917–1932.* New York: Harcourt, Brace, 1932. 3–11.

Elliott, Emory, et al. *The Columbia Literary History of the United States.* New York: Columbia UP, 1988.

Emerson, Caryl. "The Tolstoy Connection in Bakhtin." *PMLA* 100 (1985): 68–80.

Engle, Paul, and Hansford Martin, eds. Introduction by Paul Engle. *Prize Stories 1954: The O. Henry Awards.* New York: Doubleday, 1954.

———. *Prize Stories 1955: The O. Henry Awards.* New York: Doubleday, 1955.

———, ed. Assisted by Constance Urdang. Introduction by Paul Engle. *Prize Stories 1957: The O. Henry Awards.* New York: Doubleday, 1957.

Farmer, David. *Flannery O'Connor: A Descriptive Bibliography.* New York: Garland, 1981.

Feeley, Kathleen. *Flannery O'Connor: Voice of the Peacock.* New York: Fordham UP, 1982.

Fennick, Ruth. "First Harvest: Flannery O'Connor's 'The Crop.'" *English Journal* 74.2 (February 1985): 45–50.

Festinger, Leon. *A Theory of Cognitive Dissonance.* Palo Alto: Stanford UP, 1957.

Ficken, Carl. "Theology in Flannery O'Connor's *The Habit of Being.*" *Christianity and Literature* 30.2 (1981): 51–63.

Fiondella, Maris G. "Augustine, the 'Letter,' and the Failure of Love in Flannery O'Connor's 'The Artificial Nigger.'" *Studies in Short Fiction* 24 (1987): 119–29.

Fitts, Karen. "Politics and Pedagogy: The Womb as Contested Property in Flannery O'Connor's 'A Stroke of Good Fortune.'" CEA Conference. Pittsburgh, 28 March 1992.

Fitzgerald, Robert. "The Countryside and the True Country." *Sewanee Review* 70 (1962): 380–94.

———. "Introduction" to *Everything That Rises Must Converge.* New York: New American Library, 1967. xiii.

Flaubert, Gustave. *The Letters of Gustave Flaubert, 1830–1857.* Ed. and trans. Francis Steegmuller. Cambridge: Harvard UP, 1980.

Foucault, Michel. *The History of Sexuality.* Vol. 1: *An Introduction,* trans. Robert Hurley. New York: Pantheon, 1978.

———. *Language, Counter-Memory, Practice: Selected Essays and Interviews.* Ed. Donald F. Bouchard. Trans. Donald F. Bouchard and Sherry Simon. Ithaca: Cornell UP, 1977.

Freud, Sigmund. "The Uncanny." In James Strachey, ed., *The Standard Edition of the Complete Psychological Works of Sigmund Freud.* Vol. 17: *An Infantile Neurosis and Other Works.* London: Hogarth, 1955. 219–52.

Friedman, Melvin J. "Flannery O'Connor: Another Legend in Southern Fiction." *English Journal* 51.4 (1962): 233–43.

———. "Introduction." *Critical Essays on Flannery O'Connor.* Ed. Melvin J. Friedman and Beverly Lyon Clark. Boston: G. K. Hall, 1985. 1–18.

Friedman, Melvin J., and Lewis A. Lawson. *The Added Dimension: The Art and Mind of Flannery O'Connor.* New York: Fordham UP, 1977.

Gentry, Marshall Bruce. "The Eye vs. the Body: Individual and Communal Grotesquerie in *Wise Blood.*" *Modern Fiction Studies* 28 (1982): 487–93.

———. "Flannery O'Connor's Attacks on Omniscience." *Southern Quarterly* 29.3 (1991): 53–61.

———. *Flannery O'Connor's Religion of the Grotesque.* Jackson: UP of Mississippi, 1986.

———. "The Hand of the Writer in 'The Comforts of Home.'" *Flannery O'Connor Bulletin* 20 (1991): 61–72.

Getz, Lorine M. *Flannery O'Connor: Her Life, Library, and Book Reviews.* New York: Mellen, 1980.

———. *Nature and Grace in Flannery O'Connor's Fiction.* New York: Mellen, 1982.

Giannone, Richard. *Flannery O'Connor and the Mystery of Love.* Urbana: U of Illinois P, 1989.

Gilbert, Sandra M., and Susan Gubar. *No Man's Land: The Place of the Woman Writer in the Twentieth Century.* Vol. 1: *The War of the Words.* New Haven: Yale UP, 1988.

Glazener, Nancy. "Dialogic Subversion: Bakhtin, the Novel and Gertrude Stein." *Bakhtin and Cultural Theory.* Ed. Ken Hirschkop and David Shepherd. Manchester: Manchester UP, 1989. 109–29.

"God-Intoxicated Hillbillies." Review of *The Violent Bear It Away,* by Flannery O'Connor. *Time,* 29 February 1960, 118–20.

Gordon, Caroline. "Flannery O'Connor's *Wise Blood.*" *Critique* 2.2 (1958): 3–10.

———. "With a Glitter of Evil." Review of *A Good Man Is Hard to Find,* by Flannery O'Connor. *New York Times Review of Books,* 12 June 1955, 5.

Gordon, Caroline, and Allen Tate, eds. *The House of Fiction: An Anthology of the Short Story with Commentary by Caroline Gordon and Allen Tate.* 2d ed. New York: Scribner's, 1960.

Goyen, William. "Unending Vengeance." Review of *Wise Blood,* by Flannery O'Connor. *New York Times Book Review,* 18 May 1952, 4.

Graff, Gerald. *Professing Literature: An Institutional History.* Chicago: U of Chicago P, 1987.

Gregory, Donald. "Enoch Emery: Ironic Doubling in *Wise Blood.*" *Flannery O'Connor Bulletin* 4 (1975): 52–64.

Harpham, Geoffrey Galt. *The Ascetic Imperative in Culture and Criticism.* Chicago: U of Chicago P, 1987.

————. *On the Grotesque: Strategies of Contradiction in Art and Literature.* Princeton: Princeton UP, 1982.

Hassan, Ihab. *Radical Innocence: Studies in the Contemporary American Novel.* Princeton: Princeton UP, 1961.

Hawkes, John. "Flannery O'Connor's Devil." *Sewanee Review* 70 (1962): 395–407.

Heilbrun, Carolyn G. *Hamlet's Mother and Other Women.* New York: Ballantine, 1990.

————. *Toward a Recognition of Androgyny.* New York: Norton, 1982.

Hendin, Josephine. *The World of Flannery O'Connor.* Bloomington: Indiana UP, 1970.

Hicks, Granville. "Southern Gothic with a Vengeance." Review of *The Violent Bear It Away,* by Flannery O'Connor. *Saturday Review,* 27 February 1960, 18.

————. "A Writer at Home with Her Heritage." *Saturday Review,* 12 May 1962, 22.

Hoffmann, Daniel. *Harvard Guide to Contemporary American Literature.* 2d ed. Cambridge: Belknap, 1979.

Holquist, Michael. *Dialogism: Bakhtin and His World.* New York: Routledge, 1990.

HopKins, Mary Frances. "The Rhetoric of Heteroglossia in Flannery O'Connor's *Wise Blood.*" *Quarterly Journal of Speech* 75 (1989): 198–211.

Howe, Irving, ed. *Classics of Modern Fiction: Ten Short Novels.* New York: Harcourt, 1972.

————. "Flannery O'Connor's Stories." Review of *Everything That Rises Must Converge,* by Flannery O'Connor. *New York Review of Books,* 30 September 1965, 16.

Irwin, John T. *Doubling and Incest, Repetition and Revenge: A Speculative Reading of Faulkner.* Baltimore: Johns Hopkins UP, 1975.

James, William. *The Varieties of Religious Experience.* New York: Modern Library, 1936.

Janssen, Marian. *The Kenyon Review, 1939–1970: A Critical History.* Baton Rouge: Louisiana State UP, 1990.

Johansen, Ruthann Knechel. *The Narrative Secret of Flannery O'Connor: The Trickster as Interpreter.* Tuscaloosa: U of Alabama P, 1994.

Johnson, Barbara. *A World of Difference.* Baltimore: Johns Hopkins UP, 1987.

Jones, Libby F. "The Stories of Welty's 'Petrified Man.'" *Notes on Mississippi Writers* 18 (1986): 65–72.

Joyce, James. *A Portrait of the Artist as a Young Man.* New York: Viking, 1964.

Julian of Norwich. *Showings.* Trans. with the critical text by Edmund Colledge and an introduction by James Walsh. New York: Paulist Press, 1978.

Justus, James. "Fiction: The 1930s to the Present." *American Literary Scholarship/An Annual*. Ed. J. Albert Robbins. Durham: Duke UP, 1974. 279–320.

Kafka, Franz. *The Penal Colony: Stories and Pieces*. Trans. Willa Muir and Edwin Muir. New York: Schocken Books, 1961.

Kahane, Claire [Katz]. "Comic Vibrations and Self-Construction in Grotesque Literature." *Literature and Psychology* 29.3 (1979): 114–19.

———. "Flannery O'Connor's Rage of Vision." *Critical Essays on Flannery O'Connor*. Ed. Melvin J. Friedman and Beverly Lyon Clark. Boston: G. K. Hall, 1985. 119–30.

———. "The Gothic Mirror." *The (M)other Tongue: Essays in Feminist Psychoanalytic Interpretation*. Ed. Shirley Nelson Garner, Claire Kahane, and Madelon Sprengnether. Ithaca: Cornell UP, 1985. 334–51.

———. "Gothic Mirrors and Feminine Identity." *Centennial Review* 24 (1980): 43–64.

———. "The Maternal Legacy: The Grotesque Tradition in Flannery O'Connor's Female Gothic." *The Female Gothic*. Ed. Julian E. Fleenor. Montreal: Eden, 1983. 242–56.

Katz, Claire [Kahane]. "Flannery O'Connor's Rage of Vision." *American Literature* 46 (1974) 54–67.

Kayser, Wolfgang. *The Grotesque in Art and Literature*. Trans. Ulrich Weisstein. 1963. Rpt. Gloucester, Mass.: Peter Smith, 1968.

Kessler, Edward. *Flannery O'Connor and the Language of Apocalypse*. Princeton: Princeton UP, 1986.

Kierkegaard, Sören. "The Gospel of Suffering." *The Gospel of Suffering and the Lilies of the Field*. Trans. David F. Swenson and Lillian Marvin Swenson. Minneapolis: Augsburg, 1948.

Kinney, Arthur F. *Flannery O'Connor's Library: Resources of Being*. Athens: U of Georgia P, 1985.

Klinkowitz, Jerome. "Fiction: The 1950s to the Present." *American Literary Scholarship: An Annual/1980*. Ed. J. Albert Robbins. Durham: Duke UP, 1982. 301–50.

Klug, M. A. "Flannery O'Connor and the Manichean Spirit of Modernism." *Southern Humanities Review* 17 (1983): 303–14.

Kreyling, Michael, ed. *New Essays on "Wise Blood."* Cambridge: Cambridge UP, 1995.

Kristeva, Julia. *Desire in Language*. New York: Columbia UP, 1980.

———. *Revolution in Poetic Language*. Trans. Margaret Waller. New York: Columbia UP, 1984.

Laing, R. D. *The Divided Self.* London: Penguin, 1969.

Lauter, Paul. *Canons and Contexts.* New York: Oxford UP, 1991.

Lawson, Lewis. "The Grotesque in Recent Southern Fiction." *Patterns of Commitment in American Literature.* Ed. Marston LaFrance. Toronto: U of Toronto P, 1967. 165–80.

Leitch, Vincent B. *American Literary Criticism from the Thirties to the Eighties.* New York: Columbia UP, 1988.

Lester, Julius. "Black and White Together: Teaching the 'Beloved Community' in Today's Racially Divided Classrooms." *Lingua Franca* (1990): 30.

Lewis, R. W. B. "Eccentric's Pilgrimage." Review of *Wise Blood,* by Flannery O'Connor, and four other novels. *Hudson Review* 6 (Spring 1953): 144–50.

Ludwin, Deanna. "O'Connor's Inferno: Return to the Dark Wood." *Flannery O'Connor Bulletin* 17 (1988): 11–39.

MacKethan, Lucinda H. *Daughters of Time: Creating Woman's Voice in Southern Story.* Athens: U of Georgia P, 1990.

Maida, Patricia C. "Light and Enlightenment in Flannery O'Connor's Fiction." *Studies in Short Fiction* 13 (1976): 31–36.

Maritain, Jacques. "Art and Scholasticism." *Art and Scholasticism with Other Essays.* Trans. J. F. Scanlan. Freeport, N.Y.: Books for Libraries, 1971. 1–86.

———. *Creative Intuition in Art and Poetry.* New York: Meridian Books, 1953.

May, John R. "Blue-Bleak Embers: The Letters of Flannery O'Connor and Youree Watson." *New Orleans Review* 6.4 (1979): 336–56.

———. "The Methodological Limits of Flannery O'Connor's Critics." *Flannery O'Connor Bulletin* (1986): 16–28.

———. *The Pruning Word: The Parables of Flannery O'Connor.* Notre Dame: U of Notre Dame P, 1976.

Mellard, James M. "Flannery O'Connor's *Others:* Freud, Lacan, and the Unconscious." *American Literature* 61 (December 1989): 625–43.

Mitchell, Margaret. *Gone with the Wind.* New York: Avon, 1964.

Moi, Toril. *Sexual/Textual Politics: Feminist Literary Theory.* London: Routledge, 1987.

Monroe, W. F. "Flannery O'Connor's Sacramental Icon: 'The Artificial Nigger.'" *South Central Review* 1.4 (1984): 64–81.

Montgomery, Marion. "Cloaks and Hats and Doubling in Poe and Flannery O'Connor." *South Carolina Review* 11 (1979): 60–69.

Mossberg, Barbara A. C. *Emily Dickinson: When a Writer Is a Daughter.* Bloomington: Indiana UP, 1982.

Muller, Gilbert H. *Nightmares and Visions: Flannery O'Connor and the Catholic Grotesque*. Athens: U of Georgia P, 1972.

Neuleib, Janice Witherspoon. "Comic Grotesques: The Means of Revelation in *Wise Blood* and *That Hideous Strength*." *Christianity and Literature* 30.4 (Summer 1981): 27–36.

New Yorker, 14 June 1952, 118.

Nisly, Paul W. "Prison of the Self: Isolation in Flannery O'Connor's Fiction." *Studies in Short Fiction* 17 (1980): 49–54.

Oates, Joyce Carol. "The Art of Eudora Welty." *Eudora Welty*. Ed. Harold Bloom. New York: Chelsea House, 1986. 71–74.

O'Brien, Sharon. "Becoming Noncanonical: The Case Against Willa Cather." *Reading in America: Literature and Social History*. Ed. Cathy N. Davidson. Baltimore: John Hopkins UP, 1989. 240–58.

O'Connor, Flannery. *Collected Works*. Ed. Sally Fitzgerald. New York: Library of America, 1988.

———. *The Complete Stories*. New York: Farrar, Straus and Giroux, 1979.

———. *Everything That Rises Must Converge*. Introduction by Robert Fitzgerald. New York: Farrar, Straus and Giroux, 1965.

———. "The Fiction Writer and His Country." *The Living Novel: A Symposium*. Ed. Granville Hicks. New York: Macmillan, 1957. 157–64.

———. "Flannery O'Connor: An Interview." *Conversations with Flannery O'Connor*. By C. Russ Mullins, Jr. Ed. Rosemary M. Magee. Jackson: UP of Mississippi, 1987. 103–7.

———. *The Habit of Being*. Ed. Sally Fitzgerald. New York: Farrar, Straus and Giroux, 1979.

———. *Mystery and Manners: Occasional Prose*. Ed. Sally Fitzgerald and Robert Fitzgerald. New York: Farrar, Straus and Giroux, 1969.

———. *The Presence of Grace, and Other Book Reviews*. Ed. Carter W. Martin. Comp. by Leo Zuber. Athens: U of Georgia P, 1983.

———. *Three*. New York: New American Library, 1983.

Paulson, Suzanne. *Flannery O'Connor: A Study of the Short Fiction*. Boston: Twayne, 1988.

Pease, Donald. "New Americanists: Revisionist Interventions into the Canon." *boundary 2* (Winter 1990): 1–37.

Pei, Lowry. "Dreaming the Other in *The Golden Apples*." *Modern Fiction Studies* 28 (Autumn 1982): 415–33.

Phillips, William, and Philip Rahv. *Avon Book of Modern Writing I.* New York: Avon, 1953.

Poirier, Richard. "If You Know Who You Are You Can Go Anywhere." *New York Times Book Review,* 30 May 1965, 6, 22. Rpt. in *Critical Essays on Flannery O'Connor.* Ed. Melvin J. Friedman and Beverly Lyon Clark. Boston: G. K. Hall, 1985. 45–48.

Prenshaw, Peggy Whitman, ed. "Introduction." *Eudora Welty: Critical Essays.* Jackson: UP of Mississippi, 1979. xi–xviii

Problems of Dostoevsky's Poetics. 1929. Ed. and trans. Caryl Emerson. Minneapolis: U of Minnesota P, 1994.

Ragen, Brian. "The Motions of Grace: Flannery O'Connor's Typology." Diss. Princeton U, 1987.

Rahv, Philip, ed. *Eight Great American Short Novels.* New York: Berkley, 1963.

Rank, Otto. *The Double: A Psychoanalytic Study.* Chapel Hill: U of North Carolina P, 1971.

———. *The Myth of the Birth of the Hero.* New York: Random House, 1959.

Rath, Sura P. "Comic Polarities in Flannery O'Connor's *Wise Blood.*" *Studies in Short Fiction* 21.3 (1984): 251–58.

———. "An Evolving Friendship: The Correspondence Between Flannery O'Connor and Father Edward J. Romagosa, S.J." *Flanner O'Connor Bulletin* 17 (1988): 1–10.

———. "Ruby Turpin's Redemption: Thomistic Resolution in Flannery O'Connor's 'Revelation.'" *Flannery O'Connor Bulletin* 19 (1990): 1–8.

Review of *The Violent Bear It Away,* by Flannery O'Connor. *New Yorker,* 3 March 1960, 179.

Rickels, Milton. "The Grotesque Body of Southwestern Humor." *Critical Essays on American Humor.* Ed. William Bedford Clark and W. Craig Turner. Boston: G. K. Hall, 1984. 155–66.

Rogers, Robert. *A Psychoanalytic Study of the Double in Literature.* Detroit: Wayne State UP, 1970.

Rosenfeld, Isaac. "To Win by Default." Review of *Wise Blood,* by Flannery O'Connor. *New Republic,* 7 July 1952, 19–20.

Rosenfield, Claire. "Despair and the Lust for Immortality." *Nabokov: The Man and His Work.* Ed. L. S. Dembo. Madison: U of Wisconsin P, 1967. 174–92.

———. "The Shadow Within: The Conscious and Unconscious Use of the Double." *Daedalus* 92 (Spring 1963): 326–44.

Rubin, Gayle. "Thinking Sex: Notes for a Radical Theory of the Politics of Sexuality." *Pleasure and Danger: Exploring Female Sexuality.* Ed. Carole S. Vance. Boston: Routledge & Kegan Paul, 1983. 262–319.

Rubin, Louis D., Jr. "Flannery O'Connor: A Note on Literary Fashions." *Critique* 2 (1985): 11–18.

———. "Flannery O'Connor's Company of Southerners: Or, 'The Artificial Nigger' Read as Fiction Rather Than Theology." *A Gallery of Southerners.* Baton Rouge: Louisiana State UP, 1982. Rubin's essay originally appeared in *Flannery O'Connor Bulletin* 6 (1977): 47–71.

———. "Southerners and Jews." *Southern Review* 2 (1966): 697–713.

———. "Two Ladies of the South." *Sewanee Review* 63 (1955): 671–81. Rpt. in *Critical Essays on Flannery O'Connor.* Ed. Melvin J. Friedman and Beverly Lyon Clark. Boston: G. K. Hall, 1985. 25–28.

Ruskin, John. *The Stones of Venice.* London: Smith and Elder, 1853. 112–65.

Satterfield, Ben. "*Wise Blood,* Artistic Anemia, and the Hemorrhaging of O'Connor Criticism." *Studies in American Fiction* 17 (Spring 1989): 33–50.

Scarry, Elaine. *The Body in Pain: The Making and Unmaking of the World.* New York: Oxford UP, 1985.

Scheifer, Ronald. "Rural Gothic: The Stories of Flannery O'Connor." *Modern Fiction Studies* 28 (1982): 475–85.

Schmidt, Peter. "Sibyls in Eudora Welty's Stories." *Eudora Welty: Eye of the Storyteller.* Ed. Dawn Trouard. Kent: Kent State UP, 1989. 78–93.

Schwartz, Lawrence H. *Creating Faulkner's Reputation: The Politics of Modern Literary Criticism.* Knoxville: U of Tennessee P, 1988.

Scott, Anne Firor. *The Southern Lady: From Pedestal to Politics.* Chicago: U of Chicago P, 1970.

Scott, Bonnie Kime, ed. *The Gender of Modernism.* Bloomington: Indiana UP, 1990.

Segrest, Mab. *My Mama's Dead Squirrel: Lesbian Essays on Southern Culture.* Ithaca, N.Y.: Firebrand Books, 1985.

Seidel, Kathryn Lee. *The Southern Belle in the American Novel.* Tampa: U of South Florida P, 1985.

Shinn, Thelma J. "Flannery O'Connor and the Violence of Grace." *Contemporary Literature* 9 (1968): 58–73.

———. *Radiant Daughters: Fictional American Women.* Contributions in Women's Studies 66. New York: Greenwood, 1986.

Shloss, Carol. *Flannery O'Connor's Dark Comedies: The Limits of Inference.* Baton Rouge: Louisiana State UP, 1980.

Simons, John W. "A Case of Possession." Review of *Wise Blood,* by Flannery O'Connor. *Commonweal,* 27 June 1952, 297–98.

Simpson, Lewis P. *The Brazen Face of History: Studies in the Literary Consciousness in America.* Baton Rouge: Louisiana State UP, 1980.

Sloane, Thomas O. "The Strategies of Authorial Presence: Narrators and Regionalism in Flannery O'Connor and Eudora Welty." *Literature in Performance* 2 (November 1981): 1–25.

Smith, Barbara Herrnstein. "Contingencies of Value." *Canons.* Ed. Robert von Hallberg. Chicago: U of Chicago P, 1984.

Smith, Lillian. *Killers of the Dream.* New York: Norton, 1949.

Sonnenfield, Albert. "Flannery O'Connor: The Catholic Writer as Baptist." *Contemporary Literature* 13.4 (Autumn 1972): 445–57.

"Southern Dissonance." Review of *Wise Blood,* by Flannery O'Connor. *Time,* 9 June 1952, 108–10.

Spiller, Robert, et al. *Literary History of the United States.* 3d ed., rev. New York: Macmillan, 1963.

Spivey, Ted R. "Flannery O'Connor, the New Criticism, and Deconstruction." *Southern Review* 23 (Spring 1987): 271–80.

Stallings, Sylvia. "Flannery O'Connor: A New, Shining Talent Among Our Storytellers." Review of *A Good Man Is Hard to Find,* by Flannery O'Connor. *New York Herald Tribune,* 5 June 1955, 1.

———. "Young Writer with a Bizarre Tale to Tell." Review of *Wise Blood,* by Flannery O'Connor. *New York Herald Tribune,* 18 May 1952, 3.

Stallybrass, Peter, and Allon White. *The Politics and Poetics of Transgression.* Ithaca: Cornell UP, 1986.

Steig, Michael. "Defining the Grotesque: An Attempt at Synthesis." *Journal of Aesthetics and Art Criticism* 29 (Summer 1970): 253–60.

Stephens, Martha. *The Question of Flannery O'Connor.* Baton Rouge: Louisiana State UP, 1973.

Strickland, Edward. "The Penitential Quest in 'The Artificial Nigger.'" *Studies in Short Fiction* 25 (1988): 453–59.

"Such Nice People." Review of *A Good Man Is Hard to Find,* by Flannery O'Connor. *Time,* 6 June 1955, 114.

Tate, Allen. *Mere Literature and the Lost Traveller.* Nashville: George Peabody School for Teachers, 1969.

Tate, J. O. "The Essential Essex." *Flannery O'Connor Bulletin* 12 (1983): 47–59.

Thomson, Philip. *The Grotesque.* The Critical Idiom Series. London: Methuen, 1972.

Thorpe, Willard, Carlos Baker, James K. Folsom, and Merle Curti, eds. *The American Literary Record.* Chicago: Lippincott, 1961.

Tompkins, Jane. *Sensational Designs: The Cultural Work of American Fiction, 1790–1860.* New York: Oxford UP, 1985.

Tymms, Ralph. *Doubles in Literary Psychology.* Cambridge: Bowers and Bowers, 1949.

Vande Kieft, Ruth M. "The Mysteries of Eudora Welty." *Eudora Welty.* Ed. Harold Bloom. New York: Chelsea House, 1986. 45–70.

Walker, Alice. "Beyond the Peacock: The Reconstruction of Flannery O'Connor." *In Search of Our Mothers' Gardens: Womanist Prose.* New York: Harcourt Brace Jovanovich, 1987, 42–59.

Weaver, Richard. *The Ethics of Rhetoric.* Chicago: U of Chicago P, 1948.

Welty, Eudora. *The Collected Stories.* New York: Harcourt Brace Jovanovich, 1980.

———. *Conversations with Eudora Welty.* Ed. Peggy Whitman Prenshaw. Jackson: UP of Mississippi, 1984.

———. *One Writer's Beginnings.* Cambridge, Mass.: Harvard UP, 1984.

Westarp, Karl-Heinz. *Flannery O'Connor: The Growing Craft.* Birmingham: Summa, 1993.

Westarp, Karl-Heinz, and Jan Nordby Gretlund. *Realist of Distances: Flannery O'Connor Revisited.* Aarhus, Denmark: Aarhus UP, 1987.

Westling, Louise. "Flannery O'Connor's Mothers and Daughters." *Twentieth Century Literature* 24 (1978): 510–22.

———. "Flannery O'Connor's Revelations to 'A.'" *Southern Humanities Review* 20 (1986): 15–22.

———. *Sacred Groves and Ravaged Gardens: The Fiction of Eudora Welty, Carson McCullers, and Flannery O'Connor.* Athens: U of Georgia P, 1985.

Whitt, Margaret. "Flannery O'Connor's Ladies." *Flannery O'Connor Bulletin* 15 (1986): 42–50.

Wimsatt, W. K. *The Verbal Icon: Studies in the Meaning of Poetry.* Lexington: UP of Kentucky, 1954.

Woodward, C. Vann. "The Particular Politics of Being Southern." *The Prevailing*

South: Life and Politics in a Changing Culture. Ed. Dudley Clendinen. Atlanta: Longstreet, 1988. 22–23.

Woolf, Virginia. "Professions for Women." Rpt. in *Virginia Woolf: Women and Writing.* Ed. Michele Barrett. New York: Harcourt, 1979. 57–63.

———. *A Room of One's Own.* New York: Harcourt, 1957.

Wright, Richard. *Uncle Tom's Children.* New York: Harper & Row, 1969.

Yaeger, Patricia S. " 'Because a Fire Was in My Head': Eudora Welty and the Dialogic Imagination." *PMLA* 99 (1984): 955–73.

Young, Thomas Daniel, and Elizabeth Sarcone, eds. *The Lytle-Tate Letters: The Correspondence of Andrew Lytle and Allen Tate.* Jackson: UP of Mississippi, 1987.

Zuber, Leo J., comp. *The Presence of Grace and Other Book Reviews by Flannery O'Connor.* Ed. Carter W. Martin. Athens: U of Georgia P, 1983.

Contributors

Robert H. Brinkmeyer, Jr., professor of American literature and southern studies at the University of Mississippi, has published widely on modern southern literature. Besides *The Art and Vision of Flannery O'Connor,* he is the author of *Three Catholic Writers of the Modern South* and *Katherine Anne Porter's Artistic Development: Primitivism, Traditionalism, and Totalitarianism.*

Sarah J. Fodor, visiting assistant professor of English at Wheaton College, recently completed her dissertation, "'No Literary Orthodoxy': Flannery O'Connor and the New Critics." She has interviewed Reynolds Price on his new novel, *The Promise of Rest,* for the *Christian Century* and reviewed John Updike's *The Afterlife.*

Marshall Bruce Gentry teaches American literature and the short story at the University of Indianapolis. Author of *Flannery O'Connor's Religion of the Grotesque,* he has also published studies on gender dialogue in the works of E. L. Doctorow, Philip Roth, and Raymond Carver.

Richard Giannone, professor of English at Fordham University, is the author of *Music in Willa Cather's Fiction, Kurt Vonnegut: A Preface to His Fiction,* and *Flannery O'Connor and the Mystery of Love.*

Sarah Gordon, professor of English at Georgia College and editor of the *Flannery O'Connor Bulletin,* has chaired four symposia on O'Connor's work at Georgia College, including "The Habit of Art" in 1994. A widely published poet, Gordon is currently at work on a critical study entitled "Flannery O'Connor: The Obedient Imagination."

Laura B. Kennelly teaches English at the University of North Texas. Bibliographic editor of *Restoration: Studies in English Literary Culture, 1660–1700* and author of studies on O'Connor, Stevens, Swift, Byron, Dryden, and Anne

Rice, she is currently working on an edition of an American colonial manuscript entitled "Memoirs of Samuel West, 1738–1808."

Suzanne Morrow Paulson teaches American literature at Minot State University. She is the author of *Flannery O'Connor: A Study of the Short Fiction, William Trevor: A Study of the Short Fiction,* and essays on Carson McCullers.

Sura P. Rath, professor of English at Louisiana State University in Shreveport, has guest-edited a special issue of the *South Central Review* on the poetics of game-play, and is co-editor of the *Journal of Contemporary Thought.* Author of articles on Forster, Hesse, O'Connor, Rushdie, and contemporary Indian poetry, he is currently at work on a study of the carnivalization of play in fiction.

Jeanne Campbell Reesman, professor of English at the University of Texas in San Antonio and director of the division of English, classics, and philosophy, is the author of *American Designs: The Late Novels of James and Faulkner* and co-author of *A Handbook of Critical Approaches to Literature* and *Jack London.*

Mary Neff Shaw teaches English at Louisiana State University in Shreveport. Author of critical essays on Stephen Crane and Emily Dickinson, she is working on a book-length study entitled "Stephen Crane's Concept of Heroism: Satire in the War Stories of Stephen Crane."

Patricia Yaeger teaches English at the University of Michigan. She is the author of *Honey-Mad Women: Emancipatory Strategies in Women's Writing* and essays on Chopin, Faulkner, O'Connor, Porter, and Welty; co-editor of *Nationalisms and Sexualities;* and editor of *The Geography of Identity.* She is currently completing a book entitled "Dirt and Desire: The Grotesque in Southern Women's Writing."